THE
PICTORIAL HISTORY OF
MOTORCYCLING

THE
PICTORIAL HISTORY OF
MOTORCYCLING

CHARLES E. DEANE & BRIAN CRICHTON

CHANCELLOR
PRESS

First published in 1982 by Octopus Books Limited, part of Reed
Consumer Books.
This 1993 edition published by
Chancellor Press
Michelin House
81 Fulham Road
London SW3 6RB

Printed in Hong Kong

Contents

The First Seventy Years

ON 10 November 1885 a rickety looking, timber-framed bicycle, powered by a ½-horsepower, single-cylinder engine, made its maiden run in Bad Cannstatt, near the city of Stuttgart. This curious machine, the brainchild of Gottlieb Daimler, a German gunsmith-turned-engineer, heralded a revolution in transport. But a revolution of what kind? After all, the industrialized world was by this time humming with engines: the railways were more than 60 years old; steamships had progressed to the era of the luxury liner; the first manned and powered airship had already taken to the air. Even on the roads a variety of powered vehicles had made an appearance—steam carriages as long ago as the 1830s.

The revolutionary element in Daimler's machine—as in the almost exactly contemporary Petrolcycle of an Englishman, Edward Butler—was the nature of its engine, which worked on the principle known as internal combustion. Whereas steam engines tend to increase in efficiency with size (hence their success as the power units in ships and trains), Daimler's engine pointed the way towards the evolution of small engines with a high power-to-weight ratio. It was just such engines that made possible the development of *personal* transport vehicles—the motorcycle and the car—that have transformed everyday life in the 20th century.

LEFT Fresh-air transport for the Quality: a Holden autocycle with rickshaw trailer, about 1898. Colonel Holden's design was powered by a water-cooled engine in which the two cylinders had combustion chambers at both ends. Power was delivered directly from the pistons to the rear wheel by crank rods.

Daimler's *Petroleum-Reitwagen* (petrol-driven vehicle) was the progenitor of both the motorcycle and the motorcar. Its engine was based on a type developed in the 1870s by Dr Nikolaus Otto, for whom Daimler had worked for a time. The Otto Cycle, as this engine was called, operated, like the modern car engine, on a four-stroke system, the 'strokes' referring to the movements of a piston within its cylinder: a downward stroke, in which petrol vapour is drawn into the cylinder; an upward stroke in which the vapour is highly compressed; a downward stroke powered by the explosive ignition of the vapour; and an upward stroke in which the spent gases from the explosion are expelled from the cylinder. The vapour enters, and the exhaust leaves, the cylinder by means of valves in the cylinder head.

Although Daimler had clearly shown the way forward in the evolution of the motorcycle, he himself was primarily interested in motorcar manufacture: his colleague and co-builder of the *Reitwagen*, the engineering genius Wilhelm Maybach, was to design the classic Mercedes cars of the first two decades of the 20th century. It was not until 10 years after Daimler's machine had first shown its paces that motorcycle pioneers in France, Germany, and England abandoned their fruitless search for a viable steam-powered bike and turned to internal combustion. Among the leading figures in France to make the switch were Comte Albert de Dion and his partner Georges Bouton, who in 1895 built a tricycle powered by a petrol engine capable of running at an astonishing 1,500 rpm (revolutions per minute)–

BELOW This 1898 Werner ¾ hp motorcycle, with engine over the front wheel, was among the earliest French motorcycles to be imported into England.

BOTTOM LEFT The Cudell De Dion of 1898 was based on the tricycles of Comte Albert de Dion and his partner, Georges Bouton, who were among the pioneers of motorized transport in Europe.

BOTTOM RIGHT A 1910 Harley-Davidson single-cylinder, 480 cc Model 6A, one of the type known among workers at Harley's Milwaukee factory as the 'Silent Gray Fellow'. The first of the famous 45-degree V-twin, 1,000 cc models, upon which Harley's later fortunes were founded, was introduced in 1909.

RIGHT The Werner brothers were among the first motorcycle manufacturers to design a machine with the motor positioned low between the wheels. This 1903 Werner motorcycle established design principles that helped greatly to improve stability and controllability at all speeds.

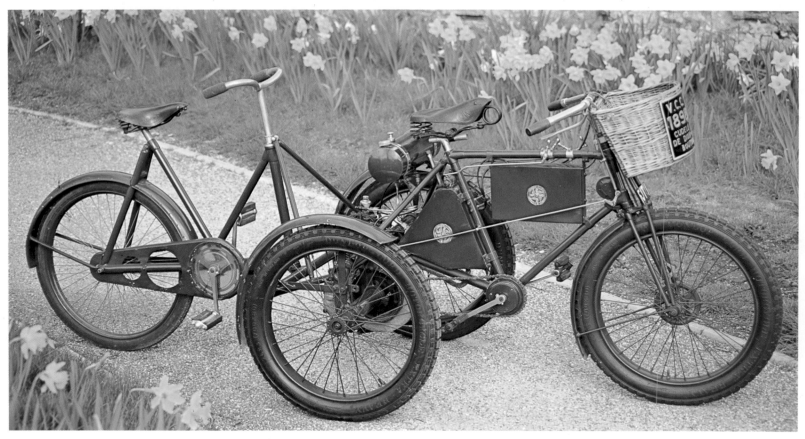

almost double the shaft speed of Daimler's engine. In Germany at about the same time the firm of Hildebrand & Wolfmüller designed a water-cooled two-cylinder petrol-engined bike; while in England Colonel Henry Holden produced a four-cylinder model—or, rather, a two-cylinder model with pistons at both ends of each cylinder.

The firm of De Dion, Bouton et Cie made an important contribution to motorcycling in the closing years of the 19th century. It began to produce 'over-the-counter' engines for a great variety of vehicles, selling them or licensing their production in England, Belgium, Germany, and the United States. (It was one of these engines that in 1898 launched the career of Louis Renault, founder of what was to become the world's first car-manufacturing giant.)

Like all other internal-combustion engines of those days, the products of De Dion, Bouton were temperamental, to put it mildly. But at least they were available, and in considerable quantities, to any would-be motorcycle manufacturer. There were customers in plenty, each with his own idea of the best way to design a motorbike. Indeed, one of the features of motorcycle design during this period was the variety of positions on the machine that were allocated to the engine. Some were mounted over or alongside the front wheel, others over or behind the back wheel, still others somewhere in between. The main problem for such manufacturers, most of whom had more enthusiasm than engineering knowhow, was how to fit a continuous drive belt to couple the engine's crankshaft to one or other of the road wheels. An even more serious problem—at least for a two-wheeler travelling at more than about 16 km/h (10 mph)—was that of stability. As the present-day rider well knows, a motorcycle with an engine mounted over one or other of the road wheels becomes unstable at speed; a front-mounted engine, in particular, tends to make the front wheel slide outwards at corners.

The matter of engine location was settled, once and for all, by Michel and Eugene Werner, two Russian exiles living in Paris. During the 1890s they had tried various engine positions, none wholly satisfactory. But in 1901 they introduced a model with the engine located low down in a specially designed diamond-shaped frame (similar to that of a pedal cycle) between the road wheels. At one stroke they had effectively conquered the problem of stability and had significantly lowered the motorbike's centre of gravity.

Many fundamental engineering problems affecting the reliability and performance of motorcycles were tackled, although not always successfully, during

the first few years of the 20th century. One of the most difficult was the problem of ignition. In most motorcycle and car engines of this time the petrol vapour in the cylinder was ignited by an apparatus called a battery trembler coil. This produced a shower of sparks in the combustion chamber at the beginning of the power stroke, one of the sparks usually serving to ignite the explosive mixture. Maximum power, however, is delivered to the crankshaft only if the gas is ignited at exactly, not approximately, the right moment—the timing being measured in minute fractions of a second. The ignition problem was solved, in principle at any rate, in 1903 by the German engineer Robert Bosch, whose high-tension magneto system was designed to generate a good, fat spark to ignite the vapour at the precise moment required. The magneto, together with the sparking plug, which had been developed the year before by one of Bosch's colleagues, was quickly adopted by all the major manufacturers, and it remains to this day the basis of car and motorbike ignition systems.

Early Racing

Until well into the 20th century the technology of the motorcycle and motorcar was pioneered in continental Europe. The backwardness of Britain in this field was due at least in part to the imposition, ruthlessly upheld by magistrates, of speed limits on public roads. An act of Parliament, limiting speeds to 6.5 km/h (4 mph), was passed in 1865; a second act, passed in 1896, raised the limit—but only to 19.5 km/h (12 mph). Such speed limits gave motorcyclists small advantage, if any, over the pedal cyclist or the man on horseback, and offered manufacturers little incentive to invest in development engineering. By contrast, the limit-free continental roads enabled enthusiasts to organize regular inter-city races, and the prestige and sales potential of the winning machines spurred the European manufacturers into investing heavily in designers and engineers. Another reason for the lack of a specifically British contribution at this stage was the activities of the British Motor Syndicate, headed by Harry Lawson, which from 1896 onwards purchased patent or distribution rights in a variety of continental powered vehicles and components, with the intention (luckily frustrated) of cornering the entire British market in motorcycles and cars.

The situation was to change swiftly, however, when in 1905 the Auto-Cycle Club organized motorcycle trials on the Isle of Man, where there was no speed limit, to select entrants for the International Cup races that by now were held annually on the Continent. The trials, and later the Manx Tourist Trophy (TT) races, set a trend that has continued to this day: the development and improvement of road bikes on the basis of racing machines that have established themselves in the arena of international competition.

BELOW This 1913 Zenith Gradua's multi-ratio belt-drive system made it an almost invincible competitor in hill-climbing competitions.

RIGHT The staid appearance of this 1913 BAT with wickerwork sidecar belies the marque's formidable TT record before World War I.

Edwardian Days

The fierce competition of the international races soon laid bare the technical weaknesses of the motorcycles of Edwardian days. The twisted rawhide drive belt, prone to stretching and sudden breakage, gave way to V-section rubber-and-canvas or leather belts. As speeds increased, the need for better suspension quite literally made itself felt: the jarring and jolting not only made the machines difficult to control at speed but also caused many frames to fracture. One early answer to the suspension problem was the front-end parallel-slider fork with compression springs, developed by Alfred Drew in 1906, which greatly improved the handling and steering properties of TT and grand-prix machines. This and other improvements in suspension quickly found their way onto road bikes.

Gearing was the next major engineering challenge to be tackled. Ordinary road bikes – and indeed many racers, too – had for long been fitted with pedals because, lacking gears, they needed the help of muscle power to get them over the steeper hills. For racing machines the problem was put into stark focus by the decision of the Manx authorities to hold the 1911 TT on the island's fearsome Mountain Circuit. The British firms of Rudge-Whitworth and Zenith had earlier attempted to solve the problem with unsophisticated, if technically sound, multi-ratio belt-drive systems. It was at this point that American motorcycle technology (until then almost unknown in Europe) intervened decisively for the first time. For some years Oscar Hendstrom and George Hendee, founders of the Indian motorcycle company, had been striving to perfect a two-speed countershaft transmission incorporating a clutch. When satisfied with its performance they integrated it with a drive chain and rear-wheel gear sprockets in place of the belt-drive system. Technically the Indian system was superior to any used by European manufacturers. That it was also superior in practice was dramatically proved in 1911, when Indian V-twin four-strokes took the first three places in the Manx TT.

Most road and racing motorbikes of Edwardian days were powered by four-stroke engines using a variety of cylinder arrangements – V-twins and parallel twins as well as single-cylinder types. The principle of the two-stroke engine was already known at this time, but research into the type had yielded little practical success. Potentially the two-stroke offered an obvious advantage: since its induction, compression, power, and exhaust cycle is completed in one revolution of the crankshaft instead of two (as in the four-stroke engine), at a given engine speed its power stroke occurs twice as often as in the four-stroke. This potential became a demonstrated fact in 1912, when Frank Applebee easily won the Manx Senior TT astride a twin-cylinder two-stroke made by Alfred Scott. (In motorcycling, as elsewhere, fashion has a habit of repeating itself: today, after being out of favour for some years, two-stroke machines, now water-cooled and with rotary valves, have re-established their former dominance of the road-racing circuits of the world.)

About this time a number of engineering companies, realizing the growing importance of the motorcycle market, began to specialize as manufacturers of components such as engines, gearboxes, front forks, and frames. Among the best and most widely used of such products were the lightweight engines of Villiers and JAP and the gears of Sturmey-Archer. The response to this ready availability of components was immediate. Scores of individuals or groups who had access to a lock-up or spare garage space suddenly formed companies and began to assemble the readymade components into market-able motorcycles. Most of them just as suddenly went out of business. For although it was possible to produce adequate 'bitsas' from bought-in proprietary components, the future lay with the companies who had the resources and vision to develop teams of specialist designers and engineers and who were prepared to test and improve their products in the hard school of international competitions. World War I effectively wiped out most of the 'bitsa' companies; indeed, even some of the greatest names in European motorcycles were crippled by the economic consequences of the war.

During the European conflict the centre of motorcycle innovation moved to the United States. In 1911 one of the greatest American motorcycle engineers, William Henderson, had swiftly gained an enthusiastic following with a machine powered by a four-cylinder in-line engine. This was a greatly improved version of a similar engine made by Pierce-Arrow, a company already established as a maker of fine cars. During the next few years four-cylinder engines were adopted by Indian, Harley-Davidson, and most other American manufacturers, including the Ace company formed by Henderson after his original firm had been taken over by Excelsior. By the end of the war the Americans were undisputed leaders in motorcycle engineering and had pioneered the use of such significant improvements as the twist-grip throttle control, the drum brake on the rear wheel, the foot-operated clutch, the starter motor, and electric lighting.

ABOVE A typical early 1930s advertisement.

TOP LEFT An AJS 348 cc, single-cylinder of 1926. That year a similar AJS lapped the TT circuit at over 113 km/h (70 mph).

RIGHT The 1920 Indian with 'flat-head', side-valve, V-twin motor.

TOP RIGHT The formidable 1,301 cc, four-in-line motor of the 1924 Henderson – a late version of a classic American motorcycle.

Between the Wars

Ironically, it was the European manufacturers who were chiefly to benefit from these improvements. In spite of its technical inventiveness, the American motorcycle industry entered a period of decline after the war–a decline foreshadowed, as we now know, on that day in 1908 when Henry Ford had unveiled his Model T. The American public was to vote decisively in favour of four wheels instead of two, and Ford's Tin Lizzie continued to sell by the million until it was replaced in 1927.

The European motorcycle and car manufacturers also benefited enormously from the tremendous technological leap forward, especially in metallurgy, that had been forced upon the contending nations by the needs of war. In particular, harder steels and a variety of light but strong alloys helped to transform the durability and performance of motorcycle engines. Harder steels made possible much stronger camshafts and valve springs; the new alloys enabled designers to make pistons from aluminium instead of much heavier iron or steel, leading to much higher engine revolutions and greater power output than ever before.

These improvements in engineering materials went hand in hand with significant advances in design technology. By the early 1920s side valves were being replaced by overhead valves operated by pushrods; this configuration in turn gave way, in the mid-1920s, to overhead-camshaft (OHC) engines–a type still to be found under the bonnet of the world's great sports cars.

The German BMW company, which had built some of the finest aero-engines during the war, produced its first motorcycles in 1923. It is an enormous tribute to the firm's quality of manufacture and to the inherent soundness of its original designs that both its engine configuration–horizontally opposed twin-cylinder four-stroke–and its use of a shaft instead of chain drive are still features of all BMW road and racing bikes.

By the mid-1920s Italian manufacturers were also beginning to make an impression on the racing scene. Moto Guzzi, in particular, was building a range of advanced lightweight OHC four-strokes. Their reliability and great speed were demonstrated in 1926, when Pietro Ghersi won the Manx Lightweight (250 cc) TT and set a new lap record of 101 km/h (63 mph)–only to be disqualified for making a false declaration about the type of sparking plug he was using.

The manufacturers were by now building enormous power into their racing engines, and multiple gears allowed riders to use this power at optimum revs whatever the road speed. Until the late 1920s, however, the hand-operated gear lever, mounted alongside the petrol tank, prevented even the best rider from exploiting fully the engine power and gearing flexibility at his disposal. One reason was that movement of even the best-designed hand levers was laborious and slow; another was that, while he was changing gear, the rider was controlling his racer with only one hand–a very dangerous thing to

do if one was dicing with the rest of the pack around a tight, bumpy corner on the Isle of Man circuit.

The answer to the problem was the positive-stop foot-gearchange mechanism invented by Harold Willis, a racing engineer at Velocette. Its decisive superiority to the hand-change method was proved for all time in 1928, when Alec Bennett's and Willis's Velocettes came first and second in the Junior (350 cc) TT. Thereafter all the successful racing marques adopted the foot gearchange, and today, of course, almost every motorbike apart from automatics and a few mopeds uses this system.

By the mid-1930s most of the engine features we find on the latest machines had been designed, tested, and race-proved by one or other of the leading manufacturers. Two-stroke engines with rotary valves had been pioneered by Scott and Vitesse. The three-cylinder, double-OHC four-stroke—a configuration that today is the special pride of Kawasaki and some Italian roadsters—was pioneered by Moto Guzzi as long ago as 1930. A year or two later another feature of the modern superbike, the four-stroke with four valves per cylinder instead of two, was introduced by Rudge.

Suspension is another area in which today's machines were anticipated, in general principles if not in refinement, by the road racers of 40 years ago. The first successful hydraulically damped telescopic front-wheel springs were fitted in the late 1930s to the works racers of BMW and Norton. Only in the field of supercharging, exploited most successfully just before World War II by Gilera, BMW, AJS, and Velocette but banned after the war by the racing authorities, has TT and grand-prix practice not found later expression in two-wheel roadsters.

By the outbreak of World War II, Britain's long record of success in the racing field had secured for it commercial domination of the motorcycling world. Many of the touring machines of that time—the Triumph vertical-twin Tiger 100, the Ariel Red Hunter, the BSA Gold Star, and the prestige machinery of Norton, Matchless, and AJS—were among the finest expressions of contemporary motorcycling technology.

The Lull Before the Storm

When peace came in 1945 the British industry shrugged its shoulders, complained about the quality of low-octane 'pool' petrol, and continued building bikes on the lines established successfully before the war. Typical of the post-war generation of British models was Norton's 1947 500 cc Model 7—a fast but noisy and bone-shaking vertical twin.

But the days of British, and indeed European, supremacy were numbered. In a symbolic sense, the watershed was the Manx race meeting of 1954. Nothing especially sensational marked the occasion. In the Senior TT Norton stemmed what in the next decade was to prove an irresistible tide of success for Italian Gileras and MV Agustas; AJS dominated the Junior TT, while the very fast German NSUs turned the Lightweight classes into a procession. But the real portent of the future was not on the circuit but among the spectators—the presence of a man who had a very special interest in the nature and performance of the racing machines. Although few knew it at the time, his interest was to prove disastrous for the traditional centres of motorcycle supremacy in Britain and elsewhere. His name was Soichiro Honda.

LEFT During the 1930s George Brough created a legend by building 'specials' powered by proprietary engines from JAP, Matchless—and even the Austin 7 car. In its gutsy, V-twin-engined form the Brough Superior roadster was capable of well over 160 km/h (100 mph), and specially prepared versions held the lap record at Brooklands before the circuit closed during World War II. This 998 cc SS100 of 1939 was the last of the line, but beautifully preserved Brough roadsters remain among the most coveted collectors' items.

WORLD RECORDS

Scientists may have split the atom but no one will ever split the bond between motorcycles and speed. Ever since the first exhaust note from an internal combustion engine barked into the atmosphere, man on two wheels has raced his fellows and taken on Time itself. The lure of speed for its own sake and within the context of competition has proved to be irresistible.

It is almost impossible to pinpoint the first universally accepted master of speed, but the word spread fast when a Peugeot rider topped 122.4kph (76mph) in 1904, on a machine weighing 45.4kg (110lb). Three years later 209kph (130mph) was allegedly reached by an American, Glenn Curtis.

In 1907 one of the most famous early racing and record breaking venues was opened, Brooklands in England. Racing did not take place until the following year but it soon encouraged manufacturers to produce machines solely for racing. North London Garages built such a machine powered by a 944cc Peugeot V-twin engine. It weighed only 53.5kg (118lb), little more than a modern 50cc moped. Rider comfort was completely sacrificed as one of many measures aimed at weight saving. The machine's design was justified when it averaged 112.7kph (70mph) in a race over 8.9km (5.5 miles) in 1910. The previous year an NLG, powered by a massive 2913cc V-twin JAP engine, had reached a top speed of 144.8kph (90mph) on the rippled concrete 4.8km (3 mile) banked circuit.

Brooklands was the only closed racing circuit of its time. The goal for absolute top speeds (i.e. record speeds regardless of the size of the machine) later followed the longest and straightest stretches of metalled public road which were few and far between in the early days of motorcycling. It was not until the mid 1950s that the vast expanse of the Bonneville salt flats in Utah, USA, was required because speeds were becoming too high for existing circuits and increasingly busy public roads.

While books about the history of motorcycling quote official records, these are not necessarily the fastest of their day. There have been instances of unofficial records being higher, and situations may arise where a country holds a national records session where speeds are higher than the

American Tom Christenson on Vink's Kawasaki which helped Vink set speed records in 1977.

current world records but, because the occasion was not run under international recognition, the higher speed does not count in the official world records' list.

Such a situation existed in 1956 when a German, Wilhelm Herz, scored the first world land speed record for motorcycles on the Bonneville salt flats, a place now synonymous with speed. The German NSU factory had sent Herz there with a completely enclosed, 499cc supercharged, double overhead cam, twin-cylinder machine. He reached 338.092kph (210.08 mph). The American Johnny Allen, using a 650cc Triumph twin-cylinder power unit, bettered the record with 345kph (214.5mph) but, because it was not ratified internationally, it stood as an American national record only and the slightly slower NSU maintained its world glory.

Apart from the necessity of having an official witness from the world governing body of motorcycle sport, the Federation Internationale Motocycliste, a world speed record must be the average speed from two separate runs undertaken in opposite directions within an hour of each other. This is true of all the capacities and classes which come under the heading of world speed records.

It is easy to become confused about motorcycle records. The world records chart which accompanies this chapter will help to clarify them, as it lists all the current holders and categories. The times and speeds shown are the average, or mean, times and speeds.

Taking an example to illustrate the point, an American drag racer, Russ Collins, has covered a standing start quarter-mile in 7.62 seconds, while the best official world record is held by a Dutchman, Henk Vink, in the 1300cc class, at a much slower time of 8.805 seconds. Vink is the world record holder because his time was recorded at an official records meeting and was the result of the average of two runs, completed within an hour. This chapter deals with both types of records, since there is no doubt that Collins has set a record with his fastest time ever clocked on a drag strip. More unusual types of records are included too, some of them open to dispute. Many would-be record holders turn to the publishers of the Guinness Book of Records to recognize their attempts and give them universal acceptance. So many

diverse records are being set with motorcycles that it seems that whoever lays the ground rules in the first place is asking to be outdone by a challenger who sees an easy way round them.

Vesco and Rayborn

At the top of the league of world record breakers stands Don Vesco, a motorcycle businessman from San Diego, California. He holds the absolute motorcycle land speed record at a mean average of 512.734 kph (318.598mph), set at Bonneville. The only man to have ridden a motorcycle at over 300 mph (480kph), Vesco's best one-way run was 512.834kph (318.66mph).

Vesco first earned a world record in 1970. Using two air-cooled 350cc Yamaha TR2 racing engines on straight petrol, Vesco attained 405kph (251.66mph). However, less than a week later the American road racer, Cal Rayborn, stole his glory on the Bonneville salt with an average of 410.98kph (255.37mph), which he then improved to 427.268kph (265.492mph) by using nitro-methane instead of petrol.

In 1973 Vesco was breaking records once again. With Yamaha water-cooled racing engines, he took both the 250cc and 350cc world records at 305.017kph (189.529mph) and 325.752kph (202.413 mph) respectively. He also added the world 750cc record to his list with two 350cc engines fitted to give 368.588kph (229.03mph).

In 1974, Vesco got his own back on his 1970 rival, Rayborn. He set a new world record at 453.372kph (281.712mph) mean speed on 1 October 1974. For this attempt, he had chosen two Yamaha four-cylinder, water-cooled, two-stroke engines. Vesco was confident that the 480kph (300mph) barrier was within his grasp and, on one trial run, calculated with the aid of his tachometer that he had reached 475kph (295mph).

Vesco had to wait several days before conditions on the 1,300m (4,300ft) altitude flats were suitable for the attempt. Any kind of wind would have been potentially dangerous. Strapped into the tiny cockpit of his 'cigar' for the first record run, Vesco, who had been training his right arm to operate the heavy throttle linkage to eight carburettors, made the 6.4km (4 mile) run-in to the electronic lights set

1.6km (one mile) apart. His elapsed time was just 12 seconds to give a speed of 452.274kph (281.030mph). The return speed was 453.372kph (281.712mph). This was considerably faster than the old world record of 427.268kph (265.492mph) set by Rayborn in 1970.

Ironically, Vesco's new record was not officially recognized, nor was Rayborn's, at the time because the FIM did not have a category for records over 1,300cc. Vesco's engines came to 1,400cc. But this was of academic importance only. The rest of the world recognized the bespectacled hero as the new speed king.

At Bonneville speed week, in August 1974, Vesco took a number of other records. On an unfaired 700cc Yamaha racing bike he claimed the American national 750cc record at 274kph (170mph). The day after his world record success, he disconnected one of the engines in his streamliner in order to better his own FIM 750cc world record to 376.981kph (234.245 mph). The difference in speed was 103kph (64mph) in favour of the streamliner, yet both power units produced almost exactly the same power and the streamliner had a disadvantage in that it had a lot more weight to pull than the unfaired bike.

After reaffirming his supremacy in 1974, Vesco did not allow himself to become complacent. A later attempt increased his record to 487.5kph (302.92mph) and this was followed by his peak of achievement in 1978, with the promise of still better to come.

The 1978 record was set with two four-cylinder 1,000cc Kawasaki engines with turbochargers. The Japanese Kawasaki factory early in 1978 was reported to have offered Vesco £36,000 for a two year contract to give them the motorcycle world land speed record and the publicity that goes with it.

Vesco's 488.94kph (303.812mph) record, set in 1975 with two Yamaha TZ750 engines, used basically the same framework and fibreglass body shell he built in 1969. In order to give his new 1978 sponsor a quick result, he continued to use the same chassis and gave the shell a new paint livery in Kawasaki's honour.

The engines were supplied by Kawasaki and fitted with turbochargers and fuel injection. Again, toothed belts connected the engines; final drive was by chain. To support the motorcycle when it was slowing to a halt, the bodyshell incorporated retractable side skids activated by compressed nitrogen. The bike was slowed by a rear disc brake and parachute.

At the top of Vesco's current list of objectives is the absolute land speed record for a wheel-driven vehicle; in other words, he wants to beat the car land speed record of 658kph (409mph) set by the American Summers brothers' four-engined Golden Rod automobile. Meanwhile, Dennis Manning has joined forces with Henk Vink to produce a Dutch-based Kawasaki attempt on the motorcycle land speed record. Thus the future of the record continues to look just as exciting as its past. As a point of interest, the fastest thing on wheels so far is a rocket-powered projectile owned by the American Gary Gabelich, who recorded 1,002kph (622 mph) in 1970.

Since the early days of motorcycle world records, supercharging as a means to get more power from an engine has been heavily relied upon. The more efficient system of turbocharging which turns waste exhaust gases into power was tried in an unsuccessful attempt at the world record by Honda in November 1971. The reason the Honda attempt at Bonneville was unsuccessful was because of the streamliner's poor handling characteristics. Vesco had produced a streamliner with good handling right from the start. It allowed him to use all his available horsepower, even during the most recent turbocharged attempt, when Vesco had more power available than ever before. Most of his major problems have been to do with getting the power from the engines to the ground: steel reinforced belts connecting the engines, chains to the rear wheel and the rear tyre, all have caused setbacks due to shredding or breaking. Vesco's painstaking approach to the art of record breaking is the sum not only of his cautious and patient character, but also of scarcity and expense of the specialized parts for record breaking.

So far, however, Vesco has met and conquered problems such as these. The Honda attempt of November 1971 almost succeeded. Honda-America ran the project with two fuel-injected 750cc turbocharged engines giving about 300bhp. Behind the controls of the 'Hawk' was automobile magazine editor, Jon McKibben, then 34, who, with university degrees in mathematics and mechanical engineering, looked at the record more as an engineering challenge than as a glory goal.

His first run through the speed trap gave 461.185kph (286.567mph), more than 30kph (20mph) faster than the record, set by Rayborn. But the return run was unsuccessful as the Hawk crashed heavily. Its handling problems caused discussion in international motorcycle circles about the theories and practicalities of two-wheel streamliners. After two years and a dozen crashes, a halt was called to the effort.

The unsuccessful Honda Hawk attempt left Rayborn's Harley-Davidson 427.268 kph (265.492mph) record of 16 October 1970 intact.

One of the most interesting points about the Harley-Davidson record is that the challenge was met with a single V-twin engine while most other potential record holders were thinking in terms of two engines. The Sportster model engine, bored out to 1500cc, was housed in a shell 5.8m (19ft) long and only 0.6m (2ft) high, designed by Dennis Manning. Total weight was about 225kg (500lb). The engine was mounted directly in front of the rear wheel, while Rayborn was almost flat on his back and unable to see straight ahead because the front tyre obscured his view. Clear plastic panels on either side of the wheel provided a view of the black stripes which marked the edges of the 16 km (10 mile) long Bonneville salt.

When stationary, pneumatically operated skids balanced the machine. They also gave the machine stability at low speed. Rayborn retracted them at 160kph (100 mph), and when the machine had slowed down after each run, he would extend the skids and lean to one side to feel for them before coming to a standstill. During a practice run when Rayborn extended the skids, one of them only partially extended. Leaning on to it resulted in the skid digging in. It lifted the rear wheel and sent the machine into a roll. Rayborn was unhurt but the shell had to be repaired.

As it turned out, Rayborn could have taken the record in third gear with a ratio still to go for. With 34 teeth on the engine sprocket and a rev limit of 7,000rpm, the American projectile was capable of about 240kph (150mph) in first gear, 370kph (230mph) in second and 425kph (265mph) in third, but 400kph (250mph) was used as the change-up point to top gear.

Early records

It was a V-twin four-stroke which, according to historians, claimed the first ever official motorcycle land-speed record. That honour went to Harley-Davidson's great American rival of the time, the Indian. On 14 April 1920 at Daytona, Florida, Ernie Walker on a 994cc model set the record at 167.565kph (104.12mph). Ten years earlier at Brooklands, Charlie Collier of Matchless fame had received world acclaim by reaching 146.19kph (91.37 mph).

Smaller capacity motorcycles fought for speed recognition. The first man to break the 100mph (160kph) barrier on a 350cc machine was the Englishman Dougal Marchant, on a Blackburne-powered 348cc Chater-Lea. His speed was 161.296kph (100.81mph) on 1 April 1924. In the same year Marchant's friend, Frenchman Bert Le Vack, on a 996cc Brough Superior, raised the motorcycle world speed record to 190.48kph (119.05mph) over the flying kilometre with a best one-way speed of 195.584kph (122.24mph). Meanwhile, in America a four-cylinder ACE in the hands of Rod Wolverton reached 214.4kph (134mph), but this was not officially recognized by the governing body of world sport at the time.

The race for records continued throughout this golden decade of motorcycling. Le Vack and his speciall prepared Brough Superior regained the record after it had been wrested from him by Claude Temple (on a 996 OEC Temple in 1926), and C. M. Baldwin (on a 996 Zenith JAP in 1928) who was the first to break officially the 200kph barrier at 200.56kph (124.55 mph). Le Vack's final achievement of the decade was 207.33kph (128.75mph) at Arpajon in France.

The last record breaker of the decade was the West German *Rekord Meister*, Ernst Henne, whose name was to remain on the record books for more than 20 years. Riding flat twin BMW machines for the German Munich factory, he was at the start of the era during which BMW laid claim to nearly 200 records of various sorts. When Henne started his promising career, his biggest challenger was the Englishman Joe Wright. They outdid each other twice: in 1929 near Berlin, Henne achieved 216.75kph (134.682mph); opening the world record scene for the new decade, Wright, riding a supercharged 996cc JAP in an OEC Temple frame, reached 220.99kph (137.23mph) at Arpajon; Henne then challenged him successfully, and finally, to get the record back in the same year, Wright took two machines to Cork in Ireland, recapturing the record by a healthy margin at 242.59kph (150.65 mph). Two years later the irrepressible Henne was in Hungary. He pushed the record to 244.40kph (151.863mph) and continued to bolster BMW prestige.

For attempts which resulted in 272kph (169mph) by 1936, Henne's now supercharged machine was completely enclosed and, like today's streamliners, his forward vision was via a cockpit screen, though underneath the bodyshell he was mounted on the bike in the conventional manner. The following year saw 8kph (5mph) added to the record, as BMW machines continued to be improved; for this attempt the machine's bodyshell had been lengthened and Henne was again wearing his aerodynamic crash helmet.

In 1937 Henne experienced one of his toughest assignments when he was challenged by two worthy and successful opponents, Eric Fernihough of Great Britain (on a 995 Brough Superior JAP) and Piero Taruffi of Italy (on a 492 Gilera). However, Henne regained the record in the same year at 279.503kph (173.68mph).

Meanwhile in America, the Harley-Davidson factory produced an extraordinary-looking piece of machinery to break the Daytona Beach record in Florida in 1937. Their 'trump card' was rider Joe Petralli who took the record with a mean speed of 219.165kph (136.183mph) and best one-way speed of 225.2kph (139.93 mph). The record, amazingly, still stands today and at the time was also the absolute land speed record for an unsupercharged motorcycle.

Petralli felt the 1,000cc V-twin engine had more to give, but Bill Harley wanted to cash in immediately on the publicity for his factory, rather than delay while further attempts at higher speeds were made. His urgency to make the most of the situation was not surprising. The Daytona record had stood for ten years at 213.62kph (132.74 mph), to the credit of the rival Indian factory. Also a twin, the Indian had eight valves and was ridden by Johnny Seymour. The Harley which took the record was developed from a new bike launched in 1937. It was a modified version of the four-speed road model 61E. The record bike featured raised compression, two carburettors and special camshaft to give 65bhp at 5,700rpm.

Today the machine is on display in the Daytona Speed Museum, resplendent in full aerodynamic dress, though most of it was removed for the record run.

The following year, 1938, saw one of the saddest chapters in the speed record story with the death of Fernihough. He was a popular and respected rider because he bought and tuned his own machines. While trying to regain the record his supercharged JAP went out of control at approximately 290kph (180mph). He died at the Gyon roadside near Budapest in Hungary. Then came the outbreak of war in 1939, which left the world land speed record situation in abeyance for almost 15 years.

The post-war era

During the Second World War the record-holding BMW factory turned its attention to munitions supply, and it was not until 1955 that the Bavarian company was back in the records game. This time Wilhelm Noll set a sidecar record at 280kph (175mph). But the 1950s were lean years for the factory both in record breaking and road bike sales. It was not until the late 1960s that BMW sales looked really healthy again. By this time other factories had taken up the world speed gauntlet and the great record-setting era of BMW was almost over. Henne's longstanding 1937 record fell to the rival German factory, NSU, in 1951. Yet BMW still have a stake in the world records as holders of the 1,000cc solo six, 12 and 24-hour records, plus the 1,000cc 10km and 100km records. These current records are a great tribute to the original 1923 design which has earned for BMW the reputation of the 'Rolls-Royce of motorcycles', and the erroneous but popular belief that BMW stands for the 'best motorcycle in the world'.

NSU, the new record holders, crossed the Atlantic for Bonneville after their 1951 *autobahn* record had been broken in New Zealand by Russell Wright on a British 998cc Vincent in 1955. Ever since, the world record has been held by riders on the Utah salt flats. NSU in 1956 were the first to break the 300kph (186mph) barrier with their new record of 338.092kph (210.1mph) and, while they were about it, made the long journey even more worthwhile by capturing the 75cc class record. Using a supercharged 50cc moped engine in a streamlined shell, their tiny projectile in the hands of Wilhelm Herz recorded 194.72kph (121mph).

Six years later a new challenger came along in the shape of British Triumph, whose factory had gained a firm sales foothold in America. Triumph took the absolute record at Bonneville in September 1962 at 361.410kph (224.57mph) with a single 650cc engine in a 5 metre (17ft) streamliner, driven by American truck driver Bill Johnson. As a result a 650cc roadster model was christened the Bonneville, and became a best seller. Triumph power set the American national land speed record in 1966 at 395.363kph (245.667mph). Bob Leppan from Detroit, USA, used two 650cc alcohol-burning engines in his Gyronaut X-I for the Bonneville attempt and was the fastest motorcyclist ever until Vesco came along in 1970.

Many of the world records mentioned so far would not have been possible without the support and forbearance of wives and girlfriends. Not all were happy to remain in the background however; some wanted to experience the thrilling taste of new speed frontiers. The fastest of them is Californian film-stunt girl, Marcia Holley. She was loaned Don Vesco's world record-breaking Kawasaki streamliner to record 369.121kph (229.361mph) at the 1978 Bonneville speed week, and became the first woman to break the 200 mph (322kph) barrier on two wheels. One of the streamliner's two 1,000cc turbocharged engines was disconnected for her record attempt.

Seven years earlier Britain's Irene Scargill became the world's queen of speed by starting a record-breaking campaign; today she holds no less than ten world records in the cycle-car class. Her exploits with an AJS Starmaker are chronicled in the world record holder's chart. Five of her records were set in 1971 and the other five in the following year when she became engaged to Des Heckle, another world record holder. Between them the couple still hold a total of 14 world records.

One-way runs

While the world records so far discussed are the mean speed of a run and a return run, other world records exist for straight one-way runs. This type of competition takes the form of sprint and drag race meetings. In a sprint a rider races the clock. In a drag race two riders race each other and it is the first one at the end of the drag strip who wins, regardless of speed or elapsed time.

Drag racing grew up in America from illegal street racing and is now one of America's most colourful sports. It is also gaining in popularity in Europe and Australasia. Because it pits two riders against each other, drag racing has much more spectator appeal than sprinting.

The sport has heroes to ride the spectacular machines, and foremost among them is the Californian Russ Collins. In 1978 he came within less than 1kph (0.5 mph) of breaking the 200mph (322kph) terminal speed barrier for the standing start 400m ($\frac{1}{4}$ mile)—the fastest speed to have been set for this category. Collins' elapsed time of 7.62 seconds was also a world's best.

His machine used two 970cc Honda four-cylinder engines arranged in a V-formation. Weighing about 409kg (900lb) the bike was 3m (10ft) long, and Collins was stretched almost to his bodily limit to reach the controls. Supercharged by an American GMC unit, the engines were linked by Hy-Vo chain with duplex chain drive to the 254mm (10in) wide rear wheel. Estimated power for this incredible piece of automation was about 600bhp.

For sheer fantasy Collins had bettered this creation three years earlier, by using *three* four-cylinder Honda engines to create a monster of 3,288cc. In Collins' eyes this machine turned from dream into catastrophic reality when it threw him off at 270kph (170mph) in 1976. But before it did, Collins had set the drag racing world buzzing by recording the first ever seven second run for the standing start 400m ($\frac{1}{4}$-mile). His time was 7.96 seconds with a terminal speed of 284.548kph (176.81 mph). On the same day he bettered these figures to 7.861 seconds and 287.944kph (178.92mph) terminal speed. Estimated power was 500bhp and the machine cost 30,000 dollars and took 4,000 hours to build. Collins used belts instead of chains for the primary drive and nitrous oxide injection to fuel the engines. The bike used 9 litres (2 gal) of fuel mixture per 400m ($\frac{1}{4}$-mile) run and Collins worked out that each run cost him between 250 and 300 dollars. After his frightful crash on this giant two wheeler, Collins took a year to recover physically and almost another year to regain his mental will to race again on an even more powerful machine. It was

during this time that he started to build the Sorcerer, working on it first from his wheelchair and then on crutches. The burning desire to go faster and faster unfortunately, but inevitably, involves some riders in personal injury. At the same time this determination can also work constructively in helping a rider to recover rapidly from his injuries, and Collins has been a prime example of this.

One 'first' which must rank as one of the greatest achievements in drag racing was the first eight-second, standing start 400m ($\frac{1}{4}$-mile) run on a 500cc machine. On 17 September 1977, Brian Chapman, a carpenter from Essex, England, took his 500cc single-cylinder Vincent down Britain's only purpose-built drag strip at Santa Pod in Bedfordshire in 8.96 seconds. This world's best was all the more remarkable when it is considered that the home-tuned engine in a home-built frame was more than 20 years old. With the record run on his nitro-methane burning supercharged mount, Chapman won the British Drag Bike Championship of that year.

Unusual records

As well as setting the conventional records so far discussed, the motorcycle world, like any other, looks for the off-beat situations to establish new frontiers. Towards the end of 1977 a motorcycle club in the Midlands of Britain decided to set a record for pushing a motorcycle. Twelve members of the club pushed a Triumph Tiger 750 round a bicycle race track for twelve hours. The distance covered was 84.17km (52.3 miles). They set the target and shortly afterwards, in December 1977, a group of schoolboys raised it to 120.7km (75 miles).

A motorcycle holds the record for getting through London rush-hour traffic. Several forms of transport, including the underground train, taxi, car and bicycle, were used in an organized contest to find out which would be the quickest form of travelling through London. The motorcycle won by a significant margin.

Even rail records have been beaten. In June 1977 Welshman Richard Parkhouse knocked 17 minutes off the London to Aberdeen record which had stood at 8 hours, 32 minutes since 1895! He averaged 104.1kph (64.7mph) on a four-cylinder 750 Suzuki over the 869km (540 mile) route.

Riding from one end of the country to the other without falling foul of the law has provided an obvious challenge to adventurous riders for decades. One of the best-known such runs is from John O'Groats in Scotland to Land's End, the westernmost tip of the British mainland.

Two Wolverhampton enthusiasts, sharing a 350cc Royal Enfield, covered the 1,453km (903 mile) distance in 23 hours in 1950. Since then, numerous riders have tackled the run in well under a day's ride.

Records for going round the perimeter of a country are also popular. Claiming the round-Australia record won an English film-maker, Julian Grant, a 20,000 dollar wager. Grant rode a 750 Honda-4 road bike on the perimeter journey in 19 days, to take the record in 1974. He made a film of the journey, which was later shown to British television audiences, and while Grant was setting the record he gained widespread publicity in Australia. Another British rider, able seaman Terry O'Grady, currently holds the record. In 1978 he covered the 15,000km (9,315 miles) of the perimeter journey in eight days, 23 hours, 57 minutes.

Climbing mountains on motorcycles is a fairly old trick, sometimes used by manufacturers to gain publicity. One of the more dramatic feats in this context was the ascent of Africa's biggest mountain, Kilimanjaro, by New Zealand scrambles rider, Bill de Garis, in April 1973. Riding a 250 CZ, he took seven days to reach the 5,895m (19,340ft) summit. The following year a party of French riders tackled the climb. One of them, journalist Christian Lacombe, on a 360 Yamaha, won a French award for a novel he later wrote about the attempt.

One man who has reached metaphorical heights in his branch of motorcycling is colourful American stunt rider, Evel Knievel. But while Knievel is the world's best-known stunt man, a series of lesser known riders have taken the world long jump record from him. On 11 September 1976, in London, Britain's youngest ever world record holder, stunt rider Eddie Kidd, then 16, took the record by clearing 33m (108ft) over 13 double-decker buses. A sour note at this successful attempt was that insufficient run-off area had been allowed. Riding a 500cc CCM, Kidd's take-off speed had been about 150kph (95mph), and when he landed he had to lay the bike down to stop himself from careering into a ditch. Two friends who tried to catch him were hit by the slewing motorcycle, each suffering a broken leg, and Kidd's father broke his collarbone in the mêlée.

Two years later, in April 1978, Kidd added another double-decker bus to his act and cleared all 14 vehicles by a 12m (40ft) margin to regain the world record at 57.9m (190ft). Television cameras filmed the jump, which was seen by 10,000 fans at the site in Radlett, Hertfordshire, England.

The following month another Londoner laid a claim to the record. Robin 'Smudger' Winter-Smith, at 26, leapt a 250cc Suzuki moto-cross bike over 31 cars to clear 57.6m (189ft), a fraction less than Kidd, but unlike his younger rival Winter-Smith did not use a landing ramp. The force of Winter-Smith's machine hitting the ground caused bike and rider to part company, whereas Kidd had stayed on his mount. Until a definite set of rules is agreed upon worldwide, who is to say which of the two is the record holder? There is also the difference in height of both riders' take-off ramps to be considered.

Another unofficial world record holder is British display rider Dave Taylor. Born in 1942, and popularly known as 'the Wheelie King', he kept the front wheel of his Yamaha 400cc moto-cross bike aloft for 10.46km (6.5 miles) of the Belgian Spa Francorchamps road-race circuit in 1976. Taylor's exciting solo display rides have gained him a few more unique world achievements: at the 1977 Isle of Man TT he lapped the 60.75km (37.75 mile) course at 113kph (70mph) standing on footrests located on either side of the fuel tank of his 650cc Yamaha twin.

One man who did not mind the risk of singeing himself or his Norton-powered AJS, but did not want to reveal his identity, set a new 'tunnel of fire' record on 4 February 1973 on the Isle of Wight. The mystery man travelled 24.4km (80ft) through the blazing tunnel—in which the temperature was estimated to be almost 540°C (1,000°F)—in only 2.5 seconds. When he emerged, his speed was estimated at 105kph (65mph). The hooded rider was then whisked away in a speedboat from nearby Wight Marina, to maintain his cloak of secrecy.

At the time of writing two American riders were waiting to hear if their claim for an absolute round the world record would be verified. They covered the 56,000km (35,000 mile) distance in 79 days. Their machine was a 1,000cc Kawasaki-4 solo with full touring equipment plus a trailer, giving their vehicle an overall length of 5.03m (16ft 6in). The trailer converted into a home for the riders, ex-Marine Colonel Ernie O'Gaffney and motorcycle accessory businessman Yan Davis, both from California. Their starting point for the 56,000km (35,000 miles) trip was New York and as their 1,000kg (one ton) vehicle moved off they straight away claimed a 'first' because the bike and trailer was the longest and heaviest in the history of the record. The fact that O'Gaffney, managing editor of a newspaper, had only learned how to ride a motorcycle six months before the trip illustrates the way in which the challenge of two wheels—or four, including the trailer—seems to bring out people's sense of adventure, and also their love of new challenges.

The kings of speed on two wheels

1920 Ernie Walker (994 Indian) at Daytona, USA: 167.565kph (104.12mph).

1923 Claud Temple (996 British Anzani) at Brooklands, GB: 174.580kph (108.98mph).

1924 Bert le Vack (998 Brough Superior) at Arpajon, France: 191.590kph (118.98mph).

1926 Claud Temple (996 OEC Temple) at Arpajon, France: 195.330kph (121.30mph).

1928 O. M. Baldwin (996 Zenith JAP) at Arpajon, France: 200.560kph (124.55mph).

1929 Bert le Vack (998 Brough Superior) at Arpajon, France: 207.330kph (128.75mph).

1929 Ernst Henne (735 BMW) at Berlin, Germany: 216.75kph (134.682mph).

1930 Joe Wright (994 OEC Temple) at Arpajon, France: 220.990kph (137.23mph).

1930 Ernst Henne (735 BMW) at Ingolstadt, Germany: 221.540kph (137.58mph).

1930 Joe Wright (998 Zenith JAP), Cork, Ireland: 242.590kph (150.65mph).

1932 Ernst Henne (735 BMW) at Tat, Hungary: 244.400kph (151.863mph).

1934 Ernst Henne (735 BMW) at Gyon, Hungary: 246.069kph (152.81mph).

1935 Ernst Henne (735 BMW) at Frankfurt, Germany: 256.046kph (159.01mph).

1936 Ernst Henne (495 BMW) at Frankfurt, Germany: 272.006kph (169.017mph).

1937 Eric Fernihough (995 Brough Superior JAP) at Gyon, Hungary: 273.244kph (169.786mph).

1937 Piero Taruffi (492 Gilera) at Breschia, Italy: 274.181kph (170.27mph).

1937 Ernst Henne (495 BMW) at Frankfurt, Germany: 279.503kph (173.57mph).

1951 Wilhelm Herz (499 NSU) at Ingolstadt, Germany: 290.322kph (180.29mph).

1955 Russell Wright (998 Vincent HRD) at Christchurch, New Zealand 297.640kph (184.83mph).

1956 Wilhelm Herz (499 NSU) at Bonneville, USA: 338.092kph (210.1mph).

1962 Bill Johnson (649 Triumph) at Bonneville, USA: 361.410kph (224.57mph).

1966 Bob Leppan (1298 Triumph) at Bonneville, USA: 395.363kph (245.60mph).

1970 Don Vesco (700 Yamaha) at Bonneville, USA: 405.25kph (251.66mph).

1970 Cal Rayborn (1480 Harley-Davidson) at Bonneville, USA: 410.98kph (255.37mph).

1970 Cal Rayborn (1480 Harley-Davidson) at Bonneville, USA: 427.268kph (265.49mph).

1975 Don Vesco (1496 Yamaha) at Bonneville, USA: 487.515kph (302.92mph).

1978 Don Vesco (1996 Kawasaki) at Bonneville, USA: 512.734kph (318.598mph).

STANDING START WORLD RECORDS

Solo   * No of cylinders.

Category	Distance (or time)	Rider	Machine	Capacity (in cc)	*	Time (or distance)	Speed in kph(mph)	Date set
50 cc	¼ mile	A. Toerson	Kreidler	49.61	1	15.5685s	93.034(57.809)	05–10–68
	1km	A. Toerson	Kreidler	49.61	1	30.3185s	118.739(73.781)	06–10–68
	1 mile	A. Toerson	Kreidler	49.61	1	44.392s	130.510(81.095)	06–10–68
	10km	R. Kuenz	Kreidler-Meo	49.80	1	3m 19.131s	180.785(112.335)	23/5–10–65
	100km	V. Kramer	Zundapp	49.81	1	37m 02.20s	162.002(100.663)	14–05–65
	1000km	D. Brandt, P. Eser, A. Lebner, V. Kramer, H. Rosenbach, G. Sandfelder	Zundapp	49.81	1	6hr 49m 10.40s	146.637(91.116)	12/13–05–65
	1hr	V. Kramer	Zundapp	49.81	1	162.609km (101.041m)	162.609(101.041)	14–05–65
	6hr	D. Brandt, P. Eser, A. Lebner, V. Kramer, H. Rosenbach, G. Sandfelder	Zundapp	49.81	1	886.792km (551.027m)	147.798(91.837)	12/13–05–65
	12hr	D. Brandt, P. Eser, A. Lebner, V. Kramer, H. Rosenbach, G. Sandfelder	Zundapp	49.81	1	1644.474km (1021.829m)	137.039(85.152)	12/13–05–65
	24hr	G. E. Marchesani, R. Patrignani, L. Pastori, G. Pernigotti, L. Spinello, G. P. Zubiani	Garelli	49.02	1	2612.022km (1623.035m)	108.834(67.626)	3/4–11–63
75cc	¼ mile	O. Buscherini	Minarelli	74.72	1	14.535s	99.649(61.919)	06–11–75
	1km	O. Buscherini	Minarelli	74.72	1	28.56s	126.050(78.324)	06–11–75
	1 mile	R. Sullivan	Yamaha	72.865	1	49.305s	117.500(73.011)	24–09–72
	10km	P. Cava	Minarelli	73.5	1	4m 32.80s	131.964(81.999)	19–11–66
	100km	P. Cava	Minarelli	73.5	1	44m 05.80s	136.064(84.546)	19–11–66
	1000km	J. P. Behra, G. Bertrand, G. Monneret, A. Nebout	Cecatto	74.70	1	8hr 47m 20.45s	113.778(70.698)	27/28–08–60
	1hr	P. Cava	Minarelli	73.5	1	135.769km (84.363m)	135.769(84.363)	19–11–66
	6hr	J. P. Behra, G. Bertrand, G. Monneret, A. Nebout	Cecatto	74.70	1	690.430km (429.013m)	115.071(71.502)	27/8–08–60
	12hr	(as above)	Cecatto	74.70	1	1359.603km (844.818m)	113.300(70.401)	27/8–08–60
	24hr	(as above)	Cecatto	74.70	1	2572.211km (1598.298m)	107.175(66.595)	27/8–08–65
100cc	¼ mile	P. Bianchi	Minarelli	99.666	1	14.785s	97.964(60.872)	13–10–73
	1km	P. Bianchi	Minarelli	99.666	1	28.195s	127.681(79.337)	13–10–73
	1 mile	P. Cava	Minarelli	99.66	1	43.485s	133.232(82.787)	03–10–71
	10km	H. P. Mueller	NSU	99.80	1	3m 20.00s	180.000(111.847)	07–08–56
	100km	S. Ciceri	Ducati	99.80	1	36m 41.60s	163.517(101.605)	30–11–56
	1000km	M. Carini, S. Ciceri	Ducati	99.80	1	6hr 28m 13.40s	154.550(96.033)	30–11–56

Category	Distance (or time)	Rider	Machine	Capacity (in cc)	*	Time (or distance)	Speed in kph(mph)	Date set
	1hr	S. Ciceri	Ducati	99.80	1	162.990km (101.277m)	162.990(101.277)	30–11–56
	6hr	M. Carini, S. Ciceri	Ducati	99.80	1	923.814km (574.031m)	153.969(95.672)	30–11–56
	12hr	Rapeau, Renaud	Prester Aubier Dunne	98.00	1	976.684km (606.883m)	81.390(50.573)	04–05–33
	24hr	J. Mathieu, M. Panin, M. Rancon, J. Rouger	Rivasport AMC	100.00	1	1935.777km (1202.836m)	80.660(50.20)	31–03–55
125cc	¼ mile	D. Heckle	Yamaha	124.889	2	13.245s	109.354(67.949)	25–09–71
	1km	D. Heckle	Yamaha	124.889	2	25.06s	143.655(89.263)	25–09–71
	1 mile	D. Heckle	Yamaha	124.889	2	36.54s	158.555(98.522)	03–10–71
	10km	H. P. Mueller	NSU	125.00	1	3m 01.00s	198.882(123.580)	07–08–56
	100km	R. Ferri	Gilera	124.70	2	30m 25.60s	197.191(122.529)	23–11–57
	1000km	D. Ambrosini, R. Ferri, R. Rizzi	Lambretta	123.00	1	7hr 32m 21.70s	132.640(82.419)	05–10–50
	1hr	R. Ferri	Gilera	124.70	2	197.774km (122.891m)	197.774(122.891)	23–11–57
	6hr	D. Ambrosini, R. Ferri, R. Rizzi	Lambretta	123.00	1	798.860km (496.389m)	133.143(82.731)	05–10–50
	12hr	(as above)	Lambretta	123.00	1	1591.617km (988.985m)	132.635(82.416)	05–10–50
	24hr	R. Rizzi, M. Brunori, M. Masserini, L. Masetti	Lambretta	123.00	1	2450.000km (1522.359m)	102.080(63.430)	19/20–04–49
175cc	¼ mile	O. Buscherini	Minarelli	174.148	1	12.415	116.660(72.489)	06–11–75
	1km	O. Buscherini	Minarelli	174.148	1	24.425	147.381(91.578)	06–11–75
	1 mile	P. Irons	Montaco	173.628	1	37.0	156.570(97.288)	24–09–72
	10km	W. Winkler	DKW	172.00	2	3m 55.57s	152.821(94.959)	27–10–37
	100km	R. Ferri	Gilera	172.80	2	28m 52.91s	207.743(129.086)	25–11–57
	1000km	G. Franzoni, A. Montanari	Bianchi	174.70	1	5hr 23m 09.80s	185.664(115.366)	19–11–57
	1hr	R. Ferri	Gilera	172.80	2	208.521km (129.569m)	208.521(129.569)	25–11–57
	6hr	G. Franzoni, A. Montanari	Bianchi	174.70	1	1114.328km (692.411m)	185.721(115.402)	19–11–57
	12hr	Cama, Gonzales, Grace, Monneret, Quintanilla	Bultaco	174.80	1	1725.158km (1071.963m)	143.763(89.330)	1/2–10–60
	24hr	(as above)	Bultaco	174.80	1	3162.628km (1965.166m)	133.776(83.125)	1/2–10–60
250cc	¼ mile	M. Hand	Honda	247.00	2	10.50s	137.95(85.718)	22–09–73
	1km	M. Hand	Honda	238.32	2	21.71s	165.820(103.036)	23–09–72
	1 mile	D. Heckle	Yamaha	246.50	2	33.26s	174.189(108.236)	29–09–70
	10km	G. Sandri	Moto Guzzi	247.00	1	3m 08.90s	190.577(118.419)	20–10–39
	100km	P. Monneret	NSU	249.00	1	31m 16.00s	191.896(119.239)	23–05–56
	1000km	T. Robb, S. Graham, B. Smith, M. Hodder	Suzuki	247.34	2	6hr 35m 19.6s.	151.786(94.315)	01–08–68
	1hr	P. Monneret	NSU	249.00	1	190.000km (118.061m)	190.000(118.061)	23–09–56
	6hr	T. Robb, S. Graham, B. Smith, M. Hodder	Suzuki	247.34	2	907.919km (564.155m)	151.319(94.025)	01–08–68
	12 hr	T. Robb, S. Graham, B. Smith, M. Hodder	Suzuki	247.34	2	1791.674km (1113.295m)	149.306(92.774)	01–08–68

Category	Distance (or time)	Rider	Machine	Capacity (in cc)	*	Time (or distance)	Speed in kph (mph)	Date set
	24hr	G. Monneret, P. Monneret, Moury, Weingartmann	Puch	248.00	2	2891.000km (1796.384m)	120.458(74.849)	16–08–51
350cc	¼ mile	M. Hand	Honda	253.1	2	10.255s	141.23(87.756)	23–07–77
	1km	J. Balchin	BSA	349.8	1	20.125s	178.881(111.152)	04–10–75
	1 mile	L. Julian	Triumph	343.47	2	32.425s	178.677(111.025)	03–10–71
	10km	W. Herz	NSU	347.285	2	2m 38.829s	226.658(140.839)	18–08–66
	100km	R. McIntyre	Gilera	349.70	4	26m 27.80s	226.729(140.883)	27–11–57
	1000km	A. Amm, E. Oliver	Norton	348.30	1	5hr 11m 05.00s	192.690(119.732)	8/9–11–53
	1hr	R. McIntyre	Gilera	349.70	4	227.519km (141.374m)	227.519(141.374)	27–11–57
	6hr	A. Amm, E. Oliver	Norton	348.30	1	1160.00km (720.791m)	193.333(120.132)	08–11–53
	12hr	F. Anderson, H. D. Dale, W. A. Lomas	Moto Guzzi	348.80	1	1975.000km (1227.208m)	164.583(102.267)	01–11–55
	24hr	E. Crooks, F. Wireway, B. Ball, H. Anscheidt	Suzuki	256.59	2	3496.521km (2172.637m)	145.688(90.526)	01–08–68
500cc	¼ mile	P. Miller	Triumph	489.25	2	9.935s	145.770(90.577)	30–09–72
	1km	J. Hobbs	Triumph	490.88	2	19.545s	184.190(114.450)	02–10–71
	1 mile	B. White	Triumph	492.448	2	28.58s	202.72(125.964)	24–09–72
	10km	W. A. Lomas	Moto Guzzi	499.30	8	2m 27.80s	243.572(151.349)	26–02–57
	100km	M. Hailwood	MV Agusta	491.89	4	25m 44.74s	233.048(144.809)	02–02–64
	1000km	G. Monneret, P. Monneret, P. Cherrier, A. Dagan, R. Leconte, B. Jacquier, B. J. Goodman, B. M. Smith	Velocette	499.5	1	5hr 54m 22.16s	169.314(105.207)	18/19–03–61
	1hr	M. Hailwood	MV Agusta	491.89	4	233.081km (144.830m)	233.081(144.830)	02–02–64
	6hr	(see 1,000km)	Velocette	499.5	1	1016.436km (631.584m)	169.406(105.264)	18–03–61
	12hr	(see 1,000km)	Velocette	499.5	1	2021.183km (1255.905m)	168.432(104.659)	18/19–03–61
	24hr	(see 1,000km)	Velocette	499.5	1	3864.223km (2401.117m)	161.009(100.046)	18/19–03–61
750cc	¼ mile	D. Hocking	Triumph	738.029	2	9.78s	148.09(92.019)	23–09–72
	1km	D. Hocking	Triumph	646.141	2	18.81s	191.387(118.922)	25–09–72
	1 mile	P. Windross	Triumph	649.30	2	28.165s	205.703(127.818)	03–10–71
	10km	S. McLaughlin	Kawasaki	748.642	3	2m 25.09s	248.120(154.175)	18–03–77
	100km	C. Neilson	Kawasaki	652.120	4	27m 52.772s	215.211(133.726)	15–03–77
	1000km	C. Neilson, W. Fulton, S. McLaughlin, R. Cleek	Kawasaki	652.120	4	4hr 51m 20.187s	205.946(127.969)	16–03–77
	1hr	G. Romero	Yamaha	694.87	4	242.0783km (150.420m)	242.0783(150.420)	03–04–74
	6hr	C. Neilson, W. Fulton, S. McLaughlin, R. Cleek, P. McDonald	Kawasaki	652.120	4	1232.673km (765.948m)	205.446(127.658)	16–03–77
	12hr	W. Cooley, K. Code, J. Hateley	Kawasaki	652.120	4	2288.129km (1421.777m)	190.676(119.481)	15–03–77
	24hr	R. Hagie, L. Hindle, H. Klinzmann, D. Cox, S. Moses, R. Milligan, R. Cleek,						

Category	Distance (or time)	Rider	Machine	Capacity (in cc)	★	Time (or distance)	Speed in kph(mph)	Date set
		M. Kidd	Kawasaki	652.120	4	4523.875km (2811.006m)	188.494(117.125)	15–03–77
1,000cc	¼ mile	H. Vink	Kawasaki	963.00	4	9.255s	156.49(97.238)	23–07–77
	1km	H. Vink	Kawasaki	963.00	4	16.68s	215.82(134.104)	24–07–77
	1 mile	J. Hobbs	Triumph	998.56	4	26.395s	219.496(136.388)	01–10–72
	10km	A. Gossutti	BMW	981.984	2	2m 50.09s	211.652(131.514)	29–10–77
	100km	A. Gossutti	BMW	981.984	2	27m 11.09s	220.711(137.143)	29–10–77
	1000km	G. Mandracchi, R. Patrignani, F. Trabalzini	Moto Guzzi	758.00	2	4hr 51m 21.40s	205.933(127.961)	30–10–69
	1hr	A. Pagani	Guzzi	797.50	2	217.040km (134.862m)	217.040(134.862)	31–10–69
	6hr	D. Beinhauer, H. Dahne, M. Milan, A. Gossutti, E. Zanini, A. Clerieuzio	BMW	981.984	2	1150.052km (714.609m)	191.675(119.101)	29–10–77
	12hr	D. Beinhauer, H. Dahne, M. Milan, A. Gossutti, E. Zanini, A. Clerieuzio	BMW	981.984	2	2290.449km (1423.219m)	190.87(118.601)	29–10–77
	24hr	D. Beinhauer, H. Dahne, M. Milan, A. Gossutti, E. Zanini, A. Clerieuzio	BMW	981.984	2	4067.203km (2527.243m)	169.466(105.301)	29–10–77
1,300cc	¼ mile	H. Vink	Kawasaki	1140.6	4	8.805s	164.49(102.209)	23–07–77
	1km	H. Vink	Kawasaki	1018.00	4	18.425s	195.360(122.391)	04–10–75
	1 mile	G. Brown	Vincent	1145.00	2	27.979s	207.067(128.665)	22–10–67
	10km	S. McLaughlin	Kawasaki	1030.5594	4	3m 6.496s	193.032(119.945)	17–03–77
	100km	S. McLaughlin, W. Fulton	Kawasaki	1030.5594	4	31m 8.080s	192.710(119.744)	17–03–77
	1000km	B. Farnsworth, S. Moses, S. McLaughlin, K. Kiefer, W. Fulton	Kawasaki	1030.5594	4	5hr 15m 41.697s	190.055(118.095)	17–03–77
	1hr	S. McLaughlin, W. Fulton	Kawasaki	1030.5594	4	191.511km (118.999m)	191.511(118.999)	17–03–77
	6hr	B. Farnsworth, S. Moses, S. McLaughlin, J. Corpe, K. Kiefer, W. Fulton	Kawasaki	1030.5594	4	1135.7758km (705.738m)	189.2958(117.623)	17–03–77
3,000cc	¼ mile	J. Hobbs	Weslake	1684.7	4	9.165s	158.03(98.195)	24–07–77
	1km	B. Jones	Volkswagen	1475.3	4	22.37s	160.92(99.991)	24–07–77

Sidecars

Category	Distance (or time)	Rider	Machine	Capacity (in cc)	★	Time (or distance)	Speed in kph(mph)	Date set
250cc	¼ mile	A. Reynard	Royal Enfield	247.821	1	14.61s	99.135(61.560)	25–09–71
	1km	A. Reynard	Royal Enfield	244.61	1	28.295s	127.23(79.057)	02–10–71
	1 mile	A. Reynard	Royal Enfield	244.61	1	42.13s	137.517(85.449)	02–10–71
350cc	¼ mile	N. Hyde	Triumph	348.00	2	13.643s	106.164(65.967)	05–10–68

Category	Distance (or time)	Rider	Machine	Capacity (in cc)	*	Time (or distance)	Speed in kph(mph)	Date set
	1km	N. Hyde	Triumph	348.00	2	26.373s	136.503(84.819)	06–10–68
	1 mile	E. Hurley	Norton	348.00	1	38.720s	149.629(92.975)	21–10–67
	10km	W. Doran	AJS	349.00	1	4m 10.98s	143.440(89.129)	20–10–51
	100km	W. Doran	AJS	349.00	1	40m 25.80s	148.400(92.211)	20–10–51
	1000km	G. Monneret, W. Doran	AJS	349.00	1	7hr 1m 39.40s	142.300(88.421)	20–10–51
	1hr	W. Doran	AJS	349.00	1	148.027km (91.980m)	148.027(91.980)	20–10–51
	6hr	W. Doran, G. Monneret	AJS	349.00	1	855.201km (531.397m)	142.533(88.566)	20–10–51
	12hr	G. Monneret, A. Barthelemy, F. Haas	Koehler Escoffier	346.00	1	1288.466km (800.616m)	107.437(66.758)	13/14–10–33
	24hr	(as above)	Koehler Escoffier	346.00	1	2376.000km (1476.378m)	99.000(61.516)	13/14–10–33
500cc	¼ mile	C. van Dongen	Honda	493.3	4	11.925s	121.45(75.466)	24–07–77
	1km	N. Hyde	Triumph	498.00	2	24.940s	144.346(89.686)	11–10–69
	1 mile	N. Hyde	Triumph	498.00	2	34.640s	167.252(103.926)	12–10–69
	10km	W. L. Handley	FN	498.00	1	3m 52.20s	155.039(96.337)	12–09–30
	1000km	A. Denly, O. N. Baldwin	AJS	495.00	1	8hr 35m 18.73s	116.434(72.349)	23–04–30
	6hr	A. Denly, L. P. Driscoll	AJS	495.00	1	707.000km (439.309m)	117.833(73.218)	28–09–29
	12hr	A. Denly, O. N. Baldwin	AJS	495.00	1	1336.000km (830.152m)	111.333(69.179)	23–04–30
750cc	¼ mile	P. Harman	Triumph	746.9	2	10.035s	144.335(89.686)	30–09–72
	1km	N. Hyde	Triumph	736.06	3	21.87s	164.609(102.283)	25–09–71
	1 mile	N. Hyde	Triumph	739.32	3	32.015s	180.965(112.446)	03–10–71
	10km	E. Oliver	Norton	597.00	1	3m 54.00s	153.846(95.595)	27–10–50
	100km	E. Oliver	Norton	597.00	1	36m 54.00s	162.612(101.042)	25–10–49
	1000km	A. Debay, R. Milhoux, A. Sbaiz	Gillet Herstal	588.00	1	7hr 28m 07.00s	133.893(83.197)	10–10–30
	1hr	E. Oliver	Norton	597.00	1	156.200km (97.058m)	156.200(97.058)	27–10–50
	6hr	(see 1000km)	Gillet Herstal	588.00	1	803.000km (498.961m)	133.833(83.160)	10–10–30
	12hr	(see 1000km)	Gillet Herstal	588.00	1	1497.000km (930.193m)	124.750(77.516)	28–10–30
1,000cc	¼ mile	J. Jansen	Kawasaki	938.1	4	11.255s	128.69(79.964)	24–07–77
	1km	N. Hyde	Triumph	823.11	3	21.285s	169.130(105.093)	29–09–72
	1 mile	G. Brown	Vincent	997.52	2	30.346s	190.916(118.630)	02–11–66
	10km	V. B. Pope	Special	996.00	2	3m 31.00s	170.616(106.016)	03–07–52
	100km	C. F. Temple	OEC Temple	994.00	2	41m 35.44s	144.263(89.641)	04–05–26
	1hr	C. F. Temple	OEC Temple	994.00	2	143.880km (89.403m)	143.880(89.403)	04–05–26
	6hr	Waterman, Taylor	Coventry Eagle	986.00	2	687.900km (427.441m)	114.650(71.240)	04–06–29
	12hr	J. D. Marwin, J. A. O. Sullivan	Harley-Davidson	986.00	2	981.070km (609.609m)	81.760(50.803)	13–07–20
1,300cc	¼ mile	A. Brown	Vincent	1147.0	2	11.746s	123.310(76.621)	21–10–67
	1km	G. Brown	Vincent	1147.0	2	21.625s	166.470(103.440)	04–11–66
	1 mile	G. Brown	Vincent	1147.0	2	31.057s	186.548(115.916)	03–11–66

Cyclecars

Category	Distance (or time)	Rider	Machine	Capacity (in cc)	*	Time (or distance)	Speed in kph (mph)	Date set
250cc	¼ mile	Miss I. Scargill	AJS	248.41	1	15.38s	94.170(58.514)	01–10–72
	1km	Miss I. Scargill	AJS	248.41	1	29.48s	122.110(75.876)	01–10–72
	1 mile	Miss I. Scargill	AJS	248.41	1	41.375s	140.012(86.999)	01–10–72
	100km	H. W. Boensch	Messerschmidt	192.50	1	55m 57.00s	107.235(66.633)	29–08–55
	1000km	H. W. Boensch, K. Eisele, F. Fend, H. Rathjen, H. Schwind, H. Stumm	Messerschmidt	192.50	1	9hr 25m 04.20s	106.182(65.978)	29/30–08–55
	1hr	H. W. Boensch	Messerschmidt	192.50	1	107.200km (66.611m)	107.200(66.611)	29–08–55
	6hr	(see 1000km)	Messerschmidt	192.50	1	637.400km (396.062m)	106.233(66.010)	29/30–08–55
	12hr	(see 1000km)	Messerschmidt	192.50	1	1276.0km (792.870m)	106.333(66.072)	29/30–08–55
	24hr	(see 1000km)	Messerschmidt	192.50	1	2473.0km (1536.651m)	103.041(64.027)	29/30–08–55
350cc	¼ mile	Miss I. Scargill	AJS	250.60	1	15.625s	92.697(57.599)	02–10–71
	1km	Miss I Scargill	AJS	250.60	1	30.11s	119.561(74.292)	02–10–71
	1 mile	Miss I. Scargill	AJS	250.60	1	43.495s	133.202(82.767)	03–10–71
	10km	Mrs Stewart	Morgan JAP	346.00	1	5m 27.60s	109.890(68.282)	23–11–29
	100km	H. C. Lones	Morgan JAP	346.00	1	55m 56.43s	107.260(66.648)	04–10–29
	1hr	H. C. Lones	Morgan JAP	346.00	1	107.305km (66.676m)	107.305(66.676)	04–10–29
	6hr	J. J. Hall	R.P. JAP	344.00	1	471.664km (293.078m)	78.610(48.846)	01–06–27
	12hr	R. Seroy	Royal Sport	342.00	1	556.347km (345.698m)	46.360(28.807)	08–06–30
	24hr	R. Seroy	Royal Sport	342.00	1	1120.240km (696.085m)	46.680(29.006)	08–06–30
500cc	¼ mile	S. Whitton	Triovad	497.00	2	72.580s	115.137(71.543)	04–10–75
	1km	A. McPhail	Triumph	498.74	2	24.5735s	146.499(91.030)	06–10–68
	1 mile	A. McPhail	Triumph	499.00	2	36.310s	159.560(99.146)	12–10–69
	10km	H. C. Lones	Morgan JAP	498.00	1	4m 40.68s	128.259(79.696)	14–08–34
	100km	H. C. Lones	Morgan JAP	498.00	1	44m 19.06s	135.386(84.125)	14–08–34
	1000km	H. C. Lones	Morgan JAP	498.00	1	9hr 1m 30.98s	110.799(68.847)	04–09–34
	1hr	H. C. Lones	Morgan JAP	498.00	1	135.872km (84.427m)	135.872(84.427)	14–08–34
	6hr	H. C. Lones	Morgan JAP	498.00	1	657.174km (408.350m)	109.529(68.058)	04–09–34
	12hr	Annino	Annino JAP	497.00	1	718.960km (446.741m)	59.910(37.226)	08–06–30
	24hr	Biolay	Monotrace	499.00	1	1279.080km (794.783m)	53.300(33.119)	14/15–05–32
750cc	¼ mile	D. Green	Triumph	648.996	2	12.66s	114.408(71.090)	25–09–71
	1km	D. Green	Triumph	648.996	2	24.61s	146.281(90.895)	25–09–71
	1 mile	D. Green	Triumph	650.00	2	36.235s	159.889(99.350)	27–09–70
	10km	H. C. Lones	Morgan JAP	741.00	2	4m 04.11s	147.474(91.636)	02–11–34
	100km	M. Sandford	Sandford	723.00	4	39m 25.01s	152.219(94.585)	19–04–34
	1000km	H. Hartmann, H. Steiner, O. Koch, Bodes, H. Polensky, A. Brudes	Goliath	735.00	2	7hr 17m 48.50s	137.057(85.163)	09–08–51
	1hr	M. Sandford	Sandford	723.00	4	152.604km (94.824m)	152.604(94.824)	19–04–34
	6hr	(see 1000km)	Goliath	735.00	2	830.774km (516.219m)	138.462(86.036)	09–08–51
	12hr	(see 1000km)	Goliath	735.00	2	1700.549km (1056.672m)	141.712(88.056)	07/8–08–51
	24hr	(see 1000km)	Goliath	735.00	2	3130.923km (1945.465m)	130.455(81.061)	09/10–08–51

Category	Distance (or time)	Rider	Machine	Capacity (in cc)	*	Time (or distance)	Speed in kph (mph)	Date set
1,000cc	¼ mile	T. Kemper Smith	Triumph	758.0	2	13.07s	110.80(68.848)	23–07–77
	1km	R. Vane	Vincent	997.524	2	25.995s	138.448(86.028)	24–09–72
	1 mile	R. Vane	Vincent	997.524	2	36.68s	157.950(98.146)	24–09–72
	10km	Mrs Stewart	Morgan JAP	996.00	2	3m 45.13s	159.910(99.363)	10–11–29
	100km	Mrs Stewart	Morgan JAP	965.00	2	36m 22.79s	164.930(102.483)	12–09–30
	1000km	Mrs Stewart, W. D. Hawkes	Morgan JAP	996.00	2	7hr 43m 05.42s	129.560(80.505)	02–04–30
	1hr	Mrs Stewart	Morgan JAP	996.00	2	163.438km (101.556m)	163.438(101.556)	07–09–29
	6hr	Mrs Stewart	Morgan JAP	996.00	2	792.725km (492.576m)	132.120(82.096)	27–03–30
	12hr	Mrs Stewart, W. D. Hawkes	Morgan JAP	996.00	2	1258.245km (781.837m)	107.350(66.704)	12–09–29
1,300cc	¼ mile	A. McPhail	Ford	1256.00	4	12.48s	116.05(72.110)	23–09–72
	1km	O. Greenwood	BMC	1298.00	4	26.507s	135.810(84.388)	22–10–67
	10km	Mrs Stewart	Morgan JAP	1091.00	2	3m 37.76s	165.320(102.725)	07–08–30
	100km	Mrs Stewart	Morgan JAP	1091.00	2	35m 49.44s	167.490(104.073)	19–12–31
	1000km	M. Sandford, Gueret, Gaudichet	Sandford	1081.00	4	7hr 30m 09.48s	133.290(82.823)	30–05–33
	1hr	Mrs Stewart	Morgan JAP	1091.00	2	164.497km (102.214m)	164.497(102.214)	28–12–30
	6hr	(see 1000km)	Sandford	1081.00	4	799.771km (496.955m)	133.295(82.826)	30–05–33
	12hr	(see 1000km)	Sandford	1081.00	4	1589.993km (987.976m)	132.494(82.328)	30–05–33
	24hr	Mrs Stewart, S. C. H. Davies	Morgan JAP	1096.00	2	2682.809km (1667.020m)	111.783(69.459)	15/16–05–30

FLYING START WORLD RECORDS

Solo

Category	Distance (or time)	Rider	Machine	Capacity (in cc)	*	Time (or distance)	Speed in kph(mph)	Date set
50cc	1km	H. van Kessel	Kreidler	49.863	1	16.2623s	221.5861(137.687)	06–09–77
	1 mile	R. Kunz	Kreidler	49.80	1	27.821s	208.247(129.399)	23–10–65
75cc	1km	M. Pasolini	Aermacchi	73.10	1	21.50s	167.439(104.042)	04–04–56
	1 mile	M. Pasolini	Aermacchi	73.10	1	35.90s	161.345(100.255)	04–04–56
100cc	1km	H. P. Mueller	NSU	99.80	1	16.20s	222.192(138.064)	03–08–56
	1 mile	H. P. Mueller	NSU	99.80	1	24.10s	222.160(138.044)	03–08–56
125cc	1km	H. P. Mueller	NSU	125.00	1	14.90s	241.610(150.129)	07–08–56
	1 mile	H. P. Mueller	NSU	125.00	1	24.00s	241.401(150.0)	07–08–56
175cc	1km	A. Venturi	Minarelli	173.62	1	18.67s	192.822(119.814)	02–10–71
	1 mile	A. Venturi	Minarelli	173.62	1	30.13s	192.287(119.482)	03–10–71
250cc	1 km	W. Martin	Yamaha	247.80	2	12.829s	280.60(174.357)	25–09–65
	1 mile	W. Martin	Yamaha	247.80	2	20.707s	279.78(173.847)	25–09–65
350cc	1 km	W. Herz	NSU	347.40	2	11.86s	303.541(188.612)	02–08–56
	1 mile	W. Herz	NSU	347.40	2	19.013s	304.720(189.344)	02–08–56
500cc	1km	W. Herz	NSU	499.00	2	10.648s	338.092(210.081)	04–08–56
	1 mile	W. Herz	NSU	499.00	2	17.07s	339.404(210.896)	04–08–56

Category	Distance (or time)	Rider	Machine	Capacity (in cc)	*	Time (or distance)	Speed in kph(mph)	Date set
750cc	1km	D. Vesco	Yamaha	747.964	4	9.299s	387.138(240.556)	28–09–75
	1 mile	D. Vesco	Yamaha	747.964	4	14.955s	387.404(240.722)	28–09–75
1,000cc	1km	R. Wright	Vincent HRD	998.00	2	12.095s	297.640(184.945)	02–07–55
	1 mile	E. Fernihough	Brough Superior JAP	995.00	2	21.38s	270.983(168.381)	19–04–37
1,300cc	1km	F. Cooper	Triumph	1298.0	4	11.94s	301.507(187.348)	25–09–71
	1 mile	F. Cooper	Triumph	1284.421	4	19.66s	294.690(183.112)	24–09–72
1,500cc	1km	D. Vesco	Yamaha	1495.928	8	7.391s	487.078(302.656)	28–09–75
	1 mile	D. Vesco	Yamaha	1495.928	8	11.884s	487.515(302.928)	28–09–75
3,000cc	1km	B. Jones	Volkswagen	1475.3	4	20.755s	173.28(107.671)	24–07–77

Sidecars

Category	Distance (or time)	Rider	Machine	Capacity (in cc)	*	Time (or distance)	Speed in kph(mph)	Date set
250cc	1km	A. Reynard	Royal Enfield	247.821	1	20.335s	177.034(110.004)	29–09–71
	1 mile	A. Reynard	Royal Enfield	247.00	1	32.392s	178.859(111.138)	27–09–70
350cc	1km	W. Bohm	NSU	347.00	2	16.60s	216.867(134.755)	26–10–51
	1 mile	W. Bohm	NSU	347.00	2	26.80s	216.180(134.328)	26–10–51
500cc	1km	W. Bohm	NSU	498.00	2	14.50s	248.276(154.272)	26–10–51
	1 mile	W. Bohm	NSU	498.00	2	23.40s	247.591(153.846)	26–10–51
750cc	1km	N. Hyde	Triumph	736.06	3	14.83s	242.751(150.838)	25–09–71
	1 mile	N. Hyde	Triumph	739.32	3	24.445s	237.006(147.269)	03–10–71
1,000cc	1km	N. Hyde	Triumph	823.11	3	13.825s	260.39(161.799)	24–09–72
	1 mile	N. Hyde	Triumph	828.82	3	25.41s	227.99(141.666)	01–10–72
1,300cc	1km	G. Brown	Vincent	1147.0	2	14.939s	240.972(149.733)	03–11–66
	1 mile	G. Brown	Vincent	1147.0	2	28.073s	206.372(128.234)	03–10–70

Cyclecars

Category	Distance (or time)	Rider	Machine	Capacity (in cc)	*	Time (or distance)	Speed in kph (mph)	Date set
250cc	1km	Miss I. Scargill	AJS	248.41	1	20.88s	172.410(107.131)	01–10–72
	1 mile	Miss I. Scargill	AJS	248.41	1	33.315s	173.904(108.059)	01–10–72
350cc	1km	Miss I. Scargill	AJS	250.60	1	22.29s	161.507(100.356)	02–10–71
	1 mile	Miss I. Scargill	AJS	250.60	1	35.87s	161.517(100.362)	03–10–71
500cc	1km	S. Whitton	Triovad	497.0	2	17.895s	201.1735(125.003)	04–10–75
	1 mile	J. Moritz	DKW	482.00	2	36.24s	159.868(99.337)	28–10–34
750cc	1km	D. Green	Triumph	650.0	2	17.885s	201.287(125.107)	26–09–70
	1 mile	D. Green	Triumph	650.0	2	29.921s	193.629(120.315)	27–09–70
1,000cc	1km	R. Vane	Vincent	997.524	2	17.695s	203.440(126.412)	24–09–72
	1 mile	R. Vane	Vincent	994.63	2	29.79s	194.470(120.838)	01–10–72
1,300cc	1km	O. Greenwood	BMC	1298.0	4	18.090s	198.999(123.652)	22–10–67
	1 mile	Mrs Stewart	Morgan JAP	1086.00	2	31.35s	184.800(114.829)	24–08–30

CIRCUITS

Anderstorp, Sweden

circuit distance 4.019km (2.497 miles)

The main straight at this circuit is also the landing strip for a small aerodrome, and lightweight aircraft are usually parked nearby. Anderstorp itself is a tiny town of 5,000 people, set in the countryside 30km (19 miles) west of Vanarmo in the Smaland region of Sweden, and the 'Scandinavian raceway' owes its existence to the efforts of the local people. Encouraged by the energy and enthusiasm of one man, Sven Asberg, who in 1966 announced that he wanted to build a race track, the local businessmen of this prosperous town decided that it was worth investing in the venture. The airstrip was no afterthought, but was designed to help business by improving trade and communications. The enterprising backers of the venture then worked hard to promote both motorcycle and car racing at the purpose-built track, and the first motorcycle race was run in 1969, for production machines.

The circuit is flat, with wide run-off areas, and set in a grassy, sandy area overlooked by a pine forest. The pit area is oddly placed, almost 1km (0.5 mile) from the start line. Anderstorp was first used in a

ANDERSTORP, SWEDEN

1 Start/finish
2 ½ Mile Straight
3 South Bend
4 Pit
5 Carousel Bend
6 Gislaved Bridge
7 North Bend
8 BP Bridge

world championship race in 1971. Relatively small crowds are usual here; after all, Sweden has only a small population, less than that of London. The area is served by several camp and caravan sites, as well as a few hotels and boarding houses. There are lakes with fishing for the visitor who wishes to spend some time in the area, and 15km (10 miles) east of the circuit is the 'High Chaparral', a tourist attraction whose theme is the American Wild West.

Assen, Holland

circuit distance 7.718km (4.796 miles)

Assen, which dates from 1925, is one of the oldest European road race venues, and regularly attracts crowds of 150,000. For the 1976 Dutch grand prix it was estimated that about 200,000 spectators were there. This round of the world championship was once known as the Dutch TT because the circuit was 16km (10 miles) long, comparable with the length of the Isle of Man TT circuit. In 1955 the currently used Drenthe circuit was constructed near Assen (in northern Holland), and another circuit is planned, as part of what will be an all-purpose motorcycle sports stadium. This new, permanent circuit, which will be ready by the early 1980s, will have a track of 5.809km (3.61 miles) with facilities for speedway, grass track, moto-cross and trials, and the complex will represent the fourth change to the circuit. Plans also include the building of a new hotel, to be race headquarters as well as to provide accommodation, in which Assen is lacking.

Most parts of the present circuit are accessible to spectators, and when the racing is not in progress there is usually some other form of entertainment going on. Sand banks offer spectators vantage points from which to watch the event, traditionally held in the last week in June. The circuit, built exclusively for motorcycles with no crash barriers, is considered extremely safe; indeed, it represents the standard by which other tracks are measured in terms of safety. Riders crank their bikes to the limits here, uninhibited by any telegraph poles or kerbs, such as are usually found on closed road circuits. The circuit is flat and affords spectators more than one view of the race track from certain points.

ASSEN, HOLLAND

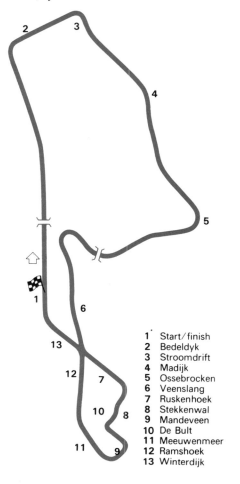

1   Start/finish
2   Bedeldyk
3   Stroomdrift
4   Madijk
5   Ossebrocken
6   Veenslang
7   Ruskenhoek
8   Stekkenwal
9   Mandeveen
10 De Bult
11 Meeuwenmeer
12 Ramshoek
13 Winterdijk

The grand prix always features a top-class entry. In the 1977 F750 round, America's first world road race champion, Steve Baker, put in a 158.09kph (98.23 mph) fastest lap.

Brands Hatch, UK

circuit distance 4.2km (2.61 miles)

Brands Hatch is probably Britain's best-known race track. It lies among the hills of the North Downs of Kent only 32km (20 miles) south-east of London, and so is ideally situated for attracting large crowds. It incorporates a short clubman's circuit of 2.0km (1.24 miles), which is used more often than the longer grand prix circuit. When racing is held on the short circuit, spectators can see the bikes nearly all the way round the course, whereas competitors disappear from view at certain points when the long circuit is used.

Brands is a very busy circuit, the scene of many vintage and club events as well as major fixtures such as grands prix, Anglo-American match races and long-distance events. The circuit has a racing school, too. Until 1952 races were held in an anti-clockwise direction and, to continue this tradition the annual Hutchinson 100, phased out after 1978, was run 'the wrong way round'. The circuit is on a slope, and the track sweeps up to Druids Bend where the bikes are cranked to their limit (sometimes a top-class rider will pass on the outside as if his machine were on rails). Then follows a downward sweep into Graham Hill Bend and, on the short circuit, thence to Clearways, a potential hazard because the bikes are cranked hard here at fast speeds. The bigger machines still have enough power to make the back wheel break traction if the throttle is opened too suddenly on leaving the corner. How this corner is taken can be crucial at the end of a race if two riders are neck and neck for the finish. The finishing line is just past the pits and main grandstands.

Originally a grass track circuit first used in 1928, the Brands Hatch site was bought by former speedway rider Joe Francis who started to put events on to a more professional footing. In the same year that he bought it, 1947, the BBC screened the first televised grass track meeting. When grass racing ended in 1949, after Whitehall finally consented to the construction of a road race circuit, the 1.6km (1 mile) oval record was held by Cyril Rogers at 97.19kph (60.39mph). In 1950, on a wet and blustery Easter Sunday, 35,000 fans turned up to watch the first road races at Brands Hatch. Many famous names were there that day and, ever since, the world's top riders have frequented this circuit which, especially in the early days, was a favourite with sidecar exponents. The circuit was improved over the years as riders like Surtees, Minter and Duke made their mark. It was acquired by Grovewood Securities in 1961, and a club house and restaurant were later added. Facilities for the public are good and the circuit brochure lists 28 hotels within a 32km (20 mile) radius of the track.

Brno, Czechoslovakia

circuit distance 10.919km (6.785 miles)

Czechoslovakia's second largest town, Brno in Moravia, is to have a new, shorter circuit, constructed to meet demands for safer racing than the present closed road circuit affords. Likened to a miniature Isle of Man TT course because it goes through three villages and includes a small mountain, the setting of the present Brno circuit is very picturesque, but the track has a reputation f r becoming very slippery when wet. The original circuit, on the outskirts of Brno, was 30km (20 miles) long, then cut to 13.941km (8.663 miles), and altered again in 1975 to its current length. Narrow built-up areas and full-bore straights make the circuit an exciting one for both riders and spectators, who have the choice of watching the riders when they seem almost in slow motion or at points of the track where they become a speed blur. It is not usually easy for spectators to get from one part of the track to another, so they have to decide where they want to be before the racing starts.

Visitors to the circuit often camp in the forested mountain and congregate round campfires on the night before race day. Foreigners often make a holiday of their visit because for most of them a visa is required before they can enter the country, and foreign tourists also have to spend a minimum amount of money per day. Brno itself is of great historical significance and has very good hotels. The nearest motorway is the Salzburg–Vienna *autobahn*.

The fastest rider at the 1978 GP, which was limited to 350cc solo machines, was South African Kork Ballington (350 Kawasaki), at 167.37kph (104mph).

Cadwell Park, UK

circuit distance 3.62km (2.25 miles)

Although it is a favourite circuit with spectators because they can get close to the action, Cadwell, near Louth in Lincolnshire, is a tricky circuit for riders. There are no real straights and the many bends require intense concentration. The bikes often 'wheelie' when they come out of the tight sections, providing spectacular entertainment for race fans. It is the oldest natural circuit in Britain with a history extending back more than 40 years. With natural gradients, the picturesque track (which includes a club circuit) was extended by 1.6km (1 mile) to its present length in 1961, when it achieved international status. A Jubilee International

BRANDS HATCH, UK   BRNO, CZECHOSLOVAKIA   CADWELL PARK, UK

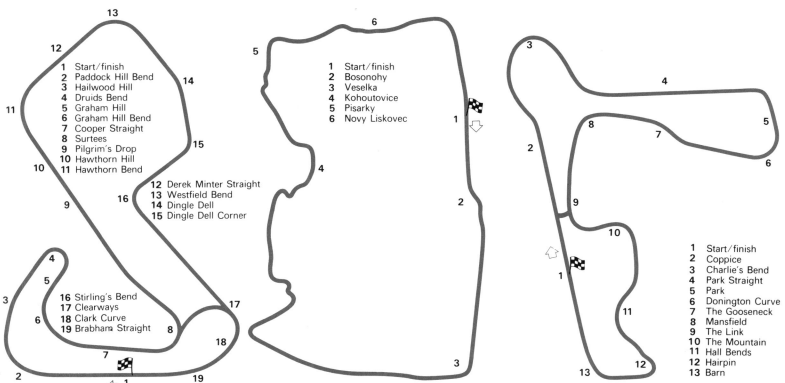

Brands Hatch:
1 Start/finish
2 Paddock Hill Bend
3 Hailwood Hill
4 Druids Bend
5 Graham Hill
6 Graham Hill Bend
7 Cooper Straight
8 Surtees
9 Pilgrim's Drop
10 Hawthorn Hill
11 Hawthorn Bend
12 Derek Minter Straight
13 Westfield Bend
14 Dingle Dell
15 Dingle Dell Corner
16 Stirling's Bend
17 Clearways
18 Clark Curve
19 Brabham Straight

Brno:
1 Start/finish
2 Bosonohy
3 Veselka
4 Kohoutovice
5 Pisarky
6 Novy Liskovec

Cadwell Park:
1 Start/finish
2 Coppice
3 Charlie's Bend
4 Park Straight
5 Park
6 Donington Curve
7 The Gooseneck
8 Mansfield
9 The Link
10 The Mountain
11 Hall Bends
12 Hairpin
13 Barn

was held here in 1976, to celebrate 25 international meetings at the track. The circuit is owned by ACU delegate Charles Wilkinson, who lives in a house inside the course and who never seems to miss an event there.

In 1961 the late John Hartle held the lap record at 117.22kph (72.84mph). Many famous riders have raced here, including Agostini, Hailwood, Read and Frith. Freddie Frith made his name here and went on to become a world champion. Perhaps the best-known local rider today is Derek Chatterton from Boston, who has frequently displayed his mastery of this circuit, and even beat Agostini at the 1971 International. At Cadwell, it seems, a 'privateer' stands a chance against the works stars.

Clermont Ferrand, France

circuit distance 8.055km (5.005 miles)

Clermont Ferrand, regarded as France's most beautiful circuit, is set in the mountains of the Auvergne region. The twisting roads leading to the circuit usually witness some over-enthusiastic riding from the motorcycling visitors who enter into the spirit of an event and try to outscratch one another. Near the town of Clermont Ferrand itself (population 140,000) and not far from Puy de Dôme, the track is considered by riders to be quite difficult to master, and it makes for exciting riding.

As with most French grands prix, a carnival atmosphere prevails, even before the race begins. Spectators either camp by the circuit or stay in a Clermont hotel. The restaurants and street cafés provide places for spectators to meet and discuss rider form and the merits of different machines.

Daytona, USA

circuit distance 6.228km (3.87 miles)

This circuit in Florida, scene of the great American road race extravaganza, the Daytona 322km (200 mile) race, is the most famous in the USA. It is an extremely fast banked circuit and the massive grandstands which flank its sides were always filled, until 1978, when only 20,000 spectators were present at the March fixture. A series of problems associated with the track led to this loss of popularity. The track was so fast that the tyre companies were having difficulty in making a cover which would last the distance. The race was altered to run two 161km (100 mile) legs, and for 1978 there was a carburettor intake restriction in an attempt to keep speeds down. Machines can easily reach 290kph (180mph) along the main straight, and it was here that Barry Sheene took a well-publicized tumble at 282kph (175mph) in 1975.

Publicity given to the event is very great, and in past years road racing enthusiasts have looked to this early season meeting as an opener, to anticipate a rider's form during the rest of the season. Daytona has its own airport, and package trips to the event from Europe are organized, with charter flights which often carry one or two motorcycles belonging to the European competitors who enter the race. As the machines travel round the speed bowl and 'infield' sections, wise spectators are seen to have binoculars with them, so that they can follow the action all the way round the circuit. This is one track where sheer horsepower really counts, and the atmosphere at Daytona is always charged with excitement. Events there attract all types of motorcycle enthusiast, from custom bike riders and would-be drag racers to full-dress tourers, and the spectators and their bikes are as much a part of events at Daytona as the racing.

Daytona beach, where the circuit is situated, is noisy and brash, and impromptu races are held on the beach. The night life is exciting but there are quiet spots in the area too. Accommodation is plentiful but should be booked in advance, and restaurants are numerous. With several museums, including the Daytona Speed Museum, and Disney World, in the area, Daytona is a great attraction for the general

CLERMONT FERRAND, FRANCE

1 Start/finish
2 Puy de Gravenoive
3 Puy de Charade

DONINGTON PARK, UK

1 Start/finish
2 Wheatcroft Straight
3 Red Gate Corner
4 Holly Wood
5 Craner Curves
6 Old Hairpin
7 Starkeys Bridge
8 Coppice Wood
9 McLeans Corner
10 Coppice Corner
11 Starkeys Straight

DAYTONA, USA

1 Start/finish
2 Infield Section
3 Outer Banked Circuit
4 Chicane
5 Lake Lloyd
6 Tunnel
7 Pits
8 Signalling Pits
9 Grandstand Area

tourist as well as the road racing enthusiast.

Donington Park, UK

circuit distance 3.15km (1.9573 miles)

The wealth and the resolve of one man are responsible for the re-establishment of racing at Donington Park, which is close to the M1 motorway at Castle Donington in Leicestershire. As a child before the Second World War, Tom Wheatcroft watched the racing at Donington (the first motorcycle races were held there in 1933), but in 1939, with the outbreak of war, it was closed and racing was not resumed afterwards. Wheatcroft, now a wealthy builder and racing car collector, decided to turn his dream of seeing racing at Donington again into reality, so in 1971 he bought the course. In spite of many delays caused by local residents who did not want the course to reopen, it did finally in 1977, after being closed for 38 years.

The circuit, which follows the lines of the pre-war circuit, is built to high safety standards, with grass run-off areas bordered by a sand-pit. In general, it has excellent pit facilities and an expert team of marshals; it seems inevitable that world championship races will be held there. The circuit also has a museum housing the world's finest collection of single-seater racing cars and, for motorcycling enthusiasts, some of the works Hondas which Mike Hailwood rode.

The Donington Park grounds are used for motorcycle rallies, and in 1978 were the setting for a contest called 'Superbike 6', held to find the best all-round British motorcyclist by putting the contenders through six different types of competition. The speed record holder is Barry Sheene, who lapped at 151kph (93.83mph) in 1978.

Dundrod, Northern Ireland

circuit distance 12.402km (7.706 miles)

This circuit is situated west of Belfast, in the rolling countryside of County Antrim. Its major annual event is the Ulster Grand Prix. Though it is not a round of the world championship since it lost its status in 1971 (when the FIM declared that riders should not be exposed to the dangers of the country's civil unrest), the event is slowly regaining its former prestige. Four thousand dedicated members of the Ulster GP Supporters Club organize all types of social activity to raise money to attract top riders. For the 1976 GP they raised £10,000, and also gained sponsorship from local firms. Unfortunately, as a racing magazine revealed at the time, they still could not afford riders of the calibre of Giacomo Agostini, who wanted £9,000

start money, and Johnny Cecotto, who is said to have asked for £15,000. The 1971 blow to the circuit resulted in no event for 1972, but since then all the efforts of the circuit's supporters have put it back into a position where it is almost ready to stage a world championship race such as a Formula 750 round.

The Ulster GP was first run at this circuit in 1953, although the circuit itself was inaugurated in 1925. Enthusiastic crowds of fans, usually around 60,000 of them, arrive to watch, even though, as often as not, they are greeted by rain. They line the stone walls, the hedgerows and telegraph poles which form the track boundaries of this very fast circuit, which has a reputation for causing engines not in top condition to blow up, the long flat-out bursts sometimes claiming lives.

A recent Act of Parliament for Northern Ireland ruled that spectators at the circuit should buy and wear a 'spectator area badge', but it seems that most people try to avoid doing so, leaving the organizers to make up the losses thus incurred with car park charges. Facilities at the circuit are poor; there is a small main grandstand which, like those of most circuits, has an admission fee; and there are refreshments, but no alcoholic drinks are sold.

There is nevertheless something special about the atmosphere at Dundrod, and most spectators, and riders who have raced

there, say that they particularly enjoyed it. The Northern Ireland Tourist Board sometimes organizes package trips to the event, to encourage visitors from the rest of the UK.

The late John Williams was one of the circuit's favourite and fastest riders. His fastest lap was 189.07kph (117.48mph).

Hockenheim, West Germany

circuit distance 6.788km (4.218 miles)

This very fast circuit was first used in 1932, and has been altered twice in recent years. The track was even faster in its original form: for example, Bob McIntyre's 1957 lap record on a Gilera-4 was 208kph (129.2mph), in the rain. At that time, the sausage-shaped track measured 7.725km (4.8 miles). In 1966 the track was modified to make room for the Karlsruhe–Mannheim motorway, which now brings huge crowds to this popular circuit. A left-hander and two hairpin bends were put in at one end of the 'sausage'. In 1970 chicanes were added to both fast stretches of the circuit, whose distance was increased slightly. Other safety measures were carried out, and many riders regard the track as one of the safest in the world. The stands accommodate 100,000 spectators, who have an excellent view of the tight

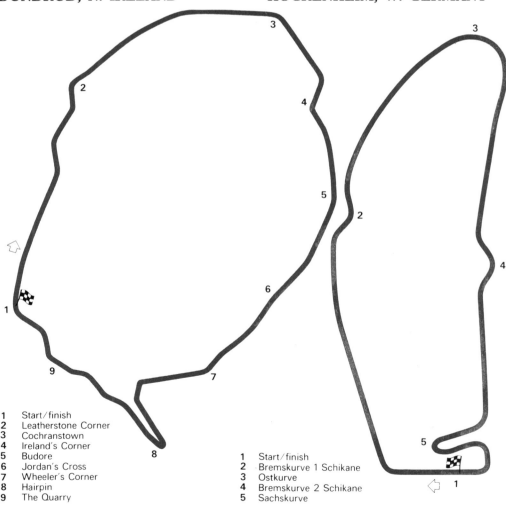

DUNDROD, N. IRELAND

1	Start/finish
2	Leatherstone Corner
3	Cochranstown
4	Ireland's Corner
5	Budore
6	Jordan's Cross
7	Wheeler's Corner
8	Hairpin
9	The Quarry

HOCKENHEIM, W. GERMANY

1	Start/finish
2	Bremskurve 1 Schikane
3	Ostkurve
4	Bremskurve 2 Schikane
5	Sachskurve

bends at the start, followed by the long straights.

For the 1975 grand prix a record crowd of 130,000 assembled to watch a battle in the 500cc class between Phil Read (MV-4) and his former team-mate Giacomo Agostini (Yamaha-4), which Agostini won by just four seconds. In 1977, the last time the West German Grand Prix was held at Hockenheim, the fastest lap was set by Barry Sheene (500 Suzuki) at 181.69kph (112.90mph). When not in use for racing, the circuit is extensively employed by the German motor industry for testing purposes.

Imatra, Finland

circuit distance 6.03km (3.747 miles)

Yellow kerbs, flower-beds, forest trees and open fields—these are all part of the scene at Imatra, in the 'land of the midnight sun'. Imatra is the most northerly circuit in the grand prix calendar, so far north, in fact, that in the height of summer the sun never sets. It is only 5km (3 miles) from the Russian border, and the whole area was once a part of Russia. Today Imatra, population 35,000, and situated in the south-eastern corner of the country, is highly industrialized, although the circuit's straight runs alongside one of the many lakes in the country, Lake Saimaa, the largest inland water system in western Europe. Bathing, water-skiing and water excursions are some of the many diversions in which a spectator can indulge after racing has finished. Extensive camping, caravanning, hostel and hotel accommodation may be found in the area.

The circuit is only used for two days a year and, to make the most of the event, the build-up to the grand prix starts a week earlier. After the Saturday practice the public can drive around the reopened circuit roads, to find their viewing places for the Sunday action. The track is a bumpy one, and Mike Hailwood has been quoted as saying that the course is 'the fastest moto-cross circuit in the world'. Imatra is unique in that it has two paddocks. The one at the start line is usually adopted by the works teams.

The fastest riders at the 1978 grand prix were Barry Sheene and Dutchman Wil Hartog (500 Suzukis), and Japanese rider Takazumi Katayama (500 Yamaha). They all set fastest laps at 168.19kph (104.51 mph).

Imola, Italy

circuit distance 5.080km (3.157 miles)

This circuit is situated in the centre of the village of Imola, in the heart of one of Italy's major wine producing areas. The nearest large town is Bologna, 40km (25 miles) away. Although the track was designed solely for motorcycle racing, the circuit has latterly been used for cars too. Most of the circuit was purpose-built, but does incorporate some public road areas. On race day nearly all the inhabitants of the village emerge to watch, finding vantage points in every conceivable place, hanging from balconies, standing on roofs and covering the natural hillside grandstand, in addition to the constructed grandstands.

Imola, a more demanding circuit than Monza, has witnessed other major events in addition to grands prix. The Imola 322km (200 mile) race is a favourite, and in 1978 the circuit was one of three venues for the AGV World Cup series. The other two circuits were Paul Ricard in France and Daytona, USA. Imola features a very fast left-hander on the lower part of the course, followed by *La Tosa* hairpin, one of the heavy braking sections. The race teams have spacious, well-equipped pits, and spectators who get on to the pit roof have one of the best views of the track. It is not too easy to move vantage points, but to get to the park circuit itself is no problem, thanks to a nearby motorway.

Apart from the racing, the area offers an excellent cuisine and, for the spectator on tour, the tiny principality of San Marino is within easy travelling distance.

IMATRA, FINLAND
1 Start/finish
2 Pits
3 Paddock

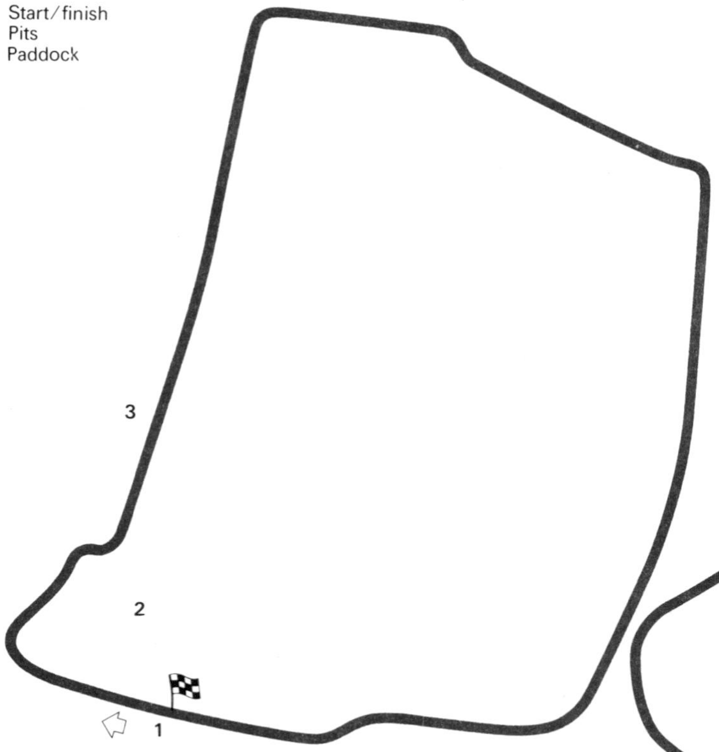

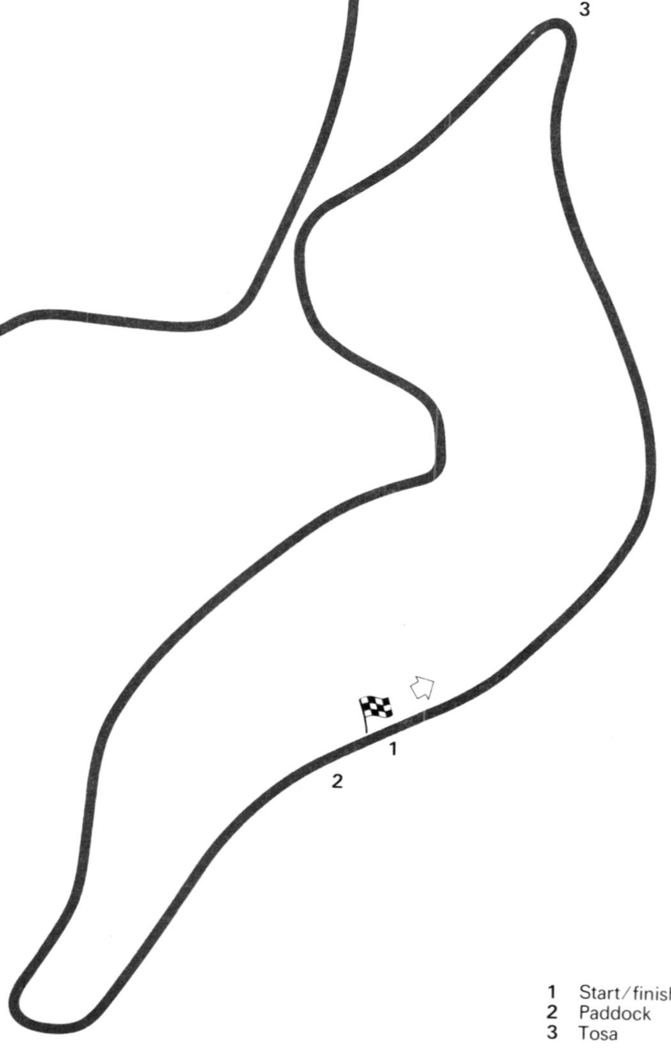

1 Start/finish
2 Paddock
3 Tosa

IMOLA, ITALY

Jarama, Spain

circuit distance 3.401km (2.113 miles)

Jarama is a purpose-built track on barren land situated beside a motorway 24km (15 miles) north of Madrid. It is the scene of the important early season Spanish Grand Prix round when Montjuich Park is not being used for the purpose. It is a tight circuit with nine major bends and a straight only 0.5km (0.3 mile) long, so acceleration is much more important than high top speeds. Facilities are good for both riders and spectators, but there were only 12,000 people present at the 1978 GP, even though motorcycle racing is popular in Spain.

In 1978 American Kenny Roberts put in a fastest lap of 130.44kph (81.05mph) on his works 500 Yamaha.

Le Mans, France

circuit distance 4.422km (2.748 miles)

Le Mans, the home of 24-hour racing, is of course the best-known circuit in the world, full of glamour and excitement, and steeped in history and tradition. Races were originally run through the streets of Le Mans and much of their reputation arose from the noise of the exhaust of the high-powered cars as it echoed off the walls of buildings in the town. Events now take place on the closed Bugatti circuit.

The French Grand Prix and the Bol d'Or 24-hour race are the most important fixtures staged here, 210km (130 miles) from Paris (though for 1978 Le Mans had neither: the 41st Bol d'Or was at Paul Ricard in the south of France). Spectators who have seen the Bol d'Or at Le Mans can testify to those who think that endurance racing over 24 hours must be fairly slow, in order to make the bikes last, that the riders go at full speed as if the race were over six brief laps. Only two riders per machine are allowed, though until 1953 the rules allowed only one. The riders wield their machines as though they were grand prix racers; sparks fly on the tight corners at night, as frames and footrests are grounded. Occasionally, a rider overshoots a hairpin bend, and under the Dunlop bridge some of the faster bikes 'wheelie' as they rush into the following downslope. The machines are big displacement projectiles, mostly four-strokes, with fantastical chassis. Rider changes and refuelling in the pits are fast and furious, and lap scorers have to work tirelessly to keep up with the race's progress.

Many of the fans who pack the grandstands camp on the inside of the track, and stalls selling clothing, books, food and drink stay open day and night to cater for the constant stream of strolling spectators. Both day and night, there is never a short-

JARAMA, SPAIN

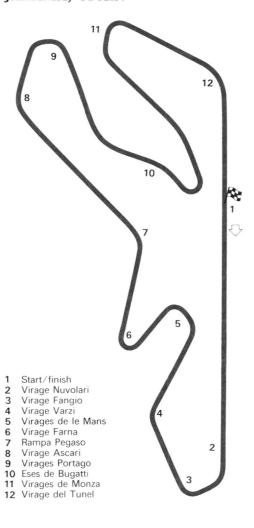

1 Start/finish
2 Virage Nuvolari
3 Virage Fangio
4 Virage Varzi
5 Virages de le Mans
6 Virage Farna
7 Rampa Pegaso
8 Virage Ascari
9 Virages Portago
10 Eses de Bugatti
11 Virages de Monza
12 Virage del Tunel

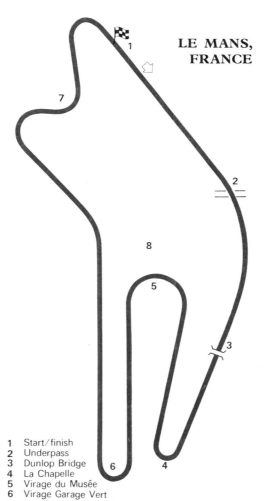

LE MANS, FRANCE

1 Start/finish
2 Underpass
3 Dunlop Bridge
4 La Chapelle
5 Virage du Musée
6 Virage Garage Vert
7 Les 'S' du Garage Bleu
8 Automobile Museum

age of wildly enthusiastic supporters only too eager to flock on to the track to congratulate the winner or the nearest rider. A large group of members of the Vincent Owners' Club, mostly British, annually assembles to provide another attraction at this event. Le Mans itself, with its pavement cafés, offers many places to eat and talk of the events at the track. Accommodation needs to be planned in advance. The entrance fee is not cheap, but most fans are quite willing to pay it: it is worth it, to be able to say they have been to Le Mans to watch the racing.

Mallory Park, UK

circuit distance 2.17km (1.35 miles)

Mallory Park, which is between Hinckley and Leicester in Leicestershire, is a small, tight circuit with plenty of scope for thrilling entertainment. There is a natural lake in the centre of the circuit and the hillside flanking the bottom straight makes this one of the best spectator venues in the country. The track also has dirt banks around most of its perimeter. However, those who wish to have a good view of the circuit must arrive early, because the best spots for viewing the track fill rapidly, leaving the latecomer to watch either machines in the distance or crash helmets in close-up. On a wet day the spectator areas and particularly the paddock become very muddy.

The long Kirkby and Stebbe straights allow fast average speeds, and for those who like a close view of the riders, almost to their facial expressions, the very tight hairpin, Shaw's Corner, is the place to go. This is where braking technique is vital: riders like Barry Sheene have it down to a fine art, braking at the last possible second to force a slower rider to accept defeat, then 'fanning' the clutch to get round the hairpin. The front wheels of the more powerful machines, on leaving the corner, often leap into the air under acceleration, much to the delight of the crowd. Devil's Elbow, a fast left-hander, is a test of machines with handling problems, and it is not unusual to see a big bike suddenly start to wobble on the exit of the corner. Gerard's Bend, a long, sweeping right-hander, invites the rider to corner as fast as he dares, and gives him time to think about it. The really top riders can overtake on the outside here. After the Stebbe straight, clever braking technique is again required to the Lake Esses (S-bends). Even though this is a fast section, the front wheels of some of the big bikes still leave the ground as they race uphill to the hairpin.

The circuit is the home of many top international races, including the Post-TT, which takes place on the Sunday after the

Isle of Man TT races. Mallory attracts top-class entries and is one of the three tracks owned by Motor Circuit Developments to stage the early season Anglo-American match race series. The track is also used as a 1.6km (1 mile) clubman's circuit, missing out the hairpin.

Montjuich Park, Spain

circuit distance 3.7km (2.3 miles)

This is a public road circuit through the beautiful Montjuich Park in Spain's industrial capital, Barcelona. Few of the many tourists who flock to the city every year, to see the museums, theatres, gardens and coloured fountains, realize that the quiet park roads are used as a race track when it is the turn of Montjuich to host the Spanish Grand Prix. In many places along the track only a piece of Armco barrier separates the bikes from the crowds, so it is possible for spectators to get very close to the action. The park, situated on a hill just over 1.6km (1 mile) from the city centre, provides an extremely demanding track for the motorcyclist, with steep ascents and downhill sections with tight

corners. Here good brakes and handling are the top priorities, and high speeds definitely take second place to these requirements. As well as for the grand prix, Montjuich is the venue for the Barcelona 24 hours meeting and for Sunday morning race meetings.

Monza, Italy

circuit distance 5.750km (3.573 miles)

The name of this circuit, Monza, has an exciting ring; its history and fame as a race track go back to its opening in 1922, when the first Italian grand prix was held there. The circuit, near Milan, is exceptionally fast, with only five bends in its composition. In spite of its reputation, however, it is now regarded as out of date: the track surface and protection facilities are not up to the standard considered adequate by today's grand prix riders, and so it is no longer a grand prix venue.

Originally 6.3km (3.9 miles) long, it was changed to its present length in 1954. The sections leading towards and away from the *Curva Parabolica* were shortened. The most spectacular bend is the *Curva*

Grande, but spectators are not allowed to watch the race at this point. Instead, most of them pack into the three stands on other parts of the circuit.

The circuit's greatest misfortune occurred in 1973, when favourite Italian rider, Renzo Pasolini, and Finnish Jarno Saarinen, the most brilliant rider of his day, were both killed in an accident. This tragedy shook the road racing world; officials at the circuit were accused of inefficiency, and Monza lost its popularity as a venue. However, in 1981, the circuit was restored to grand prix status.

Mosport Park, Canada

circuit distance 3.957km (2.459 miles)

Mosport Park near Toronto was opened 18 years ago for the specific purpose of bringing world class road racing to Canada. The circuit has fulfilled this aim and has also extended its facilities to include motocross; a 500cc world championship event was held there in 1976. Hill climbs are also held on the track perimeter, and big-bore motorcycle racing also takes place here.

The circuit, now Canada's most important racing venue, opened officially on 24

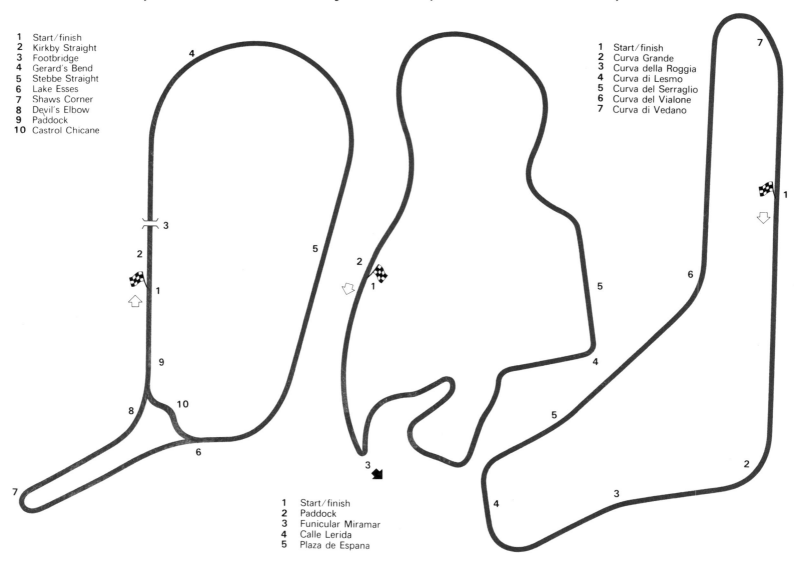

MALLORY PARK, UK

1 Start/finish
2 Kirkby Straight
3 Footbridge
4 Gerard's Bend
5 Stebbe Straight
6 Lake Esses
7 Shaws Corner
8 Devil's Elbow
9 Paddock
10 Castrol Chicane

MONTJUICH PARK, SPAIN

1 Start/finish
2 Paddock
3 Funicular Miramar
4 Calle Lerida
5 Plaza de Espana

MONZA, ITALY

1 Start/finish
2 Curva Grande
3 Curva della Roggia
4 Curva di Lesmo
5 Curva del Serraglio
6 Curva del Vialone
7 Curva di Vedano

June 1961, when 40,000 people watched a sports car event. The track quickly became a favourite with motorcyclists too, partly because it offers excellent camping facilities and a park area for off-road motorcycles and dune buggies. There is also a wide choice of hotels within a few miles of the track.

The lap record holder at the end of the 1978 season was American star Mike Baldwin.

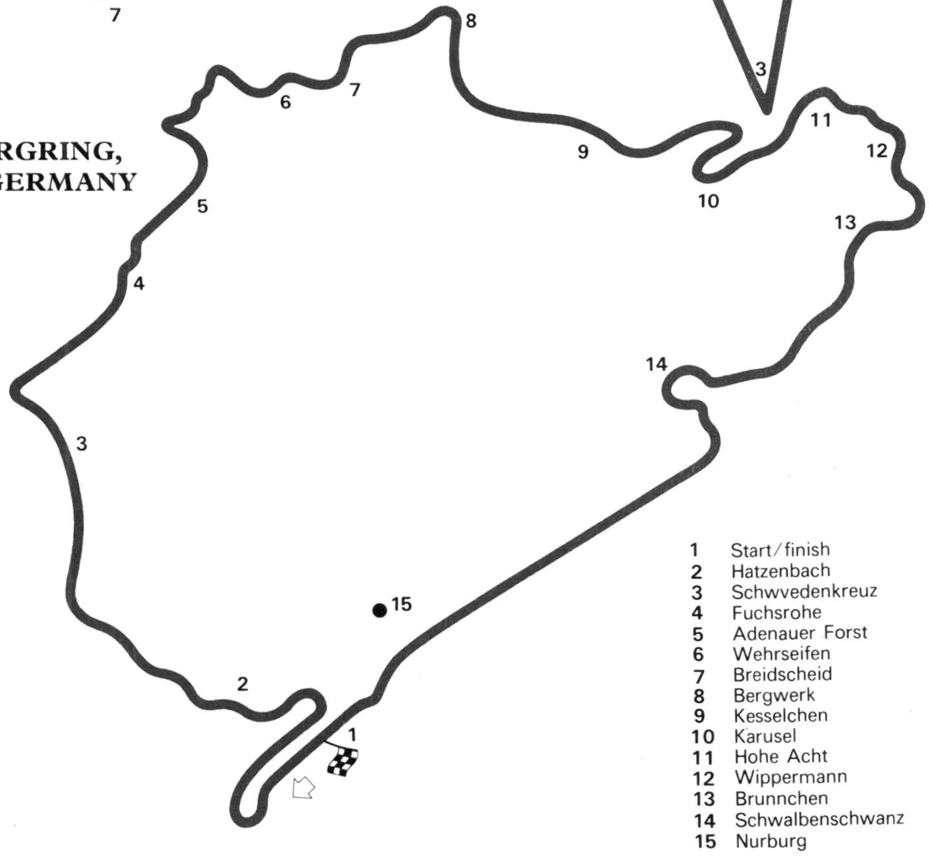

North-West 200, Northern Ireland

circuit distance 16.261km (10.104 miles)

This wide, fast, closed-road circuit on the coast of Co. Londonderry was first used in 1929, and its racing, run on a Saturday, is one of Ireland's major sporting attractions and social events. The circuit, whose paddock overlooks the sea, is basically triangular, and its fastest section leads to Portrush. In the 1978 event British rider Tony Rutter achieved a speed of 288kph (179mph) on his 750 Yamaha-4. The track celebrated its golden jubilee in 1979 when it also became the world's fastest track, as the Spa Francorchamps circuit in Belgium was then made slower. Lap speeds would be even higher at the North-West 200 circuit if it were not for the roundabout which was put in at Ballysally in 1976. Such high speeds create tyre problems, particularly blistered 'slicks', and a tyre technician from one of the leading tyre companies often attends the event to help and advise riders who all use higher tyre pressures than normal in an effort to keep the covers cooler. As well as tyre problems, the circuit has all the hazards associated with public roads, and in 1973 a modification was carried out: routing the course away from the harbour at Port Stewart.

The spectators appreciate the riders' courage and skill in these circumstances and attend the events in huge numbers: for the event in May 1978 there were reportedly 90,000 spectators, and Ulsterman Tom Herron delighted his fellow countrymen by pushing the lap record to 205.4kph (127.63mph).

Almost 500 marshals are required to staff this long course, whose revenue comes from selling programmes at £1 each. The organizers say that the 1978 event cost £30,000 to stage, and so they rely on the willingness of spectators to buy programmes.

Nurburgring, West Germany

circuit distance 22.835km (14.189 miles)

Until 1970, when the German Grand Prix was held at the Nurburgring, it took place on the south loop of the circuit over a

MOSPORT PARK, CANADA

1 Start/finish	9 Corner 7
2 Corner 1	10 Mario Andretti
3 Corner 2	Straightway
4 Corner 3	11 Corner 8
5 Quebec Corner	12 The Esses
6 Corner 4	13 Corner 9
7 Corner 5	14 Corner 10
8 Corner 6	15 White's Corner

NURBURGRING, WEST GERMANY

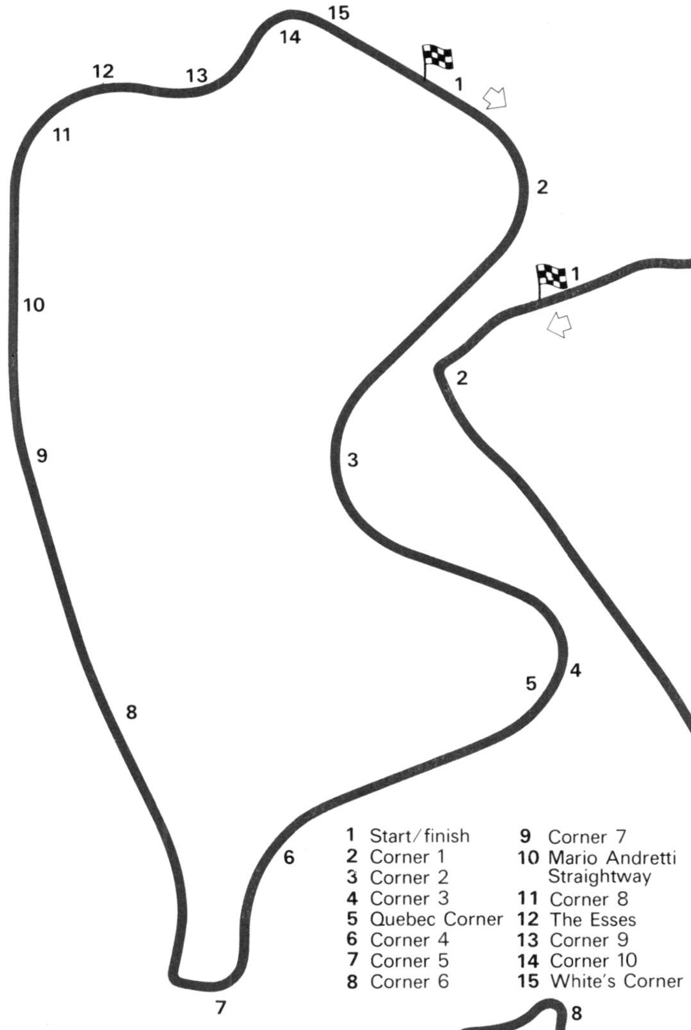

NORTH-WEST 200, N. IRELAND

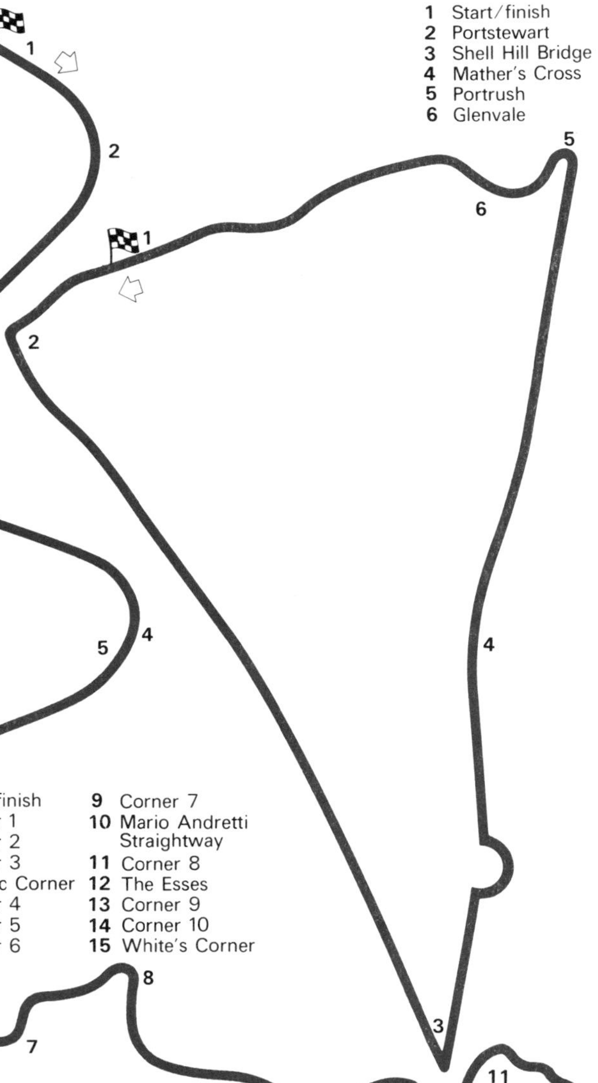

1 Start/finish
2 Portstewart
3 Shell Hill Bridge
4 Mather's Cross
5 Portrush
6 Glenvale

1 Start/finish
2 Hatzenbach
3 Schwvedenkreuz
4 Fuchsrohe
5 Adenauer Forst
6 Wehrseifen
7 Breidscheid
8 Bergwerk
9 Kesselchen
10 Karusel
11 Hohe Acht
12 Wippermann
13 Brunnchen
14 Schwalbenschwanz
15 Nurburg

distance of 7.747km (4.814 miles). In 1970 the long north loop was used for the first time since racing began at the Nurburgring in 1927. The new circuit has so many bends and is so bumpy and narrow that it presents a supreme test for a rider's

memory as well as his skill. Set in the heart of the Black Forest in the area of Koblenz, the track features more than 170 bends and the bumps in its surface often have the riders airborne. Riders respect it and spectators love it. It is generally reckoned that a rider has to put in at least 100 laps before he knows the circuit.

Italian star Virginio Ferrari was the fastest rider at the 1978 West German GP. He put in a 161.27kph (100.21mph) lap on his 500 Suzuki.

Opatija, Yugoslavia

circuit distance 6.0km (3.728 miles)

The idyllic setting of Opatija, which is right on the Adriatic coast, makes this an ideal circuit for holidaymakers: one half of the track follows the coastline and plunges down to the sea-front, and the cooler, inland part is wooded. Most spectators watch from the coastal side of the track, where they have fine views of the sea to look at when the machines are not speeding past them since, once racing starts, it is difficult to get to different vantage points.

However, Opatija, which is a closed road circuit used as a world championship venue only since the 1960s, has been criticized by riders who say that the concrete posts, metal railings, walls and mountain rock faces present safety hazards. Now the circuit is lined with straw bales at crucial points, but it took a boycott by some of the major teams at the 1973 GP before the organizers took action to make the track safer. On the other hand, the twisting circuit does provide many tests of courage and precision—corners to be

negotiated at speed but without taking chances. The small-capacity machines need all their power to climb up from the coastal section to the higher, inland part of the circuit. A paddock offers the riders covered garages to work on their machines. Camp-sites are arranged along the coastal side, and the riders themselves often use them.

Apart from the beauty of the 'Opatija Riviera', the region has other merits as a holiday centre for the road racing enthusiast: Yugoslavia's largest port, Rijeka, is only 14km (9 miles) away; the region was a favourite holiday area for the aristocracy of the former Austrian empire, and so is rich in historic interest.

Despite the difficult and twisty nature of the track, lap speeds of more than 160kph (100mph) are possible. Takazumi Katayama, the 1977 350cc world champion, set a fastest lap of 161.465kph (100.33mph) on his 350 Yamaha at the 1977 GP.

Oulton Park, UK

circuit distance 4.443km (2.761 miles)

Oulton Park in Cheshire is the major race circuit in northern Britain, and was opened in 1953. Situated in pleasant surroundings, the track is 16km (10 miles) from the M6 motorway and halfway between Chester and Crewe. It is now a favourite of

followers of the popular Anglo-American match race series held in spring. Oulton is the final venue in the series and the final points outcome is decided here. For northern fans this event marks the start of a new road race season, and a chance to see riders in their new colours and on new machines. Now that American riders are playing a more prominent rôle in European racing the event is particularly important for students of riders' form on both sides of the Atlantic. The course also features a club circuit of 2.662km (1.654 miles).

Since 1975 lap speeds at the 'magic ton' (160kph) have been recorded. Barry Sheene was the first to do it, on a 750 Suzuki and was equalled by Mick Grant in 1979.

Paul Ricard, France

circuit distance 5.15km (3.2 miles)

This circuit, named after the man who built it, is situated in the south of France between Marseilles and Toulouse, and 16km (10 miles) from the Mediterranean coast, nearly 1,000m (3,250ft) above sea level. It was first used as a grand prix track in 1973. The twisting roads leading to the circuit bring out the 'racer' in the more enthusiastic fans on their way to and from the track: impromptu 'grands prix' abound. Once at the circuit, the crowds are kept well back from the track by broad

OPATIJA, YUGOSLAVIA

1 Start/finish
2 Opatija
3 Rijeka
4 Paddock

OULTON PARK, UK

1 Start/finish
2 Old Hall Corner
3 The Avenue
4 Island Bend
5 Esso Bend
6 Knicker Brook
7 Cascades
8 Clay Hill
9 Druids Corner
10 Bailey Bridge
11 Lodge Corner
12 Deer Leap

PAUL RICARD, FRANCE

1 Start/finish
2 'S' de la Verrerie
3 Chicane
4 Virage de l'Ecole
5 Virage de la Sainte-Baume
6 Mistral Straight
7 Courbe de Signes
8 Double droite du Beausset
9 'S' de Bendor
10 L'Epingle
11 Virage de la Tour
12 Virage du Pont
13 'S' de Mejaner

SACHSENRING, EAST GERMANY

SALZBURGRING, AUSTRIA

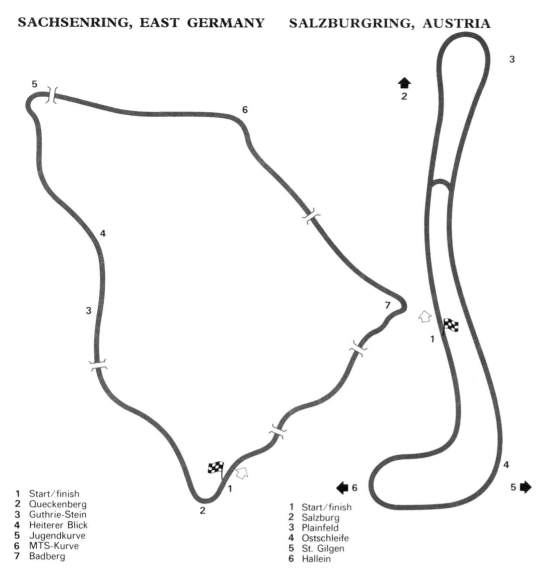

1 Start/finish
2 Queckenberg
3 Guthrie-Stein
4 Heiterer Blick
5 Jugendkurve
6 MTS-Kurve
7 Badberg

1 Start/finish
2 Salzburg
3 Plainfeld
4 Ostschleife
5 St. Gilgen
6 Hallein

Salzburgring, Austria

circuit distance 4.241km (2.635 miles)

Set in the fresh, clear atmosphere of the Austrian Alps, the Salzburgring runs through a green valley overlooked by alpine forest. The rising sides of the valley make a natural grandstand for spectators. The original Salzburg track included part of a motorway system which was too much of an inconvenience to close permanently because of the amount of traffic it carried. Funds from private sources were used to construct a new circuit 10km (6 miles) east of Salzburg (the birthplace of the composer Mozart). It is an easy circuit to reach from all directions. Accommodation is good and plentiful in the area, where tourism is promoted with alacrity.

The track, which was first given world championship status in 1971, features fast corners, which allow fast lap times, but it is lined with Armco barrier, the scourge of racing motorcyclists. In 1977, the Austrian GP was affected by a wrangle between riders and organizers over the question of safety, after Swiss rider Hans Stadelmann was killed. As a result, the 500cc grid looked very depleted, as many top names refused to start.

American star Steve Baker made his mark at the circuit in the 1977 F750 round, when he lapped his Yamaha-4 at 185.83kph (115.47mph).

San Carlos, Venezuela

circuit distance 4.135km (2.569 miles)

When Johnny Cecotto won the 350cc world championship in 1975, his native country, Venezuela, found itself on the world map of road racing. It was Cecotto's first grand prix attempt and he became a hero overnight, particularly of course in Venezuela. Interest in motorcycling in that country increased rapidly, and the San Carlos circuit was made the venue for the opening round of the following year's Formula 750 series. Unfortunately the results were declared void after a problem over lap scoring, said to have occurred because when Cecotto himself pulled out of the race, the partisan scorers decided that, if he could not win, no one would. However, in spite of this, the poor facilities and accommodation, the high humidity and temperatures of 46°C (115°F) even in March and April, the circuit has retained its prestige as a world championship venue, and the 'classic' year has begun there in 1977, 1978, and 1979.

Many top riders now start their road racing year at Daytona, USA, in March, move south to Venezuela, and then go on to Europe. The expense of travelling to San Carlos is the main objection European riders have, and the site of the track, which

run-off areas. The track itself is flat, with several bends. It became even more prominent in the motorcycling world when it ran the 1978 Bol d'Or, normally held in Le Mans. This event, the 41st held, attracted 85,000 spectators, and several other diversions in addition to supporting races were held at the same time to entertain the crowd. Paul Ricard, best known for organizing Daytona-style events, was one of the three circuits chosen to run the 1978 AGV World Cup series.

Venezuelan Johnny Cecotto put in the fastest lap at 165.504kph (102.mph) on his 750 Yamaha.

Sachsenring, East Germany

circuit distance 8.59km (5.34 miles)

Grassy slopes and green forest surround this closed road circuit which lies in Saxony, not far from Dresden. The circuit opened for racing in 1927, and was first used as a world championship venue in 1971. For the East German Grand Prix, at least 200,000 spectators always attend to watch the stars of two-wheeled sport. Even the 18,000 seats in the grandstand are sold out months in advance. Some of the more resourceful spectators without grandstand tickets have in the past erected tall poles

and scaffolding structures so as to have a panoramic view of the circuit. Many stalls and sideshows are set up round the track on the evening before the event, and on the morning of race day the circuit is traditionally washed. Between races, at the points of the track where the public is allowed to cross, the areas are covered to prevent the surface becoming dirty. Certainly, the organizers take the event very seriously.

The biggest town on the circuit is Hohenstein Ernstthal in the foothills of the Erzgebirge. Riders sweep through here and then come out of a tight left-hander to tackle the Badberg climb, which requires the correct gearing as well as a lot of power. Once the peak of the climb is reached, the track drops down to the MTS Kurve and then veers left to run parallel with a motorway. A section through forest follows before the fastest part of the course which commences after the right sweep through Heiterer Blick; gearing at the other extreme from that for Badberg is required here.

Apart from the racing, there are many other tourist attractions in the area. Karl Marx Stadt is only 25km (15 miles) away, and nearby Augustusburg has a museum of two-stroke motorcycles. And the countryside of the region is very beautiful.

was donated by Fernando Baiz, a successful racing driver of the 1950s, is 320km (200 miles) from the nearest airport, at the capital, Caracas. There was talk of building a new track nearer Caracas, but the price of land in that area makes it impossible. To get used to the high humidity (Cecotto's failure in 1976 was due to heat exhaustion), riders have been seen running about the streets of San Carlos in their leathers. Some form of carrier for water on the bikes is necessary for the South American GP, as it is for bicycle racers everywhere. The population of San Carlos itself is very small, but the crowd is almost totally Venezuelan, and when Cecotto stops most of them go home.

Barry Sheene is the fastest rider to be seen at San Carlos: in 1979 he set a record lap 158.182kph (98.29mph) on his 500 Suzuki.

Scarborough, UK

circuit distance 3.884km (2.4136 miles)

In park land at the Yorkshire seaside resort of Scarborough, this track on Oliver's Mount, a hill overlooking the town, is the only one in England using roads open to the public. The circuit runs through dense woodland, dirt banks border the narrow road and in most places fans can get close enough to the track almost to be able to touch the riders as they race by. There are no real straights and the track is so bumpy in places that the riders and their machines buck into the air; this has led to the circuit being compared with the Isle of Man TT and the Nurburgring in Germany.

Racing began here in 1946, and among the famous makes of machine seen here were the works Gileras and Nortons of the 1950s. Now used three times a year, the track provides first-class entertainment, with such famous names as Mick Grant from Yorkshire who brakes so hard that the front forks on his machine flex and shudder under the strain. He and Barry Sheene shared the 1977 lap record at 129.0kph (80.16mph).

Silverstone, UK

circuit distance 4.711km (2.927 miles)

When the Isle of Man lost its world championship status after the 1976 TT, Silverstone in Northamptonshire was chosen in 1977 to become the venue for the first-ever mainland grand prix in Britain. An estimated £120,000 was spent on improving facilities at the flat airfield circuit, ready for the 1977 season, and in particular for the four-day John Player-sponsored GP. A pit grandstand was erected, spectator banks were raised, and trees were planted to act as windbreaks. A great deal of publicity drew big crowds for the GP, and though the event has been criticized on the grounds that it does not have the atmosphere of its continental counterparts, the organizers say that the 1978 GP drew crowds of 100,000. The major stands at the circuit, which is in the Midlands of England, near Oxford, Towcester and Northampton, are concentrated at Woodcote Corner and along the pits straight. Camping is allowed at the circuit and there are 24 hotels within a 32km (20 mile) radius.

This very fast circuit is also a car Formula One world championship venue, and top drag race meetings are also held here. Before becoming a motorcycling 'classic' circuit, it had promoted international Formula 750 meetings since 1971, when it acquired grand prix status to run a round of the FIM F750.

At the 1978 GP, American Steve Baker was timed as the fastest rider to approach Woodcote at 243kph (151mph), on his 500 Yamaha. Britain's Barry Sheene (500 Suzuki) set the fastest lap in 1979 at 188.454kph (117.10mph).

SAN CARLOS, VENEZUELA **SCARBOROUGH, UK** **SILVERSTONE, UK**

1 Start/finish
2 Pits

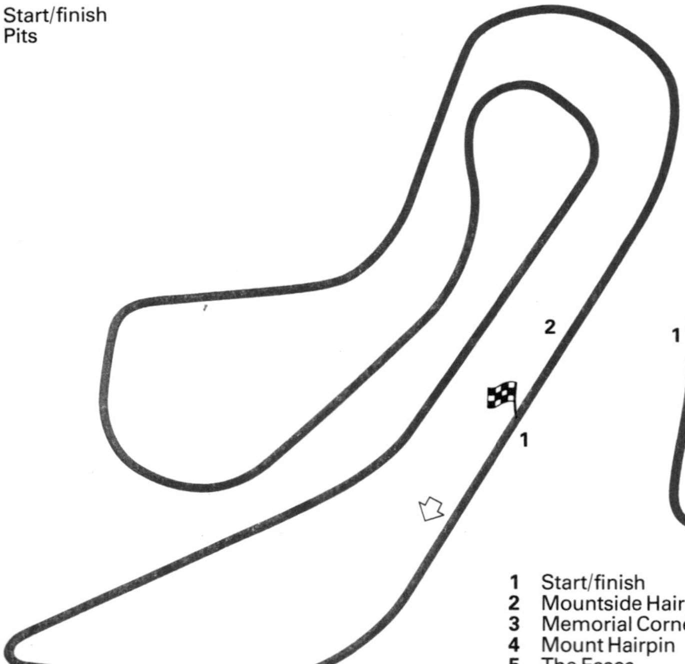

1 Start/finish
2 Mountside Hairpin
3 Memorial Corner
4 Mount Hairpin
5 The Esses
6 Mere Hairpin

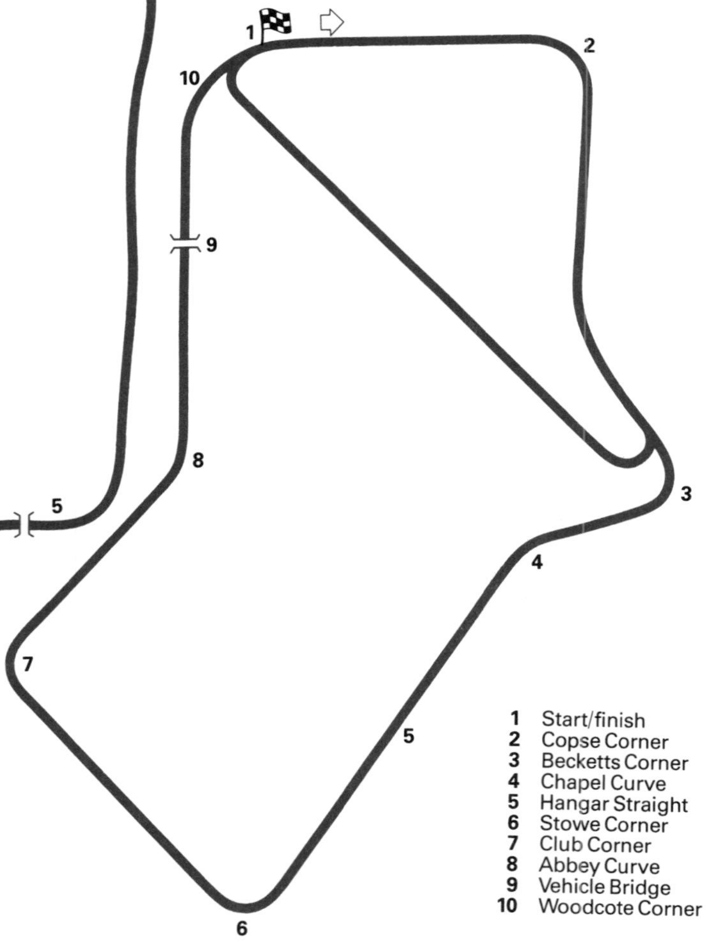

1 Start/finish
2 Copse Corner
3 Becketts Corner
4 Chapel Curve
5 Hangar Straight
6 Stowe Corner
7 Club Corner
8 Abbey Curve
9 Vehicle Bridge
10 Woodcote Corner

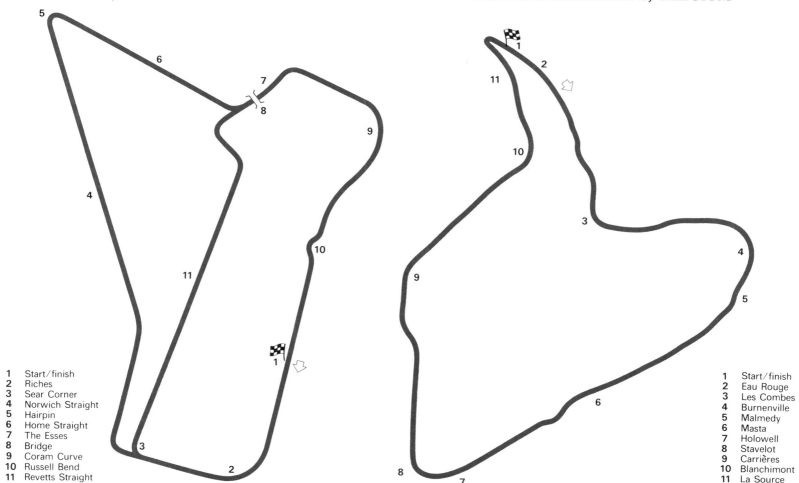

SNETTERTON, UK

Key:
1 Start/finish
2 Riches
3 Sear Corner
4 Norwich Straight
5 Hairpin
6 Home Straight
7 The Esses
8 Bridge
9 Coram Curve
10 Russell Bend
11 Revetts Straight

SPA FRANCORCHAMPS, BELGIUM

Key:
1 Start/finish
2 Eau Rouge
3 Les Combes
4 Burnenville
5 Malmedy
6 Masta
7 Holowell
8 Stavelot
9 Carrières
10 Blanchimont
11 La Source

Snetterton, UK

circuit distance 4.36km (2.71 miles)

This former airfield was converted to a race track in 1953. The flat circuit, set in a rather desolate area of Norfolk 29km (18 miles) south-west of Norwich on the Newmarket–Norwich road, is well known for the biting winds which sweep across it in early and late season. The track includes a short circuit of 3.085km (1.917 miles), which is much used during the year, not only for road racing but also for drag race events. The major event of the year is the Race of Aces which is held in July on the large circuit. Part of the Norwich Straight and the hairpin on the large circuit are used as a tarmac section for rally-cross cars. The versatile track also has a car racing school, and kart and sometimes scooter races are held here, too. The grandstands at the major vantage points are packed in summer, and though spectators are not allowed to watch along the straights when short-circuit racing is on, those watching from the Esses can see the bikes speeding down the straight into the chicane before the Esses. Despite the shortness of the new straight, some of the works bikes reach over 240kph (150mph) before they hurtle into the chicane.

A circuit of modest facilities, it is a favourite with club riders who stage many events here during the year. Because of its out-of-the-way position it is often used by riders in mid week as a test track for 'secret' new bikes. It is also used for testing cars: the enormously successful Lotus factory is nearby, and so the Lotus team find Snetterton convenient.

At the end of the 1978 season the short-circuit lap record holder was Keith Heuwen (350 Yamaha) at 152.57kph (94.80mph). On the long circuit, Dave Potter (750 Yamaha) held the record at 173.487kph (107.80mph) in 1979.

Spa Francorchamps, Belgium

circuit distance 14.098km (8.76 miles)

This circuit is extremely fast, in fact the fastest in Europe: Spa's lap record, achieved by twice 500cc world champion Barry Sheene (500 Suzuki), stood at 220.588kph (137.067mph) at the end of the 1978 season. Even the 50cc grand prix racers can average more than 160kph (100mph). It is said that most of the bends can be taken at more than 200kph (125mph), and this is what makes the average lap speeds so high, and also separates the confident riders from those with slightly less nerve. A network of roads inside the circuit gives the spectator a chance to watch the racing from different points: grandstands at the start and at Eau Rouge are favourite spots, and Burnenville also attracts a great deal of interest because a rider's technique may be studied from

there. Burnenville is an extremely fast bend, and it is not unusual to see a rider correcting a rear wheel drift while keeping the power up. At La Source hairpin one can see the riders slowing their machines abruptly, after the extremely fast corners and straights, before they start the next lap.

The speed of the circuit has led some riders to regard it as dangerous, and pressure from them and from the FIM has led to a revision of the circuit planned for the 1979 Belgian GP. It will be 7.0km (4.35 miles) long and take in 2.99km (1.86 miles) of the present track, including the start area and La Source. The Belgian government is helping to meet the cost of the new circuit. Apart from safety factors, the other reason for the modifications is to reduce administration costs. The inhabitants of nearby Malmedy and Stavelot have to be given free passes for access, and the problems of looking after such a long circuit in the heart of the Ardennes also helped to bring about the planned change. For the 52nd grand prix at Spa, the new track will be resurfaced and have an 8m (26ft) run-off area skirting the 11m (36ft) wide track. A perimeter service road will also be built. The new track does not, however, necessarily mean the end of the old, which first saw grand prix action in 1927: fans may still at times be treated to 290kph (180mph) speeds down the Masta straight.

Biographies

Giacomo Agostini

Steve Baker

'Kork' Ballington

Johnny Cecotto

Mike Hailwood

Eugenio Lazzarini

ROAD RACING

Giacomo Agostini

The most outstanding record in the history of motorcycle road racing belongs to now retired Italian star Giacomo Agostini. He won the 500cc world championship seven years running and did the same in the 350cc class. He brought his final score to 15 world titles and over 120 grand prix victories in 1975 when he won the 500cc world crown. Born 16 June 1942 at Lovere, Brescia, he first competed in motorcycling events as a hill climber in 1961. The following year he took to the track on a Morini and later joined the Italian factory team. His illustrious partnership with the rival Italian factory MV began in 1965. In the following year came the first of his string of seven consecutive 500cc titles, coupled to an unbroken string of six 350cc titles for the factory, starting in 1968. 'Ago' and MV were invincible.

The winner of ten Isle of Man TT races, his fastest laps were always over 160kph (100mph) and he won the premier class, the 500cc 'Senior' race, five years running from 1968–72. In 1972 his friend Gilberto Parlotti was killed on the Island and from then on Agostini boycotted the event, saying the course was too dangerous. It was the end of an era in TT history. That year was also a turning point for Agostini and MV. The lone factory rider was joined by British road race king Phil Read. Agostini did not want a team-mate. He won both 350cc and 500cc world titles that year, but the following season Read took the 500cc title from him. To the utter amazement of the road race world Agostini quit the Italian team.

The opinion spread that Agostini was not such a good rider after all and it was only the superiority of the three- and four-cylinder MVs which had kept him at the top. Agostini replied by joining the Japanese Yamaha team and winning the 1974 Daytona 200 race in America. It was his first race on a two-stroke. This fantastic victory silenced the tongues of denigration. Those who still had doubts were forced to dismiss them when Agostini won the Italian Imola 200 race shortly afterwards and clinched the 350cc world title. The next year he took the 500cc world crown for Yamaha. He had made his point to the MV factory of Milan where his heart still lay and for 1976 he was given the use of works MVs to race under his own private team. He alternated between the MVs and a Suzuki in the 500 class where he finished seventh in the world title chase. His reign was over and he had already made it known that he was thinking of retiring. This he did in 1977, when he decided to try car racing and concentrate on his many business interests.

Steve Baker

The distinction of being the first world motorcycle champion from America fell to Steve Baker of Bellingham, Washington State. The now-retired road racer won the Formula 750 championship when it was given world status in 1977 for the first time. He cakewalked the series that year on his 750cc Yamaha-4 sponsored by Yamaha of Canada. He won five of the 11 rounds and was three times second. Born on 5 September 1952, he first raced a 100cc Suzuki at a local dirt track meeting before becoming one of motorcycle road racing's élite. His biggest break was finishing runner-up at the American Daytona 200 event of 1974. The following year he became Canada's road racing champion. First interested in bikes as a 12-year-old when he rode his father's 80cc Yamaha, he won the Daytona event in 1977 and also finished second to Barry Sheene in the world 500cc championship. Baker made 1977, his first year in Europe, an unqualified success. The following year was not so fruitful with sixth place in the F750 series on a Yamaha and seventh in the 500 world championship on a Suzuki supplied by an Italian sponsor. It came as a shock when, a year later, Steve decided to give up racing and concentrate on his business interests thus depriving the sport of one of its most stylish and talented exponents.

'Kork' Ballington

By 1978 Kawasaki were suddenly back on top, thanks to 'Kork' Ballington—real name Hugh—who made himself a double world road race champion by taking the 250 and 350cc titles. This two-class scoop was handled with complete professionalism and cool-headedness by the Rhodesia-born rider whose background of struggles and successes formed the foundation for his triumphant year. He started racing in 1967 and moved to a British base ready for the 1973 season. Wins against riders of the calibre of Agostini and Sheene showed he was a man to be watched. He won his first grand prix, in the 350cc class, on a Yamaha in 1976 while sponsored by English businessman Sid Griffiths. Much of his early riding, however, had been done on Kawasakis. He won the 1972 South African championship on a 750cc triple and remained with the model when he first raced in Britain, competing as often as he could. In 1977 he had financial difficulties which almost made him give up, but fortunately he remained in the sport and, at the final round of both the 350 and 250cc world championships in Britain, he won both races on Yamahas. Then, while back home in Natal, South Africa, for the winter, a letter from Kawasaki arrived asking him to become a works team member. Riding the twin-cylinder water-cooled bikes in a tentative start to the 1978 season he developed a rapport with the machines which was to result in convincing victories. He won the 350cc title with three rounds to go, and this was the first time a 350

Kawasaki had even raced in grands prix. Amazingly, Kork repeated the 'double' in 1979 taking his 'green meanies' to 250 and 350 honours again. 1980 saw Kawasaki embark on an ambitious journey to overthrow the might of Yamaha and Suzuki in the 500 class with their monocoque KR500. After a year and a half of hard development, Kork was able to compete on even terms with the opposition in the blue riband class and earn respect as one of the best riders around in 1981.

Johnny Cecotto

South American Johnny Cecotto set the world on fire when in 1975 he halted an unbroken seven-year hold on the 350cc world championship by Italian Giacomo Agostini. Before 1975 Cecotto was completely unknown. It was his first time in Europe and he had only joined the grand prix series to learn the tracks and find out what was involved in world championship racing. He never dreamed that at 19 years of age he was en route to such glory. Born in Caracas, Venezuela, in January 1956 to Italian parents, he followed his father's footsteps into racing and won the 1000cc Venezuelan championship in 1973 and 1974 on a 350cc Yamaha supplied by the importer who had spotted his talent. Cecotto first became noticed internationally when he qualified on the front row of the grid for the 1975 Daytona 200 race in America. He was taken off the line because officials saw an oil leak from his 750 Yamaha-4. Made to start last, he still finished third. Moving on to Europe, he produced such good results that suddenly winning a championship seemed a real possibility, and the Yamaha factory signed him as a works rider in August. When he gained the title he became the youngest rider to win a world championship.

Cecotto started 1976 in excellent form by winning the Daytona event for Yamaha. But the year brought a series of mechanical failures and crashes, though the young star did finish runner-up to Italian Walter Villa in the 350cc world series. The next year was worse because he was the victim of a multiple pile-up in the Austrian GP. He finished the season ninth in the 350 class and fourth in the 500 series. Making up for lost opportunities and still riding Yamahas he scored his second world championship honours by winning the 1978 Formula 750 series and finishing third in the 500 championship.

After such an amazing start in the sport, the teenage World Champion slowly became disillusioned and tried his hand at car racing. With some hefty financial backing behind him, Johnny entered the tough world of European Formula Two, and some encouraging results made him a much sought after talent by 1982.

Mike Hailwood

Mike Hailwood had been called the world's greatest road racer when he 'retired' at the end of 1967. Anyone who disagreed had to think again when Hailwood returned in 1978 to have another crack at the Isle of Man TT because life in New Zealand, where he had set up his

Angel Nieto   Phil Read

home, was boring him. His return was sensational. He won the 1,000cc Formula One race on a Ducati entered by Sports Motorcycles, a dealership in Manchester. From the Isle of Man Hailwood went to Mallory Park and won the F1 race there. His Island win had been no fluke. The genius that had dominated a golden decade of road racing still flowed in his veins. The world first saw it in 1957 when the 17-year-old Stanley Michael Bailey Hailwood from Oxford, the son of a wealthy motorcycle magnate, took up the sport on an MV 125. In 1958 he raced in his first TT, gaining third place in the 250cc event. It was also the start of his domination of British road racing. At the end of the 1960 season he had won 11 out of the 12 Gold Star awards given by the Auto-Cycle Union since they introduced the scheme in 1958. His 1958 impact had been tremendous. He won 60 races and set nearly 40 records for race and lap times.

When 19 he won his first 'classic' event, the 125cc Ulster GP. In 1961 he won the 125, 250 and 500 Isle of Man TT races, the first to accomplish a hat-trick at the event. They were the first of 13 TT victories. He also started his world championship tally in 1961 with the 250cc title. The following year he joined the Italian MV team and for the next four years won the 500cc world title. In 1965 he shared his racing time between two and four wheels. Honda gained his services for 1966–7 and then pulled out of racing. Hailwood did, too, switching to cars, after fantastic seasons on the fabulous six-cylinder 250cc and four-cylinder 500cc Hondas. He made his exit complete with an MBE for services to motorcycling. While racing Formula One cars he was awarded the George Medal for rescuing a fellow competitor from a blazing car in a South African event. Hailwood himself crashed heavily in 1974 at 225kph (140mph) badly smashing his right ankle. That looked like the

end of an heroic career and for several years Hailwood, who was born on 2 April 1940, concentrated on a marine business in New Zealand. After his amazing comebacks at the Island, Mike decided finally to retire for good in 1979 and concentrated on his successful bike dealership in the Midlands. It was in 1981 that Mike lost his life in a car accident near his home, and the sport had to face a future without probably its greatest ever rider and certainly its greatest ever diplomat.

Eugenio Lazzarini

Perseverance has paid off for diminutive Italian road racer Eugenio Lazzarini. He became 125cc world champion in 1978, 13 years after taking up the sport. Although success at this level was a long time coming, when he met it he was rewarded not only for his riding ability, but also for his engineering skill, for he had built the frame which housed his Morbidelli Benelli Armi two-stroke engine. Born in 1946, this road racer from Pesaro was introduced to the sport as a teenage mechanic for the Italian Benelli factory, and has specialized in riding lightweights. In 1971 he began designing his own frames, producing a monocoque design in 1974 which he currently uses on his racers. He was near world championship success in 1975 when he finished runner-up in the 50cc series on a Piovaticci tuned by Dutchman Jan Thiel. The limelight eluded him the next year when Piovaticci, a small Italian woodworking firm, quit the sport. Lazzarini rode a private Morbidelli and finished fourth. With a works Van Veen Kreidler from Holland, in 1977 he finished runner-up behind Angel Nieto, and was also runner-up in the 125 series on a Morbidelli, behind fellow Italian Pierpaolo Bianchi (Morbidelli) who took the title for the second time. Turning the 125cc tables on Bianchi in 1978, Lazzarini again took the runner-up position in the 50cc series on a Kriedler. The following two years saw the tables turned, however, for the diminutive 110lb Italian had little success on 125s, but successfully took the 50cc World Championship on both occasions with his Kriedler.

Angel Nieto

If you ask most road race fans which rider has ten world titles, their answer is likely to be Mike Hailwood; very few people seem to remember that Angel Nieto of Spain also has that number. The reason for this is that Nieto has chosen to contest the 50 and 125cc world series, rather than the more glamorous series for larger machines. His 50cc titles came in 1969, 1970, 1972, 1975, 1976, 1977, and 1979, and his 125cc titles in 1971, 1972 and 1981. Many people would argue that winning a class for a smaller machine is more difficult than other classes, because if a rider loses his nerve, particularly on a corner, it takes much longer for the small six-speed engines to make up the loss in speed. Nieto, Spain's first ever world motorcycle champion, who was born on 25 January 1947 in Madrid, is unquestionably a brave rider. He began motorcycling at the age of 13, and in his early years gained the reputation for being 'wild', as he tried to keep up with rivals on superior machines.

Nieto joined the Bultaco factory near Barcelona and was then spotted by a rival Spanish factory, Derbi, which he joined, and to which he later returned, after a two-year contract with Ducati. In 1967 he won the 50cc national championship for Derbi, and his first world championship in 1969 was made possible by a change in rules which reduced machines to six-speed, single-cylinder engines. (He later switched to Morbidelli and Kreidler, returning to Bultaco in 1976.) His 1970 title was also for Derbi, and he was still noted as an impetuous rider, particularly when in that year he fell off his bike five times at a Spanish championship round. The following year was particularly fulfilling for him: though runner-up in the 50cc GP series, he won the 125 world crown on his home track, Jarama (where he ran a café business).

In 1972 he won both world titles, following which the Derbi factory retired from racing. His next title was for Kreidler in 1975, and in 1976 he returned to Bultaco when the factory fielded its first works bikes since pulling out of racing at the end of the 1960s. In 1978 he was runner-up in the 125 world series but only ninth in the 50cc class.

Phil Read

At the end of the 1978 road racing season Phil Read (39) announced his retirement from the sport. It was far from the first time he had declared this intention, but if he keeps to his word this time more than one generation of road race fans will mourn not seeing and reading about the Luton, England, born hero. His fantastic 22-year career on road race machines has netted him eight world championships.

A man with the taste for success, he won admiration and respect by taking the 1971 250cc world championship on his private Yamaha. He had previously won four world titles, all as a works rider for the same Japanese factory on four-cylinder two-strokes. During the making of those titles his clashes on and off the track with the late Bill Ivy who was riding for the same team lost him some fans, gained him others and kept the world road racing scene buzzing. His 1971 private effort was loudly applauded because it scuttled the might of the works factories. His professional approach to the sport resulted in

Kenny Roberts   Barry Sheene

offers from the all-conquering Italian MV factory. Read won his first 500cc world title on one of the famous screaming four-strokes in 1973, his first full year with MV. It broke a seven-year run on the title by fellow MV works rider Giacomo Agostini. A personality clash occurred between the two and Agostini quit the team at the end of the year. Read won the 500 title again the following year when his fans voted him top of the *Motor Cycle News* poll, Britain's leading motorcycling popularity census.

Then followed another controversy. An established Isle of Man TT hero, Read became one of its most outspoken critics on the grounds of safety and, along with several other top road race stars, vowed he would never race there again. He changed his mind in 1977 when Honda offered him a works ride in the new style Formula One race which constituted a one race world championship. Read won it in bad weather to collect his eighth world title. For good measure he also won the 'Senior' 500cc event on a Suzuki.

Kenny Roberts

With single-minded determination, American Kenny Roberts left his native country for Europe in 1978 with the express purpose of winning a world road racing championship. For the uncompromising way in which he claimed the 500cc title, the premier world championship, he will be well remembered in motorcycle history. Roberts was only the second American to win a world championship title of any sort, and his aggressive riding style meant that he was immediately noticed on European circuits. As well as taking the 1978 500cc crown Roberts finished second in the 750cc and fourth in the 250cc world series.

Born in Modesto, California, on 31 December 1951, Roberts took up motorcycling competition when he was 13 years old. In 1970 he moved into the professional ranks of American motorcycle competition, winning immediate acclaim as the American Motorcycle Association national novice champion. The following year he joined the Yamaha team and took the AMA national junior title; his nine victories during the season established a record. It was the first of many for Roberts who was to become the youngest ever rider to win

the AMA grand national championship with a record 2,014 points when he was 21.

In 1974 he again won the coveted American No. 1 plate, and boosted his points record to 2,286. In doing so he became the second man in AMA history to win on all five types of courses: short track, half mile, road race, TT and mile.

He completed the five sports 'sweep' the following year when his appearances in dirt events were compulsive viewing—he was the only rider using a water-cooled four-cylinder Yamaha road race engine in a dirt bike frame.

For 1979 and 1980 Roberts again campaigned his 500-4 Yamaha in World Championship grands prix and twice won the title with complete domination. Although success in 1981 generally eluded him, Roberts was still regarded with the greatest accolade of the 'racers' racer'.

Barry Sheene

Barry Sheene, MBE, has brought more glamour to road racing than any other rider. His willingness to appear on television interviews to talk about motorcycling has helped to rid it of its 'grease' stigma, and has improved the image of motorcycling sports. His own clean-cut image has helped to dispel that of the 'rocker' of the 1960s, and his sense of humour and direct personality gain respect from the older generation and idolatry from young fans. His riding is superb: he won two 500cc world championships in 1976 and 1977 for Suzuki. He is also something of a showman: to the delight of spectators, if he has time in a race he puts on a show by 'wheelieing' and playing cat-and-mouse with the other competitors. He is the lap record holder at numerous circuits and has won the British *MCN* Superbike series four times and topped the popularity poll of the British magazine *Motor Cycle News* four times.

Sheene was born on 11 September 1950 in London. His father was a successful rider and two-stroke tuner and it seemed natural for his son to follow in his footsteps. Sheene became British 125cc champion in 1970 and 1971, and his first taste of world success was as runner-up to Angel Nieto in the 1971 125cc world championship. His talent earned him a place with the Yamaha works team for 1972, and in that year he crashed at 160kph (100mph) in practice at the Italian grand prix and badly broke a collar bone. However, he won the FIM 750 series the following year. He became better known to American road race fans in 1975 at Daytona, where he crashed in practice after a tyre blew, and he was thrown off at 280kph (175mph). A film crew captured some of the action, and it was seen on television throughout the world. Even though he had multiple fractures, including a broken thigh bone which required a 50cm (18in) pin, he was back on his machine six weeks later. Six months after the Daytona crash, he had to go back into hospital after another leg fracture sustained while practising 'wheelies'. However, injuries have not stopped his progress, and may even have helped to make him more famous and respected.

Walter Villa

Italian road racer Walter Villa is one of the most popular motorcyclists of today. Four times world champion, he won three consecutive 250cc titles, 1974–6, and was also 350cc champion in 1976. A motorcycle dealer and manufacturer from Modena, Villa, who was born in 1943, began racing in 1962 and rode many types of Italian bikes. His results were good but a works ride never came his way, although he did hold a position as a development rider for Benelli until he beat one of the factory's machines on a privately entered Yamaha. (Benelli then sacked him.)

In 1974 the Italian Harley-Davidson factory which produced two-stroke motorcycles asked him to ride their machinery. Villa rewarded them with their first ever world championship. While continuing to make his own Villa two-stroke models, he stayed with Harley to become the first man to take the 250cc title for three consecutive years since the series was introduced in 1974, an amazing achievement considering the might of the ubiquitous Yamaha opposition. Villa even gave Harley a bonus with the 1976 350 title on the water-cooled two-stroke twin, which was a surprise for both rider and factory, since they were testing the model that year for a serious attempt to win the 350 title in 1977. Victory at the first round in France made them realize they stood a chance, which was just as well: in 1977 Villa actually finished 18th though he was third in the 250 class. For 1978 Villa turned to private Yamahas when the Harley factory fell into financial difficulties, but his best result was only 16th in the 250 world series. Villa will continue to build his own bikes, which he first raced in 1965, after he decides it is time to retire from full-time racing.

MOTO-CROSS

Dave Bickers

European 250cc moto-cross champion in 1960 and 1961, Dave Bickers from near Ipswich, Suffolk, England, was the first man to give a European title to a British two-stroke, winning his titles for the Essex Greeves factory. Born in 1938, at the age of ten he was already grappling with motorcycles. He first raced when he was 16 and became a works rider for DOT at the age of 18. With several British championships to his credit he left Greeves to join the Czechoslovakian CZ factory for 1966,

Roger de Coster   Joel Robert

riding one of the latest 360cc single-cylinder two-strokes in the 500 world series. At the time he forecast correctly that the reign of four-stroke engines was over. In fact 1965 was the last time a solo world championship was won on a four-stroke, by Britain's Jeff Smith on a BSA. Bickers also said that the Japanese factories would dominate the sport as they did in road racing and that 360cc machines would be the upper limit used by competitors in the 500cc world moto-cross class.

His career has so far spanned 25 years and it is not over yet. To date he has ridden solo moto-cross almost continuously, competed in two seasons of British sidecar-cross in the mid-70s, raced stock cars, and in 1978 he took on a new challenge by concentrating on enduro riding with just a little time off for stunt riding for a major film production. In all this time he has never broken a bone in his body. For 1979 Bickers agreed to become team manager of the British International Six Days Trial squad.

Roger de Coster

In February 1978 five times world 500cc moto-cross champion Roger de Coster had a horrific practice crash. It was feared that he might lose his life after hitting a tree. A three-hour operation to remove his spleen and a 5-litre (9pt) blood transfusion saved his life. Five days later he was on his feet discussing his riding programme for 1979. Within 25 days of the surgery he was back in training, and seven weeks after the crash he was winning races again. This incredible rider went on to finish third in the 1978 500cc world championship. Renowned world-wide for a silky smooth riding style in a rough, tough sport, de Coster's astonishing recovery and his determination to carry on undaunted earned him a new dimension in respect and adulation. Many thought the crash was the end of his remarkable career since he had already built up a thriving motorcycle business in Belgium.

The only man to have won five 500cc world crowns, De Coster, born on the 28 August 1944 in Brussels, maintained an interest in cycling for fitness after taking up moto-cross. His first world title came in 1971 for the Japanese Suzuki factory. It was his first year with them and it heralded

a fantastic run of success. World titles followed in 1972, 1973, 1975 and 1976, all on Suzukis. De Coster is now with the rival Honda factory, developing their grands prix machines. A perfectionist, his successes include four American Trans-AM championships. He is careful to make sure that his devotion to moto-cross is not compromised by other interests.

Robert Grogg (sidecar-cross)

One man has always stood far above the rest in the brief history of the European sidecar-cross championship; this is Robert Grogg from near Berne in Switzerland, who has won the series five times since it was introduced in 1971. No-one else has won it more than once. When on form Grogg is untouchable, and even on the rare occasions when he is not, other riders have to struggle to stay with him. Grogg is extremely modest, however, and even gets other people to receive trophies on his behalf if he can. A truck driver by profession, Grogg (born in 1949) started as a solo rider, and won the Swiss junior 500cc championship when he was 17. He then worked towards international status, but when he did not concentrate hard enough on training and failed to score enough points to retain his international licence, rather than step down the ladder he switched to three-wheelers. In his first year on a British 750cc Norton Wasp he won the Swiss championship and from then on never looked back. In 1972, in his first year of grand prix racing, he won the European series. His other European titles were gained in 1974, 1976, 1977 and 1978. Midway through the 1976 season he and his passenger Andreas Graber parted company and another Swiss ballast man, Andreas Husser, took up his position behind the passenger grab rail. The new partnership, with three Norton-powered titles, is the most successful seen on the moto-cross circuits.

Heikki Mikkola

The only man to have won moto-cross world championships in both the 250cc and 500cc classes, Finland's Heikki Mikkola has been dubbed the present-day 'iron man' of the sport because of his total commitment to reaching the winning line first. The 'Flying Finn', as he is often called, can ride a bike so hard that other world-class riders would struggle to get the best out of a machine tuned to his requirements. Born in 1944, the man from Hyvinka really hit it big in 1974 when he took the 500cc world title from Belgium's Roger de Coster who had dominated the class since 1971. Sport fans always like to see a new face at the top and Mikkola's challenge gained him a big following. The needle match continued into 1975 and this time de Coster came out on top. Mikkola switched to the 250 class for 1976 and won the title, at the same time giving the Swedish Husqvarna factory their 12th world/European title. It was his last year with Husqvarna. He had joined as a works rider in 1974 but had ridden the marque for many years before that. The Japanese Yamaha factory wanted him for 1977 to spearhead their return to moto-cross. They picked the right man. Mikkola grabbed the 500cc title for them in no uncertain terms and did the same again in 1978.

Gennady Moisseev
It seems that all Russians in motorcycle sport have a reputation for being strong, silent and mysterious, and three times 250cc world moto-cross champion Gennady Moisseev is one of them. Born in 1948 in Leningrad, Moisseev was a member of the Red Army, but because of his riding prowess he was allowed to concentrate on sport. His riding career began in 1964 and three years later he became a professional sportsman and began to make a name for himself. With Russian championships in 1970, 1972, 1973 and 1976 to his credit, he became a world celebrity in moto-cross when he took the 250cc series in 1974, only the second Russian to win a world title. The following year he was almost totally absent from the scene because of a broken arm and, since in the past Russian riders have often been seen in international racing one year and then never again, speculation grew about his return for 1976. However, he did arrive in Europe that year and soon found his rhythm again by finishing runner-up in the 250cc world series to Heikki Mikkola. Since then he has dominated 250cc moto-cross, winning both the 1977 and 1978 titles. His world championships have all been won on Austrian KTM two-strokes.

Gaston Rahier
Born in 1948, Belgium's moto-crosser Gaston Rahier has dominated the 125cc class since it gained world championship status in 1975. A little over 1.50m (5ft) tall, his lack of height has never been a handicap, and he won the world 125cc title three years in succession from 1975, for Suzuki. To retain the title in 1976, he rode a machine with a seven-speed single-cylinder two-stroke engine. Winning the championship took on more significance that year when Marty Smith, who at that time had two American 125cc championships to his credit, came to Europe for Honda to contest some of the rounds. Rahier, a courageous rider, has also won national championships: he won the 1976 Belgian 250 series by riding the final round a fortnight after breaking a wrist. Several times a member of the victorious Belgian teams in the Moto-Cross and *Trophée*

Des Nations international team events, he was runner-up in the 1978 world 125 title chase to his Suzuki teammate Akira Watanabe, the first Japanese rider to win a world moto-cross championship.

Joel Robert
With six world 250cc moto-cross titles to his credit, Belgian Joel Robert is hailed by many of the sport's pundits as the greatest scrambler of all time. Born at Grandrieu in 1943, he was able to make the motorcycle become an extension of his own personality. He could make it do almost anything he wanted. This complete mastery of machine led to tremendous admiration for the stockily built Belgian who started riding when he was seven. His father taught him and helped to shape his career. His first world championship crown came in 1964, riding for CZ. He was 21, the youngest moto-cross rider to have ever won a world title. A practical joker in the paddock, he had to accept defeat for the next three years. He made up for it by winning the title in an unbroken run from 1968–72. In 1970, when the Japanese factories were wooing riders with tempting contracts, he joined Suzuki and transferred his spectacular stunt style to machines from the Orient. His success combined with his reputation for unpredictability also pulled in the crowds. While with CZ he attacked the engine with a hammer after it had broken down for three successive GP events. And he once staged a one man strike at a Belgian international event after three false starts by throwing his bike down in the middle of the track and sitting alongside it. Still riding for fun, Robert can look back on over 50 grand prix victories and wins in most corners of the globe including America, Australia and Japan. He has been elected Sportsman of the Year in Belgium, has won four Belgian moto-cross championships and been called upon numerous times to represent his country in international team competitions.

SPEEDWAY

Barry Briggs
Barry Briggs is undoubtedly one of the finest racers speedway has ever had. Briggs, a New Zealander and four times winner of the sport's major individual prize, the world championship, gave a new word to speedway—professionalism. It was he, more than any other rider, who gave the sport respectability. He followed his childhood hero, Ronnie Moore, to England and continued where Moore left off. Briggs' first impact was in the world final in 1954 when he finished with 9 points, while Moore won it with a 15-point maximum. The first of Briggs' four wins came in 1957 after a run-off with the Swede Ove Fundin.

Peter Collins   Ronnie Moore

The following year he won again, with Fundin second, but this time he did not have to resort to a run-off. It was not until 1964 that Briggs won again, beating off the threat of a first world championship win by a rider from behind the Iron Curtain. The great Igor Plechanov finished runner-up on 13 points, with Briggs on 15. Briggs' last win, in 1966, was a significant one for speedway, for he won on a new machine, one that was to dominate speedway for a further decade—the Czechoslovakian Jawa. Briggs was instrumental in bringing the two-valve Jawa to world class status, and he became the British concessionaire for Jawa. After Briggs' development work the Jawa overtook the venerable British JAP engine, until it too was overtaken by the British Weslake. Now Jawa is again a prominent make, and has won world championships with its four-valve machines.

Peter Collins
Peter Collins was the undisputed number one speedway rider in England in 1976. It was 'PC', as he was known worldwide, who put an end to England's dearth of world championship titles. Before 100,000 people at the vast Chorzow stadium in Poland, he became only the third Englishman to take speedway's major crown, since the series began in 1936. PC was the first Englishman to win for 14 years, since the great rider with the same initials, the late Peter Craven, won in 1962. England's only successes prior to that were another Craven win in 1955 and Tommy Price in 1949.

Collins, born 24 March 1954, started racing for the Second Division side Rochdale in 1971, after having second-half meetings at Crewe in 1970. He was an immediate success and was a hit with Division One club, Belle Vue, the same season, when he completed 11 matches for them. He has been their number one ever since. Record breaking comes naturally to the brilliant Collins. And one record that will take a long time to emulate is his performance in the world team cup for England. He scored maximums in each of the cup finals for three years running, in 1973, 1974 and 1975.

Ove Fundin
The first of the 'Super Swedes' was Ove

Fundin, who for many years held the outright record of five world championship wins. In many experts' eyes, Fundin is simply the best rider of all time. His record can support such a claim, with world final wins in 1956, 1960, 1961, 1963 and 1967. It was not until 1977 that anyone equalled these record five wins: this was Ivan Mauger.

Fundin's world final record bears scrutiny: in 1954 (his first final) he came last with 2 points; in 1955 he had 10; in 1956 he came 1st; in 1957 2nd; in 1958 2nd; in 1959 2nd; in 1960 1st; in 1961 1st; in 1962 3rd with 10 pts; in 1963 1st; in 1964 3rd with 13 pts; in 1965 3rd with 13 points; in 1967 1st; in 1968 7 pts; and in 1969 9 pts. He therefore had 5 wins from only 15 appearances and, had it not been for a border guard who stopped him going into Poland for the European final, he would have been at the world final again in 1970.

Fundin was one of the great con men of the game. He liked to turn up at important meetings, saying he was either unfit, had had no practice, or was using a slow bike. Then, after his rivals had written him off, he would go out and beat them all! Fundin, born in Transa on 23 May 1933, was the maestro at the famous Norwich track.

Ivan Mauger

When Ivan Mauger won the 1979 world speedway championship final one fine night in Katowice, Poland, he rewrote the history books. It was the mighty New Zealander's sixth world title win which beat the number of titles won by the legendary Swede, Ove Fundin.

Mauger, born in Christchurch on 10 October 1939, took his first world title in 1968. He dominated the world championship for the next three years, and is the only rider in the history of the world championship to win three finals in successive years. In 1970 Mauger also became the winner of the first world final ever held behind the Iron Curtain, when he overcame the odds to win in Wroclaw, Poland.

After finishing runner-up to his own protegé, Ole Olsen of Denmark, in 1971, he was back on the winning trail again in 1972. However, it took him another five years to add his historic fifth title, and on this occasion many 'experts' had to eat their words after saying he was too old to win another title.

Ronnie Moore
The 'wall of death' rider who became a double world speedway champion is the legendary New Zealander Ronnie Moore. (He was in fact born in Tasmania and only later became a naturalized New Zealander.) His parents ran a wall of death show, which toured Australia and New Zealand, and it was here he received his rudimentary motorcycle training and skill. This skill was to take him to world championship titles in 1954 and 1959.

Moore's career really started when, at the age of 17, he was signed up by Wimbledon Dons. Four years later, in 1954, he became the sport's youngest world champion. He was impervious to injuries, and in that final he rode with a broken leg, heavily strapped up with steel. In 1959 he won the world final at Wembley, and once again he was injured, with a fractured foot.

'Mirac', as he is sometimes called, retired in 1963, but made a comeback for Wimbledon in 1970, and showed he still had what it took to be a top rider, making the 1971 world final. He then announced his retirement from the international scene. His story does not end there, however. In 1975, at the age of 41, he rode for the Ivan Mauger/Barry Briggs world champions troupe at Newcastle, New South Wales. In a crash, he fractured his skull and was taken to hospital in a coma. Luckily he recovered and fears that he would be paralysed were unfounded. Today, having retired once more, Moore is content to work at his own motorcycle business.

Egon Muller
Egon Muller has proved himself to be one of the great characters of motorcycle sport. This extrovert West German from Kiel really is a superstar, not just on his speedway and long track bikes, but also as a singer and night club owner. He is a real attraction for the many girl fans of speedway and long track.

His first major title was taken in 1974 when he won the world 1,000 metre long track title in Scheessel, West Germany, from New Zealand's Ivan Mauger, who was second, and Alois Weisbock, Muller's fellow countryman, who was third. Muller went from strength to strength, retaining his 1,000 metre title in 1975 in Gornja Radgona, Yugoslavia, when Mauger was again second and Ole Olsen was third. Three years later Muller was at the top

again, claiming his third world title in 1978 at Mühldorf, West Germany, before 30,000 people. Muller, who was born on 26 November 1948, weighs only about 50kg (8 stone) and his diminutive stature, together with his tremendous ability on two wheels, has made him one of the greatest attractions on continental long tracks—and one of the highest paid.

Ole Olsen
Ole Olsen is speedway's 'great Dane', and Denmark has been put on the world speedway map by this great rider. But for his impetuosity, Olsen would have won more world titles, but he still has three of them, gained in 1971, 1975 and 1978.

Olsen, born in Haderslev on 16 November 1946, went to England as a youth and rode for Newcastle Diamonds in 1967. At that time Ivan Mauger was their kingpin and he took the young and promising Olsen under his wing. Mauger obviously spotted talent, and the Dane fulfilled his promise when he beat his master in Sweden in 1971 to take his first title. After a long spell with Wolverhampton in the British League he demanded to go to the team of his choice, Coventry Bees. He worked wonders with this Midland team, and under his leadership it took the title in 1978. He masterminded his country's first win in the world team cup the same year too, at Landshut, West Germany. Through his leadership, his country is now producing several fine young prospects for future world honours. Olsen is an innovator too: he introduced the Masters speedway championship which holds a £10,000 first prize, but promoters in England, the leading speedway nation, have vetoed his approaches to run a round on one of their tracks, so it is confined to his own track in Vojens in Denmark, and Sweden and West Germany.

ICE RACING

Sergei Tarabanko
Sergei Tarabanko is one of the world's leading ice speedway exponents; living up to his western nickname: 'Sergei—the sure guy'. Tarabanko, a Moscow sports teacher, is a master of ice racing, considered the most dangerous motorcycle sport. He has won the world title, against mighty opposition, in 1975, 1976, 1977 and 1978. The USSR riders dominate this specialized branch of motorcycling and are the toughest bunch around, often racing in temperatures of −40°C (−40°F). But even Tarabanko, born on 25 August 1949, has some way to go to equal the feats of the greatest ever Russian ice racer, Gab Kadyrov, who won six world ice titles, in 1966—the year that Tarabanko started racing—1968, 1969, 1971, 1972 and 1973.

Martin Lampkin   Malcolm Rathmell

TRIALS

Martin Lampkin

Martin Lampkin, born 28 December 1950 in West Yorkshire, England, is to trials riding what fellow Yorkshireman Geoff Boycott is to cricket: more used to winning than losing. The youngest and most successful of the three Lampkin brothers who have all made a significant mark in trials, Martin achieved a unique hat-trick when he won the world's most testing trial, the Scottish Six Days in 1976, to follow up the victories by brothers Alan (1966) and Arthur (1963). His obvious 'feel' for this highly specialized annual event in Scotland's rugged Western Highlands is evidenced by his further wins in 1977 and 1978, so completing only the third hat-trick since 1932.

Riding for the Spanish Bultaco factory, a company to which he has remained loyal for most of his professional career, he became world champion in 1975, the first year the previously named European Championship had world title status. It was a close thing, for after the 12 gruelling rounds, he only managed to beat his Bultaco team-mate, Finnish champion Yrjo Vesterinen, by one mark. Lampkin's subsequent world championship positions have been third, fourth and second—but it has been at home, in major British events, that he has achieved a reputation as the best rider since Sammy Miller. Though occasionally beaten in non-championship trials, in the big, prestigious events Lampkin was untouchable. He took the trials world's triple crown in 1977 with a grand slam in the Scottish Six Days, the Scott Trial and the British Experts—and then repeated the feat 12 months later.

Sammy Miller

Born on 11 November 1933, Sam, 'The Maestro' to thousands of motorcycle enthusiasts the world over, is really the first and last word in the history of trials competition. Name it, and he is almost sure to have done it. Now a relative 'oldie', Miller is still riding and adding to the incredible figure of 910 trials victories he had achieved by the beginning of 1979.

It was at a grass-track meeting in Ulster that he had his first taste of competition. He took to road racing—and was only a hair's breadth away from pulling off a famous victory in the 125cc Isle of Man TT.

Sammy Miller won no fewer than 11 consecutive British titles, from 1959–69, (six of them for Ariel, two European championships, five Scottish Six Days Trials, seven Scott Trials) and respect from all those who saw him or rode with him.

Having done so much to immortalize the British four-stroke, Miller then became the architect of the two-stroke generation in trials. Signing for Bultaco as development rider in 1965, he put his first bike together in just 12 days—and started out on another victory run that brought him the remaining five British championships.

When the Japanese factories invaded the 'feet-up' game in the early 70s, Miller continued his development rôle for Honda, helping to develop the bike that was to win one more British championship—for his team rider Rob Shepherd, in 1977. It was the first four-stroke success in the British championship since Miller's own Ariel win in 1964. The wheel had turned full circle. Sam's Honda team management rôle disappeared with Honda's financial cutback, and the Irishman quickly found himself doing it all over again—with the Italian SWM concern. But by the end of 1978 SWM, too, had drawn in its belt, and he was dropped again.

The rider/author/development engineer/businessman did not stay idle for long. He started working with another Italian factory, Hiro, to build *their* first trials iron.

Malcolm Rathmell

Irony surrounds the trials career of Malcolm Rathmell, for this four-times British Trials Champion originally intended to become a moto-cross professional. Born on 18 June 1949, at Otley, Yorkshire, Rathmell first came to prominence towards the end of the 1960s, as a trials rider for the Triumph and Greeves factories, but he persuaded Greeves to lend him a scrambles machine. Rathmell's early results—second and third placings in the British 250cc Moto-cross Championship and several notable Grand National wins—indicated a racing star in the making, and when the Barcelona Bultaco factory stepped in to sign him in 1970, they offered him a moto-cross contract.

The high spot for this likeable rider was a ninth place in the world 250 Moto-cross GP in Spain—but he continued to ride British trials in the winter. He astounded the critics by winning the British Experts Trial just a few weeks after breaking his wrist in the torturing Yorkshire classic, the Scott Trial. At last, Malcolm Rathmell was established as a trials rider. He stayed with Bultaco for four years, winning the European Championship in 1974, two British crowns (1972 and 1974), and enjoying a host of other successes as a member of the formidable Bultaco team with Martin and Alan Lampkin, including the Scottish Six Days Trial in 1973.

Switching to the rival Montesa factory at the start of 1975, Rathmell took the British championship in both 1975 and 1976, and the Scott Trial in the same years. The Japanese Suzuki concern, hungry for trials success, persuaded Rathmell to join them in 1978 on a contract reputedly worth £80,000 over two years—considerably more than any trials rider had ever been paid before. The partnership never really clicked though, and he left to rejoin Montesa for the 1979 season.

Yrjo Vesterinen

Born 7 December 1952, near Helsinki, Finland, Yrjo (pronounced oo-ree-ah) Vesterinen has become a phenomenon in trials, and one that British fans would rather forget, for he is the man who finally broke the British domination of trials that began in European competition in 1965, and continued for 11 years.

Finland, though a country with a total population no bigger than that of London, has repeatedly produced world champions in motorcycle sport, and Vesterinen is only continuing what was begun by the late Jarno Saarinen (world 250cc road race champion) and Heikki Mikkola (world 500cc moto-cross champion). He started an illustrious riding career by riding moped trials in the Finnish forests and scrubland as a 13-year-old. Vesterinen's amazing talent quickly established him as Finnish champion, then Nordic champion.

Snapped up by Bultaco competitions chief, Oriol Bulto, in 1973, he came within an ace of taking the world championship in 1975, its year of inception, failing by one point to beat Britain's Martin Lampkin. Twelve months later Vesterinen became the first non-Briton to win either a world or European trials title, beating Malcolm Rathmell by six points, after the tiring long-distance trek around the world for the 12 championship events. Those who looked upon this foreign intrusion into a British domain as a flash in the pan were disappointed. Vesterinen proved good enough to go on to a hat-trick of world titles by winning in 1977 and again in 1978.

Vesterinen is remarkable in trials events in that he has brought a deep-thinking, psychological approach to the sport for the first time. His cool approach even when under pressure tends to make his opponents uneasy. His balancing ability is brilliant and he is a master tactician. However, he still has weaknesses, and has never been able to come to terms with the most exacting of all trials—the Scottish Six Days.

Bikes for Everyone

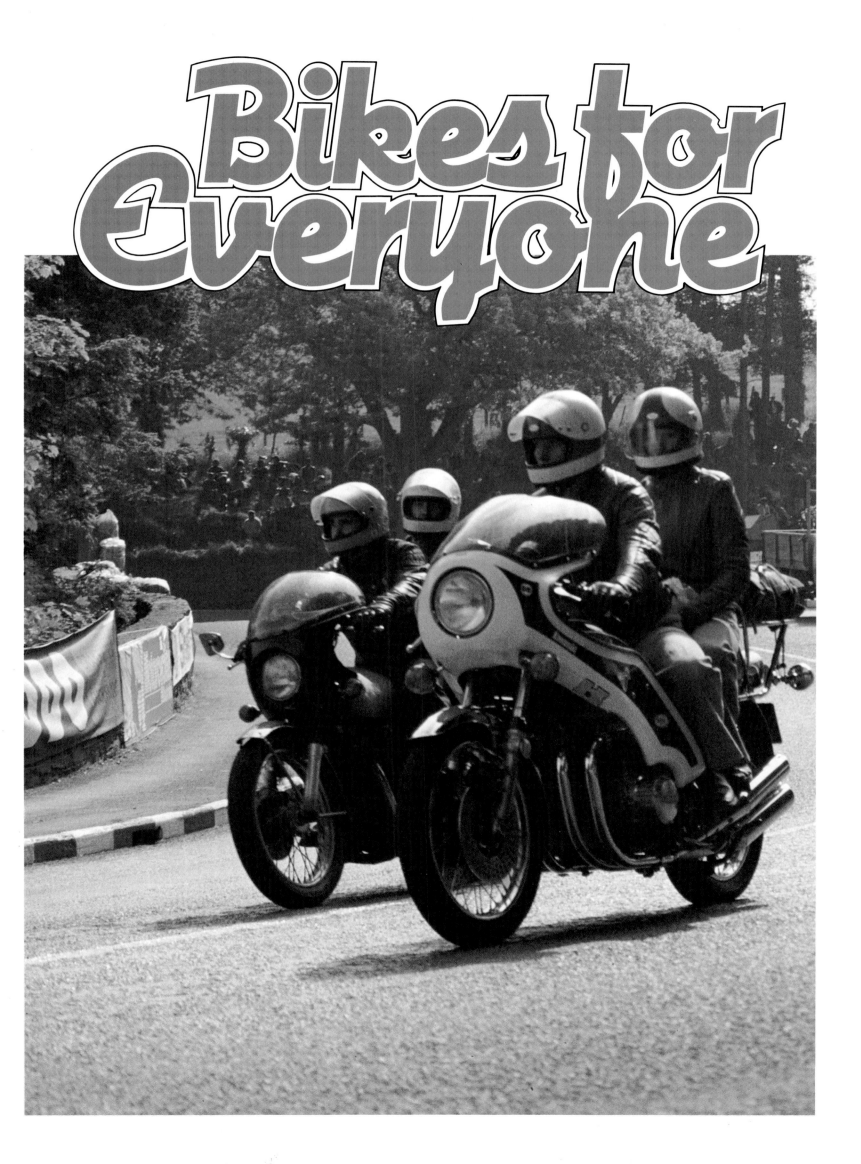

IT has been estimated that, since the birth of the motorcycle 90-odd years ago, at least 2,000 companies (and possibly many more) have ventured into motorcycle manufacture, and that somewhere in the region of 560 of these were registered in Britain alone. In a highly competitive market, only those companies with imaginative managements, innovative design engineers, and successful competitions shops have endured. Survival has hinged on sporting successes and on continual development of new models that have kept pace with–or preferably anticipated–changes in fashion. Over the years, the overwhelming majority of motorcycle manufacturers have failed on both these counts. Most have gone bankrupt, while a fortunate few have managed to sell their assets to more profitable competitors.

Until about 25 years ago the British motorcycle industry, as we have seen, was the most successful in the world, not only in terms of the technical excellence and sporting prowess of its products but also in terms of the total number of manufacturers producing sound and saleable motorbikes for the international market. Today the British industry is in ruins. There are many reasons for this, and by no means all of them have to do with the quality of the machines produced.

The beginning of the decline can be traced back to World War II, which put paid to a number of established companies with excellent reputations: Rudge, Sunbeam (unless one counts the post-war BSA-built Sunbeam S7 and S8 models), Brough, New Imperial, and many others failed to survive the war. The best placed were those companies which had worked during the war on government contracts (not necessarily building motorbikes) and who consequently had sufficient capital after 1945 to invest in post-war production to meet a steadily increasing demand for relatively cheap two-wheeled transport.

By the early 1950s Villiers, Excelsior, and British Anzani were building proprietary lightweight, two-stroke engines from 98 up to 250 cc, and this enabled a number of small motorcycle companies to establish themselves in the ride-to-work, lightweight touring motorcycle market. Excelsior themselves, Norman, Dayton, DMW, Greeves, Sun, Francis-Barnett, and James were among the best-known firms to use these proprietary engine-gearbox units in a range of machines that were almost identical in performance, with only their colour schemes, small variations in design of frames and suspension, and the name plates on the fuel tanks to prove that they were built in different factories.

The Villiers 8E and 9E single-cylinder two-stroke and 2T twin-cylinder engines were to remain for some years the mainstays of the lightweight motorcycle industry in Britain. Even companies as renowned as DOT and Cotton, which had done well in pre-war TT races with their highly successful four-stroke racers, had to rely on Villiers engines to continue production after the war. Only the large manufacturers such as BSA, Triumph, Norton, Ariel, Royal Enfield, Velocette, AJS, and Matchless could afford to build lightweight motorcycles powered by engines of their own design.

Perhaps the most successful of all these lightweights was the BSA Bantam. The design for this machine was claimed from the German DKW factory as part of Britain's war reparations, and thousands of pale-green, 123 cc, single-cylinder, two-stroke, three-speed models were churned out by the Armoury Road factory.

In order to keep pace with competitors, BSA had to revamp the Bantam a number of times, first increasing the capacity to

148 cc and, finally, to 175 cc. The last of the line, the Bantam D14, had a four-speed gearbox, contact-breaker/coil ignition, a generator for battery lighting, full swinging-arm suspension at the rear, and front telescopic forks.

Another success story also came about through the claiming of designs under the guise of war reparations. Ariel motorcycles of Selly Oak, Birmingham, was granted rights to manufacture the German Adler 250 cc two-stroke twin engine. Ariel incorporated this in a monocoque, pressed-steel-construction frame, truly unique for its period, which had a dummy fuel tank in the usual position and the real one situated beneath the saddle (an idea quite recently adopted by the Japanese because, by lowering the machine's centre of gravity, it improves low-speed handling). The entire engine, apart from the frontal area, was enclosed in panelling, and the rider was protected against the weather by leg-shields and a windscreen. The Ariel was well in advance of fashion in other respects: its flashing indicators, electric clock, and other fittings were not to become standard items on motorbikes until the Japanese invasion a decade hence.

With some justification, Ariel called this machine the Leader. It was, however, a little too far in the lead: its reception from an ultra-cautious motorcycling public was decidedly cool, and it was not until it had been stripped of all its panelling and called the Arrow that it was finally accepted as a 'real' motorcycle. For a period of four or five years in the early 1960s the Arrow and its tuned sports version, the Golden Arrow, sold well in Britain. But they found few buyers abroad and, with growing competition from imported machines and the need to develop internationally saleable products, they were finally abandoned by Ariel's parent company, BSA.

The most depressing characteristic of the British motorcycle industry in the 1950s and early 1960s was its complacency. Until this period, things had gone very much its way, in both the British and the international markets: it seemed to assume that whatever it built would be eagerly accepted by a transport-hungry world.

PREVIOUS PAGE Spectators assemble for the TT week at the Isle of Man, where enthusiasts off circuit demonstrate the qualities of their machines just as the competitors do. Here people have a chance to see many different marques and to compare their performance.

LEFT This Norton Dominator 77 of 1953 was one of a long line of post-war vertical-twin Nortons, from the four-stroke Model 7 of 1947 to the 850 cc Commando of the 1970s.

ABOVE The 'scooter' boom of the early 1960s was led by the Italian Vespa and Lambretta machines. Although scooters have been overtaken in popularity by the moped, this 1970s Vespa shows the almost ageless quality of its 20-year-old design.

Above all, it failed to invest adequately in new engineering and design technology: the Bantam and the Arrow – both essentially 'borrowed' from the Germans – were scarcely complimentary to British innovatory prowess. Not surprisingly, the next development – the scooter boom – caught the British industry unprepared.

By the late 1950s the German NSU company had virtually killed off the Excelsior and other British auto-cycles with its astonishingly lively 50 cc single- and two-speed mopeds, which sold in huge quantities to workers fed up with pedalling a bicycle to and from their places of work.

Hard on the heels of NSU's invasion an almost toy-like machine, with tiny wheels and a panelled body, arrived from Italy.

The scooter, as this type of machine came to be called, was pioneered by two Italian manufacturers. The first of the type, the Vespa (Wasp), carried its 125 cc two-stroke engine with built-in gearbox beneath the off-side of two bubble-shaped panels enclosing the rear wheel. A unique design feature used the transmission casing as the pivoting-arm suspension on which the rear wheel was mounted. The second Italian scooter, the Lambretta, also had a small-capacity two-stroke power unit with shaft drive to the rear wheel.

By the mid-1950s the British manufacturers woke up to the fact that Vespa
and Lambretta were carving chunks out
of their motorcycle sales, and hurriedly
embarked on a crash scooter-building
programme. They met with scant success:
they were too late and, in any case, few if
any of the British models could hold a
candle to their Italian rivals. BSA built a
Sunbeam scooter based on a modified
Bantam 175 cc two-stroke engine. Triumph
used the same engine in their Tigress
scooter, which was also available with a
250cc, twin-cylinder, four-stroke power
unit. Velocette's contribution was powered
by a two-stroke engine with twin, horizontally opposed cylinders; it was a clumsy
giant compared with the nippy Italians.
Even the Dayton and DMW scooters, using
the highly efficient Villiers engine-gearbox
units, failed to make much impression on
the market. By now both the Vespa and
Lambretta had not only reached a very
high level of development: equally important, they had become highly fashionable in a predominantly middle-class
market, acquiring a social cachet their
British rivals could not aspire to.

Ironically, yet another blow to the
British motorcycle industry was itself
British: Alec Issigonis's Mini. One of the
most significant cars of the post-war era,
the Mini was introduced in 1959 and soon
demonstrated that its 850cc engine had
only a marginally greater thirst for petrol
than some of the large-capacity motorcycles – and, moreover, the car cost only a
little more than the big two-wheel roadsters. Many motorcyclists switched allegiance and bought a car.

The Japanese Invasion

Meanwhile, on the other side of the world,
the Japanese motorcycle industry was
flourishing. The multi-million population
of Japan had an insatiable appetite for
lightweight, powered two-wheelers of any
description, and, consequently, anybody
with enterprize and a reasonably well-
equipped engineering workshop could
make their fortune.

Soichiro Honda was just such a person.
In 1946 this 40-year-old Japanese engineer
bought a cheap lot of army-surplus
stationary two-stroke engines and with

RIGHT An important recent development in the
ultra-lightweight market is the 'sports'
moped – its attraction for young riders being
that in looks (if not in performance) it was
obviously kin to the motorcycle proper. One of
the most successful examples of the type is the
Yamaha FS1E, a 50 cc, single-cylinder two-
stroke with a four-speed gearbox and a top
speed of about 73 km/h (45 mph).

12 other workers set up shop to convert the engines so that they would fit onto and drive push bikes. By 1949 Honda had designed his first complete motorcycle, a small-capacity two-stroke which he named the Dream. Constant re-investment of profits ensured that within two years Honda was building and selling more than 250 machines a week. In 1951 he abandoned two-stroke designs to produce his E-model

LEFT An evening meeting of members of the South London branch of the BSA Owners' Club. Motorcycle clubs, especially those devoted to individual marques no longer in production, have become popular in Britain since the war. Typical activities include rallies, in this country and abroad, and expert restoration of old machines.

BELOW Suzuki's A100M is an example of the sports-moped class, its 100 cc motor giving improved acceleration and top speed. Japanese sports mopeds have a high standard of finish and include wing mirrors and flashing indicators among items fitted as standard equipment.

four-stroke Dream, the first in a long line of four-strokes to be produced over the next 25 years.

In spite of financial problems, Honda realized that he had to gamble everything if he hoped to capture the largest share of the home market. He designed and produced his first step-through utility motorcycle, the Cub, in 1952, and the following year he embarked on a massive re-tooling programme which brought him to the verge of bankruptcy. Fortunately his company survived the crisis and by the end of 1953 was manufacturing up to 1,000 Benly 90 cc single-cylinder, four-stroke motorcycles a month.

Honda then set his sights on the world export markets. Hence his visit in 1954 to the Isle of Man, where no one, least of all the British manufacturers, realized what was in his mind as he studied the racing machines of the most successful motorcycle-manufacturing countries. He decided that grand-prix racing was the finest publicity platform for any motor-

cycle manufacturer who wished to sell his products worldwide.

The small-capacity motorcycle market in Europe, with the exception of Italy, was wide open for exploitation, and, by 1958, Honda motorcycles had designed, built, and tested the 50 cc step-through C100 and sold well over 20,000 of the machines in a year. Some filtered through to Britain, where Hondis, the importers, attempted to set up dealerships to handle the unusual-looking product. Later Honda was to establish subsidiaries of the parent company in both Britain and the United States instead of relying on the services of importers.

Honda was also developing his light-weight racing motorcycles with which he hoped to capture world titles and acclaim. The Honda race team arrived for its first Isle of Man TT in 1959 with a batch of machines almost totally unsuited for racing on the tricky circuit. Knobbly tyres had to be changed for proper racing covers, and after a reliable if somewhat unspectacular race week the Japanese mechanics, engineers, and riders returned home with many lessons learned.

The following year Honda again competed in the Isle of Man 125 cc TT and, although the Italian MV Agustas remained invincible, five of Honda's six machines finished the tough course, close behind the leaders. At the same time Honda was marketing a range of unorthodox-looking 125 and 250 cc motorcycles in Britain. The angular finning of the 125 cc OHC C92 Benly and CB92 Sports Benly attracted curious glances from British motorcyclists. Square-sectioned rear suspension units on pressed-steel swinging-arms looked decidedly exotic when compared with European tubular frame designs. The absence of damping on the roadster models made them extremely uncomfortable to ride and their poor-quality Japanese tyres proved a nightmare on wet roads. Only the Sports CB92 125 cc twin and the Sports CB72 250 cc OHC twin machines came anywhere near matching the European-built motorcycles in road-holding.

But there was one thing that amazed the European motorcycling public. The Japanese motorcycles had flashing indicators, electric starters, toolkits, and equipment such as wing mirrors that had rarely before been fitted on European machines except as optional extras. They proved an irresistible sales attraction.

The British industry failed to perceive the threat materializing before its very eyes and, as other Japanese manufacturers sought world export sales, the British lightweight motorcycle market began to be dominated by Honda, Suzuki, and Yamaha machines. One by one the smaller British factories closed down: James, Francis-

Barnett, Norman, Dayton, Sun, Ariel, Royal Enfield . . . the melancholy list grew longer each year.

Britain still dominated the large-capacity motorcycle market through the 1960s with machines powered by essentially obsolescent overhead-valve, four-stroke, vertical-twin engines. Exceptions to the rule were the much more refined German horizontally opposed, twin-cylinder, shaft-driven BMW motorcycles and the magnificent American Harley-Davidson V-twin machines. Each was excellent in its own, very individual way, but too expensive for any but the most dedicated enthusiast to contemplate buying.

LEFT The Triumph Bonneville, probably the most popular machine the company ever made, was built around a vertical-twin four-stroke motor Triumph introduced in the 1930s and eventually built in capacity classes from 350 to 750 cc. This Bonneville 750 of the early 1970s has a five-speed gearbox and a top speed of about 177 km/h (110 mph).

LEFT BELOW In 1970 Britain's answers to the Honda 750 were the BSA Rocket-3 and the almost identical Triumph Trident, with three-cylinder, triple-carburettor, 750 cc engines. Although less sophisticated (and less commercially successful) than the Honda, the Rocket and Trident were superior to it in roadholding and handling. The Rocket-3 shown here, differed from the Trident in the less upright position of its motor.

RIGHT ABOVE A 1973 version of the Honda 750-Four introduced in 1969. Its 750 cc overhead-camshaft engine had four cylinders, each with its own carburettor, an electric starter, and a five-speed gearbox, and took the Honda to a top speed of 193 km/h (120 mph). Stopping power was provided by a single-disc front brake.

RIGHT BELOW The Norton Commando 750, introduced in 1968, brought a new smoothness to the ride of British motorbikes, rubber mountings isolating the frame from the engine and transmission and so reducing the effect of the vibrations of its vertical-twin motor.

Power and Speed

As far as the British manufacturers were concerned, as the market demanded faster, more powerful motorcycles, they simply modified or rejigged existing designs either by overboring them (that is, enlarging cylinder diameters) to increase capacity or by fitting twin carburettors, increasing compression ratios, and modifying camshaft profiles to improve engine breathing. Thus the 'soft', touring Triumph 650 cc Thunderbird became the high-performance, sports 650 cc Bonneville; the touring Norton Dominator was transformed into the Super Sports 650 Dominator, and the BSA A10 650 twin was uprated to become the Road Rocket and later the highly regarded but regrettably short-lived Rocket Gold Star.

Unfortunately, the typical 180° vertical-twin motors of such machines were poorly balanced: as engine revolutions increased, so vibration became ever more pronounced. The result was that light bulbs would break, and number plates, mudguards, and even major components of the frame would split under the stress.

Norton attempted to deal with the

problem in 1968, when it introduced the 750 cc Commando in which the complete engine and transmission, including the rear swinging-arm suspension, were attached to the main frame by large rubber mountings. This isolated the rider from the vibration, and to a limited degree the system worked; but the special rubber bushes which absorbed the vibration had to be renewed every 16,000 km (10,000 miles) or roadholding deteriorated drastically. (Ironically, the only manufacturer fully to overcome the vibration problem of the classic British vertical twin was Yamaha with its 650 cc model. By 1975, after its frame had been remodelled by Percy Tait—once Triumph's chief test rider—the Yamaha XS650, had emerged as a much smoother and more refined vertical-twin than anything British manufacturers were able to offer.)

Triumph and BSA went one better, late in 1968, with the introduction of the 750 cc three-cylinder Triumph Trident and BSA Rocket-3. The machines were almost identical except for 'badge engineering' and had basically the same pushrod-operated overhead-valve motor designed by Doug Hele. They were highly successful, especially in the United States, where a rapidly expanding motorcycle market was demanding smoother and more sophisticated machines.

Then, in 1969, Honda stunned the opposition by introducing a brand-new, four-cylinder, OHC, five-speed motorcycle, the CB750. It was said that the project had taken Honda only six months from drawing board to the first production models, whereas the much less sophisticated and technically inferior Triumph and BSA triples had been under development

for five years. The CB750 was smooth, powerful, and fast, and its specification (apart from its open-chain drive) was years in advance of anything on the road at that time. Four cylinders, four carburettors, electric starting, five-speed gearbox, front hydraulic disc brake, flashing indicators, full instrumentation including console with warning lights for oil pressure, generator, main beam, and indicators, had until that time been unheard of on a mass-produced motorcycle.

Honda launched the model with brilliantly aggressive salesmanship. To prove beyond doubt that the new machine was fast and reliable as well as technologically very advanced, Honda entered a specially prepared version of the CB750 in the Daytona Classic 200 race—and won. The modern era of the large-capacity superbike had been well and truly launched.

BELOW This Kawasaki KH250 was the smallest of a range of three-cylinder, air-cooled, two-stroke Kawasakis of up to 750 cc.

RIGHT In the mid 1970's, Yamaha stunned the biking populus with their 250 and 350 cc two-stroke roadsters. The RD350LC had a top speed of 110 mph and lightning acceleration.

BELOW RIGHT This is the machine which marked the zenith in the 'age of the superbike', the Kawasaki Z1300.

MODERN CLASSICS

SUPERBIKES are nothing new. From time to time throughout motorcycling history machines have emerged whose advanced specification, exceptional quality of construction, or spectacular performance has placed them ahead of their contemporaries – and beyond the reach of all but the most dedicated enthusiast. Some obvious landmarks in this category are William Henderson's trend-setting in-line four-cylinder giant of 1911, the legendary Brough Superior of Brooklands fame in the 1920s and 1930s, and, in the years immediately after World War II, the somewhat unsophisticated but rocket-fast HRD-Vincent Black Shadow.

Yet sheer performance statistics are not the sole criterion of a classic machine. Between the heyday of the Black Shadow

produced by the British motorcycle industry, especially after March 1975, when the T160 Trident was fitted with disc brakes at front and rear and an electric starter. Both models offered high-speed cruising in reasonable comfort, and in their three-cylinder engine configuration they anticipated a trend that was later to find more successful expression in some Japanese and Italian superbikes, as we shall see in the following pages.

Norton, meanwhile, responded to the threat of Honda's CB750 by overboring the engine on their Commando to 850cc. By the mid-1970s the Norton, too, was fitted with an electric starter, hydraulic disc brake on the front wheel, flashing indicators, and many of the other items offered – and relentlessly promoted – by

learned the Japanese lesson in time but were prepared to take on Honda and the rest and even to challenge them in engineering excellence. Today, there can be little doubt that the Japanese continue to lead the world in motorcycle research and technological innovation, while the quality of finish on their machines – and even their superbikes are essentially mass-produced – remains astonishing. But, for many people, the finest Italian motorcycles offer not only great power and speed but also the ultimate experience in pure handling and in that essential but indefinable quality of 'feel' that makes the true aficionado totally at one with his machine.

One of the few large-capacity motorcycle manufacturers that remained almost uninfluenced by Japanese thinking until quite recently is the German car and motorcycle firm of BMW. During the middle years of the 1960s BMW almost ceased motorcycle production, mainly as a consequence of the sales slump that occurred in the United States and Europe. But the firm's fortunes recovered during the early 1970s with a fine new range of 500, 600, and 750cc models. While they have not neglected recent trends in superbike engineering and design, the most striking characteristic of BMW motorcycles is the sheer quality of their construction and finish; although not perhaps the most exciting of the big machines, they have a fair claim to the title of 'the motorcyclist's Rolls-Royce'.

This last observation serves to remind us of changes in what might be called the sociology of the motorbike. The modern classics described on the following pages are special in more ways than those of sheer size and performance. After all, there are still plenty of enthusiasts around who are capable of transforming the performance of quite ordinary roadsters by judicious tinkering of one kind or another. The significance of the present generation of superbikes lies in the fact that they are aimed directly at a section of the public that motorcycle manufacturers have never before catered to on this scale. The machines offer not only tremendous road performance but a high degree of mechanical refinement, luxury, and comfort – at a price that places them beyond the reach of the traditional motorcycling public. We have to think of the modern superbike as a direct competitor of the high-performance sports car, and this is a development that may have profound implications for the motoring world in general.

Meanwhile, the struggle for supremacy continues, with bigger, faster, more powerful, and more expensive superbikes being unveiled every year. Let us have a closer look at a few of them.

and the introduction of the trend-setting Honda CB750 in 1969 was the brief ascendancy of the big-engined Triumphs, BSAs, and Nortons. Among the best of these machines was the Triumph 650 Bonneville, introduced in 1959. Although its acceleration and top speed were fairly modest compared with the performance of present-day superbikes, its handling qualities and speed of response to the rider – especially after its suspension had been refined by Doug Hele – are still recalled with enthusiasm by its many admirers. Beautifully maintained 'Bonnies' are still to be seen on the roads of Britain and elsewhere – especially in the United States, where the exploits of American riders on earlier Triumphs at Bonneville Salt Flats, Utah, had been acknowledged in this model's name.

Although they never inspired the same affection as the Bonneville, the Triumph Trident and the very similar BSA Rocket-3 were arguably the best machines ever

ABOVE the 1948 Series C Vincent Black Shadow, one of the original 'superbikes'.
PREVIOUS PAGE The Executive version of the flat-four Honda Gold Wing 1000 cc version.

Honda, but it came up with nothing to match the highly efficient, very complex, but reliable Japanese motor. It was rather like offering cosmetics when major surgery was needed. Already by the late 1960s the quality of the big Japanese machines had won for them the lion's share of the crucially important North American market; now they were poised to conquer Europe as well.

Honda had set the pace, but now Kawasaki, Suzuki, and Yamaha were following close behind in the race to produce bigger, faster, and more sophisticated superbikes. The only significant European challenge to the Japanese big four came from the Italians and from the German BMW factory at Berlin.

In the superbike field the Italian manufacturers, unlike the British, not only

Honda CBX-B

To fellow designers at Honda, the CBX was christened 'Irimajiri's folly' when it was announced, as the high-technology, six-cylinder superbike embodied much of designer Soichiro Irimajiri's work from his successful multi-cylindered racing machines of the 1960s. The CBX was never the fastest bike in its class, but its sheer excess of specification put it head and shoulders above its rivals: a showcase for its mentor's work.

The early CBX Hondas with 105bhp on tap were immensely fast, nevertheless, but their huge engines slung sideways under a diamond-type frame, did little to help the handling of the bike. Then, in the early 1980s, Germany announced that it would prohibit the importation of any machine over 100bhp, so it was a good excuse for Honda to change the image of its range leader. The CBX-B was announced as a 'Sports Tourer' and featured an engine of just under 100bhp, a superb fairing and a revised rear suspension system. Instead of the usual twin spring/damper units, the CBX-B featured Honda's Pro-Link design

as used on their successful motocross bikes with a single larger unit mounted behind the engine.

The heart of the CBX-B remains the same with the short-stroke 1,047cc engine breathing through six carburettors and 24 valves operated by twin overhead camshafts. A lot of thought has gone into the motor to keep it compact. The alternator is mounted behind the cylinders rather than on the end of the crankshaft to make the engine narrower, while the whole power plant is suspended from the frame rather than sitting in it so that the front down tubes can be dispensed with and a shorter wheelbase be incorporated.

Power is transmitted through a wet-multi-plate clutch and five-speed gearbox to a final drive chain, while three disc brakes take care of the stopping. The twin front discs are interesting in that they are ventilated and the first of their type to be featured on a road machine.

In spite of losing a few bhp and gaining a few pounds in weight, the 'Touring' CBX is still a very quick machine with a

top speed of just under 135mph and the ability to cover a quarter mile from a standing start in 12secs. The penalty for such a responsive engine is in fuel consumption for, if the engine is kept near its 9,500rpm red line, it will reward its rider with something less than 30mpg; not quite in keeping with its tourer image, either.

The handling of the bike has been transformed with its stiffer monoshock rear end and, although far from being an easy bike to throw around, the Pro-Link system keeps things stable near the limit and it doesn't become hard work like its predecessor.

The finish of the big Honda is exemplary and the fairing in particular is impressive in that it affords a good deal of weather protection without being either bulky to ride behind in heavy traffic nor unsightly to look at.

Whether folly or not, the Honda is a magnificent example of Japanese high technology, and even if the CBX-B is not the fastest bike around, the sound and feel of its engine still set it apart from the rest.

Kawasaki GPz1100

Kawasaki Heavy Industries keep a very tight rein on their motorcycle operation and they don't allow them as much money for development as Honda, for example. That is why the large Kawasakis since the famous 903cc Z1 have retained simple two-valves-per-cylinder engines rather than multi-valved designs favoured by Honda and Suzuki. However, that has not stopped Kawasaki from being at the forefront of performance motorcycles.

The first mass-production motorcycle equipped with fuel injection, the 1,089cc, four-cylinder engine produces a massive 108bhp to give the bike incredible acceleration and a top speed of just on 140mph. The performance gain over its predecessors has not merely been through continual development of the bike's bullet-proof engine, but also the gradual paring of weight from the machine as a whole. Incredibly, the GPz1100 weighs 522lb which is around 50lb less than most of its rivals.

Yamaha XS1100

Yamaha's early 500, 650, and 750 cc twin-cylinder, four-stroke roadsters were far from inspiring in either outright performance or handling, and had only moderate commercial success. But there were greater things to come: the eight-valve, 500 cc, four-stroke twin was more than a match for anything else in the capacity class on the market, and the XS750 three-cylinder, double-OHC, shaft-driven superbike competed well with the CB750 Honda and BMW R75/7.

At the Paris Motorcycle Show of 1977 the company announced the ultimate in Yamaha motorcycle design for the 1978 season – the XS1100. This 1,100 cc, four-cylinder, double-OHC, five-speed, 95 hp machine has all the trimmings, including shaft drive, cast-alloy road wheels, electric starter, and quartz-halogen headlights, and with a top speed of 225 km/h (140 mph) and a standing 400 m ($\frac{1}{4}$ mile) of less than 12 seconds, it offers virtually race-track performance to the superbike owner.

Laverda Formula Mirage

The Laverda has always been unique in the world of three-cylinder motorcycles for, whereas machines like the Triumph Trident have featured pistons connected to the crankshaft in phases of 120°, the Laverdas have had them set in a strange 180° pattern. You don't need a mathematics degree to work out that it is an odd configuration but it can be explained easily as a normal four-cylinder engine with an end cylinder missing. If you think of that when you next hear one, too, it will all fall into place. The company used this system to combat a high-frequency vibration they said would otherwise occur, but that didn't stop their own bike from having its own unique 'shakes'.

Whatever, the Laverda triples were no slouches and indeed the 100bhp plus Formula Mirage had a top speed of well over 140mph and acceleration to match. Thus, it came as some surprise when, for the 1982 range of bikes, the company switched after seven years to 120° engines.

Ducati 900ss Hailwood Replica

In the world of motorcycling, the Italian industry has a certain charisma. Although the Latin manufacturers are overshadowed by the Japanese in terms of advanced technology, their bikes are still able to compete with the oriental opposition with their exemplary simple and lightweight design and inherrent fine handling characteristics. When one talks of roadbike handling, the Ducatis are the yardsticks by which others are judged.

Even though the Japanese can produce any variation on a multi-cylindered theme with excellent results, there are many traditionalists on two wheels who believe that a 90° vee-twin mounted with the cylinders longitudinal in the frame is *the* perfect configuration; the Ducati 900SS Hailwood Replica has just that.

Designed by renowned engineer Fabio Taglioni, the bike's 864cc motor features desmodromic valve operation in which the valve is opened and closed mechanically, rather than left to bounce shut with a spring as is the case with every other automotive engine, be it for bikes or cars or whatever. The advantage with the 'desmo' system is that at high engine speeds the valve cannot get out of frequency with the rest of the engine and damage the piston. The disadvantages are that maintenance of the adjustment is required at very short intervals.

With just 68bhp on tap a lot of the big 'Duke's' performance can be attributed to its paltry 420lb weight, and the bike can reach 130mph. The same figures are also responsible for the machine being able to return over 55mpg, which is far better than any other bike with comparable performance. The Hailwood Replica is a faired version of the 900SS, similar to the mildly tuned bike Mike Hailwood raced on his comeback to the Isle of Man in 1978. That year he humbled the Japanese opposition which had around 40bhp extra to propel them, but then that was typical of the man as well as of his machine.

Moto Guzzi 850 Le Mans III

Unlike Ducati who use their 90° vee-twin engine longitudinally in the frame, Moto Guzzi for the past decade and a half have used their vee-twin transversely with the cylinder heads just in front of the rider's knees. Top of the Moto Guzzi range is the Le Mans III which, as its title implies, is the third in a range of sports bikes named after the famous 24-hour bike race.

The Le Mans features an 844cc engine which is every bit as robust as its appearance suggests and, breathing through two valves per cylinder, operated by pushrods and rockers, the unit produces 78bhp. This may seem strange when earlier versions were said to have had well over 80bhp, but it is only now that the Italian industry quotes in proper brake-horsepower rather than their own *cavallinos*, themselves notable for being weaker than our 'horses'. Power is fed through a twin-plate dry clutch to a five-speed gearbox and thence to a shaft drive. The whole engine/transmission unit is mounted low in the frame making for a sub-

sequent low centre of gravity and fine handling.

The braking system on the Le Mans is like all other Moto Guzzis being the company's patented 'integral linked' system. The normal brake lever on the handlebars works just one of the bike's twin front discs, while the brake foot pedal takes care of the other front and rear disc together. Pressure is in the proportion 75% to the front and 25% to the rear.

The idea with the integral system is that, except under emergency conditions, all braking can be safely accomplished merely by using the foot pedal. In practice, however, a bike rider will still instinctively use the same combination of hand and foot, and the riders are very few who use the brakes in the manner in which they were designed. However they are operated, though, the Brembo brakes are exceptional in all weathers.

The suspension on the Le Mans is conventional but that should not detract from its effectiveness in any way. The

whole machine is built low and the rider, leaning forward to the racing style bars, has no trouble controlling the bike.

Mounted with the cylinders across the frame, the Le Mans feels very lumpy at idle and tends to shake if the throttle is blipped open. That shaking is lost once under way, however. With gearing more suited to high-speed cruising, the Le Mans is not the quickest of machines away from standstill and if full acceleration is needed a lot of violent clutch slip is called for. The low seating position angles the rider perfectly into the wind so that fast speeds can be held with little strain, while the small fairing deflects wind.

A top speed of just under 130 mph can be obtained by the 485lb bike while fuel consumption can be extremely frugal around 50mpg if the throttle hand is restrained from holding the two 36mm carburettors open for too long.

Some Italian bikes can be criticised for having a poor finish, but the Moto Guzzi Le Mans III is the exception.

Hesketh V1000

The 1980s are seeing a small revival in the British Bike industry after a period of stagnation which has seen the once biggest motorcycle-producing nation pale into a faint shadow of its former self. Heading the revival is the Hesketh V1000.

Lord Hesketh comes from a wealthy family which, amongst other things, owns Towcester race course. Lord Hesketh became famous for his unsponsored British Formula One team which gave James Hunt his first Grand Prix victory and put him on course for the World Championship in 1976. When racing became too expensive, Lord Hesketh turned to engine rebuilding for all manor of racing engines, but most notably Cosworth F1 motors. It was during this period that Lord Hesketh decided to build his own superbike from the ground up.

To begin with, it was decided that the bike should be of the classic vee-twin design so it became a 992cc unit with cylinders arranged in a 90° vee. Weslake, the famous tuning company of Rye, Sussex, helped with the cylinder-head design.

The finished motor is a very sophisticated unit indeed and features four valves per cylinder operated by twin chain-driven overhead camshafts. Breathing through twin Del'Orto carburettors and running with a high 10.5:1 compression ratio, the Hesketh engine produces a healthy 86bhp at 6,500rpm and, more importantly, a whopping 69lb ft of torque at 5,000rpm.

The engine is powerful and very much looks the part, dominating the whole bike, with the huge crankcase in particular catching the eye.

The chassis is formed around the engine (rather than the engine sitting in the frame) with a neat and basic design. For cost's sake, a simple rear suspension has been used with twin spring/damper units rather than a complex monoshock layout, but there is one rather important feature. The swinging-arm pivot is concentric with the power take-off point in the gearbox casing so that chain tension stays the same however much the suspension is compressed.

Obviously, arch patriot Lord Hesketh

wanted to keep as much of his bike British, but he has compromised in the most sensible way by using Italian suspension and Japanese instruments and switchgear, simply because they are the best around. The brakes are Italian Brembos, too, although the temptation to use Campagnolo wheels was averted and British Astralite units used instead. To complete the specification, a powerful German Bosch headlight is fitted.

The solid engine helps contribute to a dry weight of 506lb, which is heavy compared with the Ducati, for example, but a bit less than the Japanese multi-cylindered bikes. With a small frontal area, the Hesketh should reach a speed of over 120mph and be able to return over 40mpg at least.

The Hesketh V1000 is one of the most expensive motorcycles available, but close up you can see exactly where your money has been spent. The finish on the bike is superb and represents British engineering at its best.

Honda CX 500T Turbo

Suzuki GSX 1100SZ Katana

The mighty Research and Development unit at Honda with monotonous regularity turns .out new models and starts new trends whether it be for road or track. In recent years there has been an upsurge of interest in turbochargers with everybody looking on the exhaust-driven super-charger unit as being everything from a source of boundless energy for an engine to an answer to the fuel crisis. Correctly or mistakenly, the Japanese industry has backed turbos and of course the first production turbocharged bike has come from Honda. If there is a future with the turbo, then it will be with middleweight four-cylinder bikes, so why did Honda choose their mild-mannered 500 tourer, the vee-twin CX500? In typical Honda authority, they announced because it was the most *difficult* . . . So, in proving that they can turbocharge an 80° vee-twin, everyone will know that a turbo Honda multi would have to be good. The CX500T bears little resemblance to its sedate stablemate apart from cylinder capacity of 497cc. Using fuel injection,

turbocharging and a multiplicity of advanced electronics to keep the whole plot running sweetly, the 500T has 80bhp at its disposal, 30bhp more than the ordinary CX. The engine is mounted in a Pro-Link frame with a neat full fairing, but weighs a disappointing 499lb, putting it out of the mid-range weight class. Top speed is an impressive 124mph with spark-ling off-the-mark acceleration just a little slower than Honda's own four-cylinder 900. What is poor, however, is the fuel consumption which only just betters 30mpg on average and can drop alarming-ly to little over 20mpg if the bike is pressed hard. Where the bike scores over every other machine, whatever capacity, is its pick up from low engine speeds in high gears where, after a little initial turbo lag, it rockets away. Handling is excellent while braking is aided by anti-dive forks.

In some ways, the bike is better than a 1,000cc machine, but there are penalties. Certainly, with this bike and with turbo-chargers in general you *don't* get some-thing for nothing.

In an effort to make their machines 'different', Suzuki decided that the stan-dard look of their bikes should change and commissioned a European design team to come up with a new image. Their new range was the Katana (which is a Samurai double-edged sword). Sold alongside the ordinary range, the Katanas have a little extra power, suitably reinforced chassis and that unique styling. The GSX1100SZ Katana has a 1,075cc four-cylinder engine with four valves per cylinder in what Suzuki call their TSCC head (twin swirl combustion chambers); they purchased the rights to the design from car makers Fiat who named it after their designer, Piata. In the Suzuki, the motor produces 111bhp, enough to give the 510lb bike a top speed of just over 140mph and accelera-tion over a quarter mile from a standing start in just over 11 seconds: superbike performance, indeed.

The styling is, of course, very much to personal taste, but underneath the bike is just about the fastest thing money can buy in 1982.

Harley-Davidson FXB-Sturgis

Massive bikes with big, 'soft' engines are one of the most enduring traditions of the North American motorcycle–a tradition established before World War I by such famous names as Harley-Davidson, Indian, Henderson, Ace, and Excelsior. Of these, only Harley-Davidson has survived; indeed, it is now the only major motorcycle manufacturer in the United States.

The company was founded at Milwaukee by William S. Harley and Arthur Davidson in 1903, and in 1909 it began to build the large V-twin, four-stroke-engined machines on which its subsequent fortunes and world-wide reputation were based. In terms of post-World War II trends, Harleys have remained unique, and that is one reason why the Japanese motorcycle invasion of the United States in the 1960s, although

damaging to the company, could not destroy the special corner of the market the Harley had created for itself.

The Sturgis, named after a famous American bike rally, is something of a departure for the company in recent years and features rubber driving belts. However, that solid vee-twin motor with push-rod valves still dominates the bike as indeed it does all other Harleys. In Sturgis form, the engine displaces 80cu in, or 1,340cc in metric language. However you convert the figure, it is the largest engine available in a mass-produced motorcycle.

Power is taken from the engine to the gearbox by the first of the cogged rubber belts which are not only quieter and cleaner than chains but last a lot longer, too. Considering the bike weighs 572lb, the belts must be up to the job.

The Sturgis is one of the many roadster-style Harleys available and uses highway pegs. These are suspended from the front downtubes and enable the rider to lay back in the traditional American way. A 'sissy-back' seat is used for the pillion to lean on and further adds to the bike's casual character.

In fact, anybody who pays the high prices for the famous Milwaukee monsters and expects sizzling performance is missing the point. The Sturgis, like its stablemates, has adequate performance, surprisingly good dry-weather roadholding, excellent fuel economy and poor brakes. What is exceptional is its reliability and character. Harleys are called 'the Great American Freedom Machines' and are most at home cruising on endless freeways.

BMW R100RS

While its machines are no longer contenders in the major road-racing grands prix except in sidecar combination form, BMW (the initials stand for Bayerische Motoren Werke) can claim a long and distinguished history in the field of speed. As early as 1932 a specially prepared machine powered by a 750 cc, horizontally opposed twin motor established a world motorcycle speed record of more than 244 km/h (152 mph); four years later a BMW with a supercharged 750 engine raised the record to almost 280 km/h (174 mph). The years immediately before World War II also saw the company establish its reputation for building superb racing machines, BMWs made their first appearance on the Isle of Man TT circuit in 1937, and two years later the racers crowned their efforts by taking first and second places in the Senior TT,

the first supercharged machines to win the 500 cc class.

When BMW introduced its first motorcycle in 1923, it was a 496 cc, horizontally opposed, four-stroke, twin-cylinder machine with shaft drive to the rear wheel, and it was fitted with a primitive version of the modern disc brake. Fifty-five years later BMW is still building horizontal twins with shaft drive, proving that the initial design concept was not only sound but years ahead of its time. The power unit has of course undergone continuous development, one of the major changes in more recent years being an overhead-valve system instead of the older side-valve arrangement.

The RS100R has an engine of 980 cc, a five-speed gearbox, swinging-arm rear suspension and telescopic front forks,

hydraulic disc brakes on front and rear wheels, and all the attributes of the big modern roadster, enabling it to keep pace with fierce superbike competition. Introduced in 1976, it is very much a purist's motorcycle. It has evolved by retaining the best of the old ideas and blending them with the latest design concepts. Standard fittings include an aerodynamically designed full fairing and a race-style seat, and little luxuries such as an electric clock, a cigar lighter, and a first-aid kit. The machine has a maximum speed of approximately 200 km/h (124 mph). Although it falls short of some other superbikes in absolute speed, the RS100R will cruise effortlessly for hours on end at over 160 km/h (100 mph) and is unquestionably one of the finest touring machines in the world.

SPORTING MACHINERY

To survive commercially, the infant motorcycle industry had to prove to the buying public that motorcycles (or tricycles) were robust inventions capable of travelling long distances at reasonable speeds and with acceptable reliability. The result was a series of inter-city races on open roads between Paris and Marseilles, and Paris and Vienna, plus the establishment of the International Cup races. All of these conferred great prestige on a winning make of machine and the country in which it was manufactured. The motorcycles used were roadster or prototype roadster models similar to those which the ordinary public could buy at that time.

In fact, there was to be a great affinity between the development of road machines and those used in competition right through to the 1930s and, in the case of the British motorcycle industry, well into the 1950s. What was learned on the race tracks, and in trials and enduros (long-distance cross-country events), was applied sooner or later in the form of improvements to roadster machines. This in turn meant that, with only slight modifications, many roadster machines could be used for competing in motorcycle sport.

Then specialization in design began to creep into all sections of motorcycle sport: the four-stroke engine was superseded by the two-stroke in practically all forms of motorcycle competition, while the frame designers attempted more extravagant innovations to keep the high-performance two-stroke power firmly on the ground.

The outcome of the last 25 years of development in sports motorcycles has been the evolution of a variety of 'breeds' almost wholly unsuitable for anything other than the specific purpose for which they were designed. What was once a fairly inexpensive amateur all-round sport has become a very expensive, highly specialized professional occupation, and only at the motorcycle-club level does the true spirit

LEFT Belgium ace Roger DeCoster aboard a two-stroke CZ, the Czech-built machine that revolutionized the moto-cross scene when it ousted the long-established, heavyweight four-strokes.

of the amateur rider survive. In closed-to-club events, whether they be grass-track meetings, scrambles, or trials, club members will ride any machine they can lay their hands on so long as it has two wheels and a motor that works. If the bike happens to bear a plausible resemblance to a machine specially built for the type of event, so much the better.

So, what is the difference between a trials motorcycle, a moto-cross or enduro machine, a grass-track or speedway bike? Some use almost identical power units, but there the similarity ends . . . .

RIGHT Sammy Miller, probably the greatest trials rider of all, demonstrates on a Honda the kind of control that enabled him to win almost 900 events over 20 years. Miller not only helped trials to achieve international status but was responsible for many of the frame and engine features that are now commonplace on most trials bikes.

BELOW Honda was late to enter the sport of moto-cross but rapidly made up ground with its two-stroke 'fire engines'–this one a 1977 401 cc model. Note the tremendous clearance between the wheels and the mudguards, an indication of the amount of wheel travel and suspension movement required to absorb the violent impact of leaps and bumps encountered on the rough circuits.

ABOVE Typical—although exceptionally successful—examples of trials machinery in the 1960s, these magnesium-engined Royal Enfields of 350 (left) and 500 cc brought one-time British champion Johnny Brittain many notable victories. The development of high powered but flexible two-stroke engines in lightweight frames, pioneered by Sammy Miller and others, quickly made such heavy four-stroke models obsolete.

Trail Motorcycles

Trial or trail? Many newcomers to motorcycling are confused by these two terms, principally because the machines used for each purpose appear to be very similar.

The difference between the two sports is straightforward: trials riding is a competitive activity, whereas trail riding is a hobby which allows the motorcyclist to get off the tarmac and venture out into the country on the numerous 'green' roads. In Britain the members of the Trail Riders' Association spend weekends away from the congested highways enjoying the pleasures of the open countryside.

The machines they ride have a reasonably high ground clearance, and knobbly trials tyres are fitted to the large wheels to give extra grip. Wide handlebars also give the trail bike a likeness to a trials iron. But there the similarity between the two ends.

The power unit of the trail bike usually has totally different characteristics, with maximum power being produced higher up the rev scale. The trail motorcycle also has a closer-ratio gearbox and less steering lock. The electrical equipment is usually very comprehensive, with flashing indicators, main and dipped beam headlights, stoplight, and full instrumentation including tachometer. This means that the weight of the trail motorcycle would also make it quite unsuitable for trials competitions.

Trail motorcycles are now being built by the majority of the world's large manufacturers and vary in capacity from 50 cc two-stroke mopeds to 550 cc four-strokes. They have been increasing in popularity throughout the world owing to their on-and off-road capabilities which make them equally suitable for road or rough riding.

Trial Motorcycles

Trials riding, which takes place at relatively low speeds, is possibly the safest of all motorcycle sports. For years, the motorcycles used in the sport bore a close resemblance to the roadsters from which they were developed. Large-capacity, low-revving, four-stroke roadsters were fitted with larger wheels and knobbly tyres for extra clearance and grip, and heavy steel mudguards were replaced with light alloy. The bikes were given a small fuel tank and seat, wide handle-bars for better control, and a wide-ratio gearbox.

It was a design philosophy which worked admirably in its day. The British motorcycle industry reigned supreme and the large Norton, Royal Enfield, AJS, Velocette, BSA, and Ariel four-stroke singles dominated the sport. Then, in 1962, Sammy Miller, the top trials rider of the 1960s and possibly the greatest ever, designed the Bultaco Sherpa, the first purpose-built two-stroke trials motorcycle, which changed trials riding from an amateur pastime into a professional sport. Miller set the trend and the rest of the motorcycle trials world followed. The four-stroke engine was dead and the lightweight two-stroke was champion of a rapidly expanding motorcycle sport.

Basically, a trials motorcycle can be defined as a machine which has a ground clearance below the bottom of the crankcase/frame of at least 25 cm (10 in); an engine varying in capacity from 125 to 400 cc and developing maximum torque (pulling power) at the lower end of the engine rev scale; and a wide-ratio gearbox of four, five, or six speeds, which allows the rider to make maximum use of engine flexibility on steep inclines or in on-road use between trials sections. Fully silenced and equipped with speedometer and optional electric lighting for road use, the trials motorcycle is registered and taxed.

Although the cost of trials machinery has risen considerably since the introduction of 'works replicas' (versions of competition machines specially built for sale to the general public), trials riding is still a cheap form of motorcycle sport.

RIGHT Dutch moto-crosser Ken Van der Vos aviates on his Husqvarna, a very competitive two-stroke machine from Sweden. Husqvarna, together with Greeves and CZ, launched the modern moto-cross revolution in the 1960s when they introduced the highly tuned two-strokes.

BELOW Typical of the early race-winning two-strokes is this 250 cc Greeves, seen at a Glastonbury moto-cross meeting in 1965. The rider is Dave Bickers (ex-European champion).

ABOVE American star Rex Staten with his Yamaha motocrosser. Motocross differs in the USA where, apart from holding some events indoors, the circuits are designed more for high and spectacular leaps like this one.

Moto-Cross Motorcycles

While trials and trail riding are both reasonably sedate off-road motorcycle activities, moto-cross—or scrambling, as it used to be called in Britain—is one of the toughest sports yet conceived by man. It was pioneered in the 1920s by British motorcycle enthusiasts, who would ride their machines to off-road circuits, strip off all unnecessary weight in the form of lights, mudguards, and other superfluous fittings, and then race up to 50 km (about 30 miles) across rough tracks and heathland to the finishing flag.

The development of the telescopic front fork helped to establish scrambling as a serious form of motorcycle sport, and the advent of hydraulically damped swinging-arm rear suspension allowed manufacturers to build motorcycles which could be ridden at high speed with reasonable stability over rough ground.

In the early days British manufacturers relied on the large-capacity, single-cylinder four-strokes, just as they had done when building their trials machines. Brute strength and courage were needed by the riders of the 1950s to handle the massive 500 cc, four-stroke AJS, Matchless, Norton, and BSA scramblers which

dominated the scene. There was a 250 cc class, but it was very much the 'junior' class with its low-powered two- and four-stroke machines. Then, in the 1960s, Greeves of Britain, Husqvarna of Sweden, and CZ of Czechoslovakia produced a new generation of 250 cc two-strokes which were highly tuned and were built into light-weight frames with specially developed suspension systems to cope with moto-cross conditions. Racing suddenly became more spectacular and the 250 cc class was rejuvenated. Overbored versions of these lightweights were soon competing on equal terms with the giant four-strokes, and when 350 and 400 cc two-strokes appeared, the big, heavy four-stroke was abandoned.

Moto-cross machines are totally un-suited for road use and so are not equipped with electrics other than ignition systems. They do not have to be registered or taxed and consequently may be used or raced only on private land.

Although they are of the same capacity classes as most trail and trials machines, the highly tuned moto-cross motorcycle engines produce considerably more power. The machine is lighter and has a more flexible suspension system, with far greater travel of front and rear forks, to absorb the fierce bumps and leaps encountered on the moto-cross race circuit.

The greatest strides in the development of moto-cross machines in the past five years have been in frame and suspension design. Cantilever frames with inert-gas shock absorbers permit greater travel of the rear wheel, ensuring that in spite of extremely rough terrain the tyre remains firmly in contact with the ground to transmit full power and maintain speed.

Enduro Motorcycles

In events such as the International Six Days Trial (ISDT), where speed and reliability are necessary to avoid strict time penalties at checkpoints, competitors ride a special breed of motorcycle which has the performance of a moto-cross machine and also the equipment needed to comply with road traffic regulations. This is the enduro motorcycle.

A fully equipped enduro motorcycle carries a spare chain, spare brake and clutch levers, spare inner tubes, a com-pressed-air bottle for rapid inflation of punctured tyres, and of course a com-prehensive toolkit. The competitor also normally carries a number of other useful spares in the pockets of his riding suit, and must be capable of carrying out all manner of mechanical repairs en route.

Enduro machines are built in all capacity classes from 50 cc upwards and compete in the ISDT in different categories according to engine size. These motorcycles are of little practical use to the average road rider and, although they resemble trail bikes, most large-capacity machines are little more than thinly disguised moto-cross racing irons.

Similar machines are used in the United States for desert racing, and it is because of the growing interest in this type of off-road racing that the Japanese manu-facturers have turned to building enduro motorcycles to compete in events such as the ISDT. However, it is the East German MZ two-strokes and Czechoslovakian JAWA/CZ enduro bikes that have domin-ated the sport in Europe for the past 10 years or so.

ABOVE This Czech 344 cc Jawa two-stroke is something of a wolf in sheep's clothing. Its lighting and other equipment make it 'street-legal' (permitted to travel on public roads), but its engine and suspension are of virtually moto-cross specification. This combination of characteristics identifies it as an enduro machine – the Jawa model that won the 1973 International Six Days' Trial championship.

BELOW Similar in general design to a speedway motorcycle and using the Weslake four-valve 500 cc motor that has been a dominant force in world speedway racing, Don Godden's grass-track bike features swinging-arm rear suspension (speedway frames are solid) and a two-speed gearbox (speedway machines have only one gear). Godden, an outstanding grass-track specialist, also races very successfully on a similar machine at Continental long-track meetings, where speeds of up to 145 km/h (90 mph) are reached on the 800 m ($\frac{1}{2}$ mile) tracks by machines which have no brakes.

Grass-Track and Speedway Motorcycles

Anybody seeing a grass-track racing machine for the first time could be forgiven if they called it a speedway bike. The styling is very similar, with high, wide handlebars and spindly frame design, and the power units fitted are the same methanol-burning JAWA, JAP, Cole, or Weslake 500 cc single-cylinder four-strokes as are used in speedway.

A grass-track racer has, however, a number of items which are necessary to cope with the difference between a flat speedway cinder track and the bumpier and often faster grass circuit. For a start, grass-track frames have swinging-arm rear suspension, and both front and rear wheels are fitted with small brakes. Also, instead of having a single-speed transmission, as on speedway machines, grass-track racers are equipped with two-speed gearboxes.

Similar to speedway events, grass-track races usually comprise a four-lap dash around a closely marked circuit; but, instead of there being only four riders on the start line at a time, there may be anything up to a dozen or more. Since the riding technique is similar to speedway, it is not surprising that many speedway riders, including Don Godden and Peter Collins, are also grass-track champions.

The most popular and successful grass-track motorcycles are built by Elstar Engineering and ex-grass-track champions Don Godden and Alf Hagon, while complete speedway machines (including the engines) are manufactured by Weslake Engineering and the JAWA factory.

Whereas speedway is run along professional lines on permanent shale tracks, grass-track racing remains essentially an amateur sport run on stubble fields or meadowland, usually provided by a farmer who is also a motorcycle enthusiast.

Dragster Motorcycles

To attempt to describe a dragster or sprint motorcycle is an impossible task. Designs and specifications vary endlessly according to the finances, mechanical ability, and aspirations of the designer and builder of the machine. What these motor-

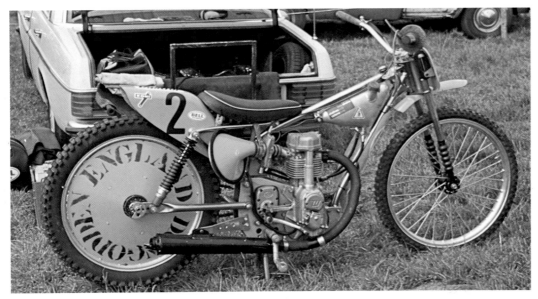

cycles do have in common is a long, low chassis with no rear suspension and a huge, flat-sectional rear tyre to gain maximum adhesion on the drag strip. As for the rest of the machine, some have gearboxes, others do not; some use a single-speed with slipper clutch, others use more conventional transmissions. Some riders believe that the brute power of a multi-engined machine more than compensates for all the extra weight, while others adhere to the contrary theory that light weight and just one powerful motor are all that is needed for maximum acceleration.

The object of the exercize in building these high-powered monsters of the motorcycle world is to get from point A in a straight line to point B a quarter of a mile (400 m) away in the fastest possible time, and to blow the competitor alongside you 'into the weeds'. There are classes for production motorcycles in sprinting and drag racing, but for most spectators the real excitement comes from watching the supercharged, multi-engined specials.

Road-Racing Motorcycles

Something of the history of the development of road-racing machines appears in the next chapter, but we should say a word here about the different types of event in the road-racing calendar.

Road racing, the fastest and most glamorous of the motorcycle sports, has more classes based on engine capacity than any of the others. Capacity classes date back to the years before World War I; the first Senior and Junior TTs, for instance, were held on the Isle of Man in 1911. Over the years, as the performances of racers have increased, the classes have proliferated. Today there are world grand-prix championships for machines of 50, 250, and 500 cc. These form the very heart of the road-racing scene – the world of grand-prix stars such as Barry Sheene, Angel Nieto, Kenny Roberts, Randy Mamola, Kork Ballington, Marco Lucchinelli, and the rest. In addition, there are the Formula One championship; the Internationale Coupe d'Endurance series of long-distance events such as the *Bol d'Or*; the Formula 1, 2 and 3 Manx TT championships, with different capacity limits for two-stroke and four-stroke machines; and a variety of events for production machines (more or less modified roadsters).

The quest for speed is never ending, and present-day racing motors develop prodigious power. The 500 cc racers, for instance, produce up to 130 hp – as much as most 3-litre car engines, and double that of a 500 cc roadster.

ABOVE A standing-start quarter-mile (400 m) in 8 seconds or less is the aim of the riders who race the nitro-methane-burning, supercharged dragsters seen at Santa Pod raceway. This twin-engined Kawasaki was one of Europe's most successful dragsters and belonged to Dutchman Henk Vink. Terminal speeds of over 285 km/h (177 mph) are achieved at the end of the drag strip.

BELOW The start of a 750 race in the United States. One of the differences between these machines and ordinary roadsters is that they develop about twice as much power as a roadster engine of equal size.

Swiss rider Rolf Biland (No. 2), world sidecar road racing champion of 1978, pushes off at the start of the 1978 Italian GP with his controversial monocoque machine whose brilliant engineering helped him win the title.

How a Motorcycle Works

The engine

The principle of operation of all internal combustion engines is basically the same. A mixture of petrol and air is ignited in a confined space. As the fuel burns it expands rapidly and causes the pressure in that confined space to increase. It is this rapid increase in pressure which is used to create movement which, in turn, can be used to propel a motorcycle.

Basically an engine consists of a cylinder with a close-fitting piston inside it. The principle is not unlike that of a gun, where the cylinder represents the gun barrel and the piston the bullet. Unlike the bullet, however, the piston is fitted with a pivoting rod and this in turn is connected to a pin which is offset mounted on a wheel.

When the piston is at the top of the cylinder the pin, which is joined to the piston via the connecting rod, is at the top of the wheel. As the piston moves down the cylinder the wheel is cranked around, passing through 180 degrees as the piston reaches the bottom of the cylinder. At this point the piston cannot travel any further and it is said to have reached the bottom of its stroke.

The wheel that the crankpin is attached to is fairly heavy and once it has started to rotate it will not stop when the piston reaches the bottom of its stroke. Instead the inertia stored in the wheel carries it on, and the piston is pushed up the cylinder via the connecting rod. When the piston has travelled from the top of the cylinder to the bottom, or vice versa, it is said to have completed one stroke.

From this action comes the term 'four-stroke' to describe a certain type of engine. On its first stroke the piston in a four-stroke engine moves from the top of the cylinder to the bottom, and as it does so a valve located in the top of the cylinder opens. A mixture of petrol and air is drawn into the top of the cylinder, past the open valve, due to the vacuum which the descending piston creates.

When the piston reaches the bottom of the cylinder the first, or induction, stroke is said to be finished and the inlet valve closes.

A mixture of petrol and air is now trapped in the space above the piston and as the flywheel continues to rotate it pushes the piston back up to the top of the cylinder. This compresses the mixture into the space left at the top of the cylinder, which is known as the combustion chamber. The second, or compression, stroke is now completed.

The third stroke is called the 'power stroke' because an electrical spark is now introduced into the combustion chamber which starts the fuel/air mixture burning. The rapid expansion of the mixture forces the piston down the cylinder bore. But the piston is stopped at the bottom of its power stroke because it is still connected to the flywheel.

The flywheel continues on its circular path and the piston is once more pushed up the cylinder bore towards the cylinder head. This is the exhaust stroke, and at the start of it a second valve located in the cylinder head opens and the burning gases above the piston are forced out of the combustion chamber. That completes one cycle. The inlet valve then opens to start the procedure all over again. There is thus only one power stroke for every four strokes of the piston, which results in two complete revolutions of the flywheel. To recap, the strokes are: 1 induction, 2 compression, 3 power, and 4 exhaust.

This is, of course, a simplified descrip-

LEFT This finely restored early Omega, a collector's item today, shows that its frame is virtually a reinforced pedal-cycle design.

The shape of the smallest from the BMW factory, West Germany's largest motorcycle manufacturer: the 450 cc R45 flat twin.

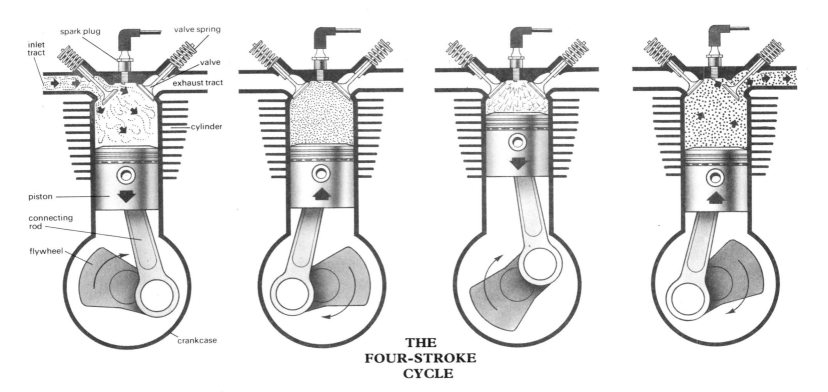

labels: inlet tract, spark plug, valve spring, valve, exhaust tract, cylinder, piston, connecting rod, flywheel, crankcase

THE FOUR-STROKE CYCLE

Induction
The inlet valve opens to allow the petrol/air charge to be drawn in by the vacuum created by the descending piston.

Compression
The inlet valve is now closed as the piston begins its upward path, thus compressing the fresh mixture.

Power
Just before the piston reaches the top of its stroke the spark plug fires. This ignites the mixture which rapidly burns and expands, thus forcing the piston down as illustrated.

Exhaust
Now the exhaust valve opens, allowing the ascending piston to expel the spent mixture. Energy stored in the flywheel will then bring the piston down again to recommence the induction stroke.

tion of the four-stroke cycle and there are a number of other technical terms used to describe four-stroke engines, for example 'high compression' or 'low compression ratio'. The compression ratio of an engine is determined by the volume above the piston when it is at the bottom of its stroke, compared to the volume above the piston when it is at the top of its stroke. If the space above the piston at the bottom of its stroke (known as bottom dead centre, or BDC) is ten times greater than the volume left at the top of the stroke, (known as top dead centre, or TDC) the engine is said to have a compression ratio of ten to one.

Naturally, if this compression and the combustion pressure are not to be lost, the piston must fit tightly in the cylinder bore. It is not practical to try to make the piston an exact fit in the cylinder, so the piston is fitted with thin cast-iron rings which are square in section and fit into grooves in the piston. They are naturally springy and force themselves against the cylinder wall at all times, thus effecting a gas tight seal between the piston and the cylinder bore. A large piston may have several rings fitted to it.

Engines are generally graded by capacity. Such terms as 500cc or 750cc refer to the total volume, measured in cubic centimetres, through which the piston moves. If an engine has two or more cylinders the total sum is always quoted.

The bore of an engine is simply the diameter of its cylinder, while the stroke is the distance moved by the piston from the top of the cylinder to the bottom. An engine with a large bore and a short stroke can still give the same capacity as an engine with a small bore but a long stroke. From this come the terms 'long stroke' and 'short stroke' motor. An engine with a cylinder bore the same size as its stroke is said to be 'square'.

When two or more cylinders are used they are often placed side by side. Most two-, three- and four-cylinder machines are arranged in this way, with the pistons connected to a common crankshaft. However, they can be pushed 'fore and aft' into a V-formation, or laid right over to face one another, as in the flat engine layout of the BMW.

With a V, or a flat-twin, engine the connecting rods can share a common crankpin, or they may be separate. In a twin-cylinder engine with vertical bores the two pistons may go up and down together as in Triumph twin-cylinder engines, or one may be up while the other is down. The first type is known as a 360 degree twin, while the latter is referred to as a 180 degree twin because the crankpins of the crankshaft are 180 degrees apart.

The connecting rod which couples the piston to the crankshaft has a small bearing at the piston end and a much larger bearing at the crankpin end. Hence the terms 'little end' and 'big end'.

The bearings which support the crankshaft are known as 'main bearings'. The number of main bearings in an engine varies according to the layout of the crank-

shaft and the number of cylinders that it has to serve. Sometimes an engine can be classified by the number of main bearings it uses. For example, a four-cylinder engine may be described as a five main-bearing unit. This means that there is a main bearing on either side of each piston position. Another type of four-cylinder engine may only have three main bearings, one at each end of the crank and one in the centre.

Two main types of bearing are used for the big end of the connecting rods and the main bearings. The most common bearing is known as a shell. This is a thin semi-circular strip of steel, coated with a soft 'white metal' bearing surface. Two half shells are used to make up one complete bearing and this arrangement must be used when a solid, or one-piece, crankshaft is employed. The outer section of the shell is held firmly in the crankcase and the crankshaft rotates within it. The crankshaft does not actually run against the soft white metal bearing surface. Oil, supplied under quite high pressure, is forced between the two surfaces keeping them apart.

When oil pressure drops, as indicated by an external oil pressure gauge, it may be due to worn main or big end bearings leaking the oil out from between the shell and the crankpin.

The second type of bearing used on motorcycle main and big end bearings is the ball, or roller, race. This type of bearing consists of two hardened tracks

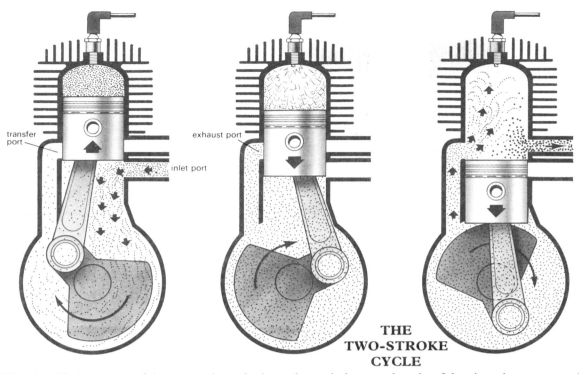

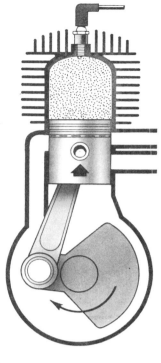

THE TWO-STROKE CYCLE

This simplified sequence of the two-stroke cycle shows that each downward stroke of the piston is a power stroke, unlike the four-stroke engine which powers on alternate downward strokes.

The piston is compressing the petrol/air charge ready for ignition. At the same time the ascending piston uncovers the inlet port, allowing the partial vacuum created in the crankcase to draw in the next fresh charge.

The spark plug fires, igniting the mixture and forcing the piston downwards. As the piston descends it forces the fresh charge into the transfer port.

Now that the piston is at the bottom of its stroke the exhaust port is open, allowing the burnt gases to escape. They are helped on their way by the incoming charge under crankcase compression via the transfer port.

At this point all the ports are closed by the piston which has its fresh charge trapped in the combustion chamber. The ascending piston will compress the mixture which also contains some oil for bearing lubrication. As the piston moves up, the inlet port will once again be uncovered as in the first diagram.

which are kept apart by a series of hardened steel balls or rollers. Due to their construction, these bearings cannot be split into halves as can shell bearings. For this reason a one-piece crankshaft cannot be used. A crankshaft for an engine with more than one cylinder has to be made in sections, which are pressed together with the ball-bearings sandwiched between them.

In many two-stroke engines this type of bearing is preferred, but the construction is simplified one stage further. The connecting rod is machined so that it also becomes the outer race of the bearing, with the pin of the crankshaft acting as the inner race. Also, since side loadings are minimal, the balls are replaced with rollers.

Unlike the shell bearing, the roller main or big end does not require oil to be supplied at high pressure, hence its popularity with two-stroke designers.

This, then, is the basic theory of the four-stroke cycle and the way the main components of an engine are laid out. But, for all this to function correctly, the valves must open and close at the right time and in the right order, and the mixture must be ignited at the right moment.

Valves are opened and closed in a controlled manner by a simple cam. In its most basic form a cam is a circle of metal with a bump on one side, making its profile something like an egg. If the cam is rotated about its centre and a component known as a 'cam follower' is placed where it will

be in constant contact with the outer edge of the cam, the cam follower will rise and fall as the bump on the cam meets it. This motion can be transferred to the valve by rods and levers, or the cam can be mounted directly above the valve and operate straight on to it.

With a multi-cylinder engine several cams are mounted on a single shaft and the complete assembly is known as a 'camshaft'. The camshaft may operate the valves in a number of ways, and each system is named after its method of achieving valve lift. The 'push rod' engine, for example, has its camshaft mounted around the base of the cylinder and long rods, known as push rods, transmit the action of the cam follower up to a 'rocker' arm which in turn operates the valve.

The single overhead-camshaft engine eliminates the push rods by mounting the camshaft just above the cylinder head, where it can operate directly onto the rockers.

With a double overhead-camshaft engine the rockers are eliminated by having the cams operating directly onto the valves. Two separate cams are needed for the inlet and exhaust with this system.

Once a mechanism is designed to open and close the valves it needs to be 'timed' to match the needs of the engine. The inlet valve needs to start opening as the piston begins its downward inlet stroke, and must close at the completion of that stroke if the inlet charge is not to be forced back up the inlet port whence it came. This is achieved

by gearing the camshaft directly to the crankshaft with the camshaft turning half as many times as the crankshaft. This means that the inlet cam will only rotate once for every two rotations of the crank. If the bump of the cam only covers 45 degrees of its rotation then the total lift will take place during 180 degrees of crankshaft rotation: or one stroke of the piston. The same applies to the exhaust cam which can be mounted on the same shaft as the inlet, but in a different position relative to the crankshaft rotation.

Getting the mixture in and out of the cylinder is one thing, firing it at the right time is another. With an engine turning over at anything up to 10,000 times in one minute (10,000rpm) the timing of the ignition is critical. The answer is to use an electric spark which jumps between two electrodes mounted in the combustion chamber. These electrodes are fitted to a body, which can be removed from the cylinder head via a threaded section. This component is known as a 'spark plug'.

There are various systems used to produce this high voltage spark at the plug but all basically rely on an ignition coil of one type or another. An ignition coil consists of two sets of wire coils, one known as the primary coil and the other as the induction coil. When a low voltage is passed through the primary coil windings it creates a magnetic field around the secondary, or induction, coil. If the primary current is then switched off, the magnetic field around the secondary coil breaks down and

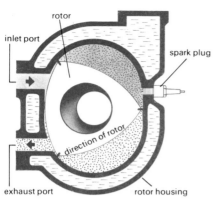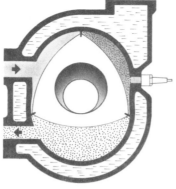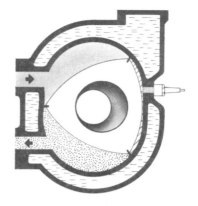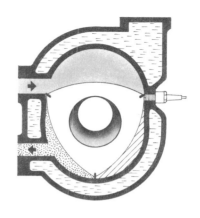

WANKEL (ROTARY) ENGINE CYCLE

With this type of engine the spark plugs fire three times per complete revolution of the rotor. The design has potential because of its simplicity and inherent smoothness, but so far, motorcycles offered with this type of power unit have enjoyed little commercial success. The DKW is the only model currently available to the public.

Induction
Having passed the inlet port, rotor face A has completed the induction stage, the petrol/air mixture having been drawn in by the partial vacuum created.

Compression
The fresh charge is now under compression. Meanwhile, rotor face C is undergoing induction and B exhaust.

Ignition/power
Now fully compressed, the charge is ignited by the spark plug.

Exhaust
The burning gases expand and will soon be expelled via the exhaust port which at this stage is servicing rotor face B.

Induction

Compression

Power

Exaust

a high voltage is 'induced' into that coil. A heavily insulated wire carries that high voltage from the coil directly to the spark plug, where it jumps from one electrode to the other, on its way to 'earth'.

The critical point for timing the arrival of the spark, therefore, is the breaking of the primary circuit in the coil. Although this breaking of the primary circuit can be done with an electronic device, the most common method is to use a 'contact breaker' set. This is simply two hardened contact point faces which remain together until one is lifted from the other by means of a cam. At this point the circuit is broken and the spark is induced. Since the contact breaker cam only needs to operate at the top of the compression stroke it requires the same two to one gearing as the camshaft. Quite often the contact breaker cam is driven directly from the valve camshaft.

Ignition timing is simply a matter of positioning the points relative to the breaker cam so that they open at the recommended time which, in practice, is a little before the piston reaches TDC. However, as engine speed increases, the piston spends less time at TDC. For this reason the ignition point has to be advanced as the engine speeds up. This is normally taken care of by an automatic device, which moves the contact breaker cam in relation to the crankshaft.

The power generated at the crankshaft has to be carried to the back wheel before it can be used to propel the motorcycle, and the first stage in this operation is the

primary drive. Power is taken from the crankshaft either by chain or gears and used to turn the clutch drum. The clutch, which is simply a device for transmitting movement in a progressive manner, operates by friction. The outer section of the clutch is turned by the chain or gears from the crankshaft and this in turn drives a number of plates which are free to slide inside the drum. These driving plates are separated by driven plates fitted in between each of them. A powerful spring (or springs) clamps the assembly together and allows it to rotate as a unit. When the clutch handlebar lever is pulled in, the spring pressure is released and the two sets of plates are allowed to separate. The driving plates will turn with the engine while the driven plates will turn with the gearbox input shaft. As the clutch lever is released the spring pressure brings both sets of plates together until the friction between them increases and the drive is taken up. When the clutch is fully home the drive is 100 per cent.

Since the driven plates in the clutch power the inner drum of the clutch, this in turn has to be connected to the gearbox input shaft. This is the first stage in transmitting the power through the gearbox.

The gearbox is simply a means of increasing the leverage of the engine. It achieves this by making the crankshaft turn many times compared to the number of turns received at the gearbox output shaft. In understanding how a gearbox

works, it is probably the term 'changing gear' that leads to more confusion than anything else. In a constant mesh gearbox, the type used on all motorcycles, the gears are never actually changed from one mesh to another.

Two shafts run side by side and these can carry anything up to six sets of gears which are always in mesh with each other. On one shaft the gears are all rigid, while on the other the gears are free to rotate around that shaft. By locking any one of those gears to the mainshaft, any power fed into the fixed, or layshaft, will be fed to the mainshaft via the locked gear.

When it is necessary to change gear, the mainshaft gear is unlocked and another gear is 'selected' for locking to the mainshaft. This gear selection is normally carried out by moving a selector 'dog' which is splined to the mainshaft. This selector dog has driving 'ears' which locate in the side of the gear to be selected. In this way two gears which lie side by side can share the same selector dog, simply by fitting selector ears to both of its sides. When a bike 'jumps out of gear', i.e. the drive ratio alters without the selector pedal being pressed, the gears in fact remain engaged; it is the selector dog which has jumped out of engagement.

As the final link in the transmission of power to the rear wheel, the output shaft from the gearbox has to be connected to the back driving wheel. The most common method of achieving this is to fit a chain sprocket to the end of the shaft and take a chain to a sprocket located on the back wheel.

A more complicated, but reliable, method of final drive is the shaft. With a shaft drive the output shaft is connected to a universal joint and then to a long shaft reaching down the side of the rear wheel. From here the motion is turned through 90 degrees via a bevel gear set and the rear wheel is driven.

Whichever system is used the transmission of power has to be 'damped' somewhere along its line by the fitting of a transmission shock-absorber. To connect the torque from the engine straight to the rear wheel would produce too sudden a loading on the gears and chains in the system. A damper must be used and this normally takes the form of a rubber cushion either fitted to the rear wheel sprocket, where it connects to the back wheel, or to the clutch driven drum.

The two-stroke motorcycle uses the same gearbox and transmission system as the four-stroke, it is only the engine which is radically different. The two-stroke power unit has no valves to control the induction and exhaust strokes and starts a power stroke every time it reaches TDC.

When the two-stroke engine was first designed it was hoped that, by producing twice as many power strokes as the four-stroke engine, it would produce twice as much power. However, due to the charging and exhaust systems used it proved a simple, but not very efficient, engine.

With a two-stroke power plant the crankcase which houses the flywheel acts as the induction chamber. As the piston moves up the cylinder bore the vacuum created underneath it draws mixture into the crankcase, but through a port uncovered by the piston instead of through a valve. Since the induction stroke is obtained when the piston travels up the cylinder, engine compression takes place at the same time.

As the piston is forced down the bore under combustion pressure, the mixture previously drawn into the crankcase is compressed and forced into transfer ports located at the side of the barrel. This carries the mixture up the side of the motor and into the combustion chamber above the piston. Just prior to the opening of the transfer ports the exhaust port in the barrel is uncovered by the descending piston and the pressure of combustion releases most of the exhaust gas out into the exhaust pipe. The incoming fresh charge is then used to push out the remaining mixture, but before it can follow the exhaust gases out into the pipe, the port is closed off by the piston moving back up the bore on its compression/induction stroke.

From this it is obvious that the successful operation of the engine depends to a large extent on the correct timing of the port openings. However, since the piston has to be used to control all the timings, the time that the ports are open is reduced as the speed of the piston increases. Hence the port timings can only be 'right' for any one engine speed.

When a two-stroke engine is running at low speed a lot of the exhaust gas remains in the combustion chamber where it pre-heats and dilutes the incoming inlet charge. The result is low pressure in the power stroke, and sometimes even a failure to fire at all. This explains the uneven running of a two-stroke engine at low speed.

The second major difference in the two-stroke power unit is the lubrication system. Because the crankcase has to be used as a pump, to draw in and transfer the fresh petrol/air charge, it cannot be partially filled with oil to lubricate the bearings and the piston. Until recently the oil was simply mixed with the petrol and 'open cage' type rollers were used so that the oil carried in the mixture had a fair chance of

FIVE-SPEED GEARBOX

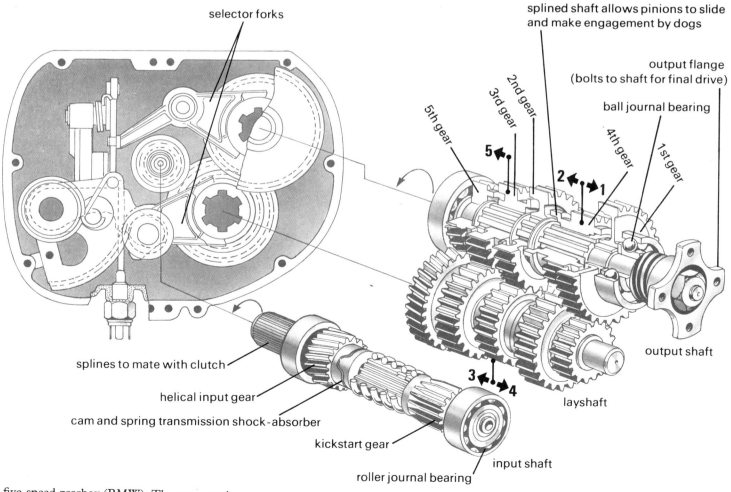

A five-speed gearbox (BMW). The gears are in constant mesh.

finding its way into the bearings.

The major fault with this system, simple though it is, is that closing the throttle cuts off not only the supply of fuel to the engine, but also the lubricant. Naturally a high proportion of the oil is carried through the transfer ports and into the combustion chamber, where it burns with the mixture, but reduces the combustion pressure and therefore the efficiency of the engine.

When a two-stroke engine is running under a light load the mixture of oil required to lubricate the piston and bearings can be as little as one part oil to 75 parts petrol. However, when operating under maximum power the mixture ratio would need to be in the order of one to 20. This means that a mixture of the latter ratio must be used at all times to safeguard the engine when full power is used, but since most of a motorcycle engine's life is spent producing only half power, a lot of oil is burnt in the combustion chamber without making any useful contribution to the motor's lubrication needs.

Modern two-stroke engines do not use the petrol/oil mixture method of lubrication. Instead an oil pump is fitted to the engine which supplies oil to the bearings and the pistons direct. The pump is geared to the engine speed so that the oil supply is automatically reduced as the crankshaft speed drops. With this system, if the throttle is closed when the engine is turning at high rpm, the oil supply is not cut off.

However, the engine's need for oil is not only dependent on its speed of rotation. At moderate rpm, with a wide throttle opening and the engine pulling strongly, more lubricant will be required. To meet this need for extra lubricant the oil pump is designed to have a variable 'stroke'. This stroke is controlled by the throttle cable so that when the throttle is wide open the stroke of the oil pump is at its maximum. Closing the throttle will reduce the stroke of the pump and therefore its oil output.

This complete system of engine speed and throttle linked control means that the right amount of oil is supplied to the engine under all operating conditions. When the pump speed is low but extra oil is needed, the stroke is increased so that more oil per working cycle is injected into the engine. When the pump speed is high but the engine load is light, the stroke is reduced, thus injecting less oil but more often so that once again the engine's needs are catered for.

Obviously both these systems are total loss, that is, once the oil has done its job it is pumped into the combustion chamber and from there out into the exhaust port. However, with the pumped system the oil consumed by the motor need not be any greater than that burnt by a conventional

four-stroke with slightly worn piston oil control rings.

The third type of engine used in motorcycles is the 'Wankel' power unit. This motor bears no resemblance to either the two- or four-stroke engines. There are no pistons, connecting rods, flywheels or valves. The Wankel engine consists of a three-faced rotor mounted inside a cylinder. This three-faced rotor is mounted offset on its rotational, epicyclic geared axis so that all three points of its edges are always in contact with the roughly oval-shaped cylinder in which it runs.

On one side of the cylinder are mounted the inlet and exhaust ports. As the rotor turns it moves up towards the top half of the 'oval' and creates a depression which draws petrol and air mixture into the engine. As the rotor continues to turn, one of the points passes the inlet port and traps the mixture in the top half of the oval section. This mixture is carried around the cylinder until it is compressed against the sidewall opposite the inlet and exhaust ports.

This side wall is fitted with a spark plug which then fires the mixture. Combustion pressure acts on the face of the rotor, forcing it round until eventually the exhaust port is uncovered. The exhausted gases are then forced out into the exhaust port by the rotor face closing up against the cylinder wall.

While all this is taking place on one face of the rotor the other two faces are also working. During combustion the second face of the rotor has already drawn in a fresh charge while the third is on the exhaust pulse. You can see from this that for every complete revolution of the rotor there are three power pulses, or 'strokes'.

Lubrication of this engine follows the same principle as the two-stroke power unit: either a petrol/oil mixture or an oil pump feeding directly into the inlet manifold rather than straight into the bearings.

If the piston engine has problems, then the Wankel engine also has its share of crosses to bear. First, the rotor has to have at its three points a gas tight seal against the walls of the cylinder. If a seal is less than perfect the combustion mixture can leak out into the chambers on either side of it, thus reducing the efficiency of the power pulse, and also diluting the charge in the chamber next to it.

Cooling is also a major problem. For an effective charge of the chamber, the incoming mixture needs to be kept cool to maintain its density. However, the hot rotor face is presented to the fresh charge just after pumping out the exhausted mixture. This would not be such a problem if the rotor did not tend to run so hot. With only three small points in contact with the cylinder there is very little area making actual contact which would provide a path

for conducted heat. Thus most of the cooling is done by the incoming mixture which, as already mentioned, reduces the efficiency of the charge.

For use on motorcycles, the Japanese Suzuki company complicated the design still further. Motorcyclists tend to rely on engine braking when riding in poor weather conditions, but the nature of the design in the Wankel motor does not provide this. The answer Suzuki came up with was to fit a second ignition system which would fire the mixture early and try to make the rotor run backwards!

When the throttle was closed the carburettor still allowed a small amount of mixture into the engine, also the ignition system was changed for the 'pre-ignition' set up. In practice this resulted in heavy fuel consumption in an engine already noted for using rather a lot of petrol. In spite of spending over a million pounds in development of the Wankel-powered Suzuki RE5, the bike was discontinued shortly after its introduction.

Whatever the design of engine, if it runs on petrol it must be fitted with a carburettor. A carburettor is a device for mixing together petrol and air. The carburettor's main job is not only to supply this mixture in the right quantity, according to the rider's demands, but also in the right ratio, and the right ratio will depend on many things.

For a petrol engine to develop maximum power it will need approximately 15 parts of air to every one part of petrol, by weight. When running for maximum economy this ratio will need to be wider to give a 'weaker' mixture. However, when starting an engine from cold the carburettor will have to change the ratio once again to a 'richer' mixture with less than 15 parts of air to one of fuel.

Although all this sounds complicated the basic principle is quite simple. Petrol will not actually mix with the air, so the term 'mixture ratio' is a little misleading in this respect. What the carburettor does is to break the petrol up into tiny droplets which are carried in the airstream. This action is exactly the same as that of a perfume atomizer.

Air passing at speed over a small bore tube causes the air in the tube to be drawn out. This creates a partial vacuum which draws the fuel up the tube. When the fuel reaches the top of the tube it breaks into droplets and is carried away into the airstream.

The small bore tube which supplies the fuel to the engine has a restriction in it which limits the amount of petrol that can be drawn off for a given air speed. This restriction is known as the 'main jet'. The reservoir for the tube is called the 'float bowl'. With a carburettor the fuel is kept level with the top of the tube, instead of it

A CONSTANT VELOCITY (OR DIAPHRAGM) CARBURETTOR

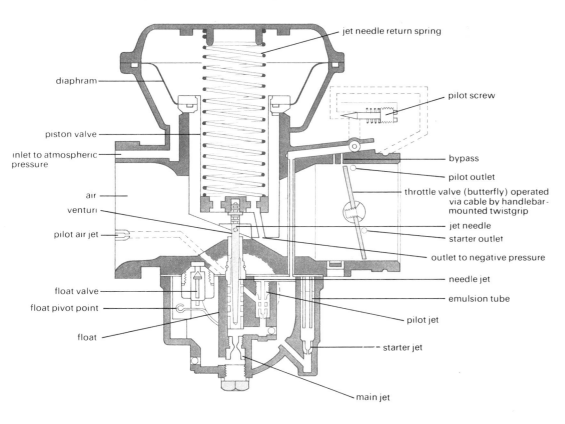

- jet needle return spring
- diaphram
- pilot screw
- piston valve
- bypass
- inlet to atmospheric pressure
- pilot outlet
- throttle valve (butterfly) operated via cable by handlebar-mounted twistgrip
- air
- venturi
- jet needle
- pilot air jet
- starter outlet
- outlet to negative pressure
- needle jet
- float valve
- emulsion tube
- float pivot point
- pilot jet
- float
- starter jet
- main jet

A SLIDE-TYPE CARBURETTOR

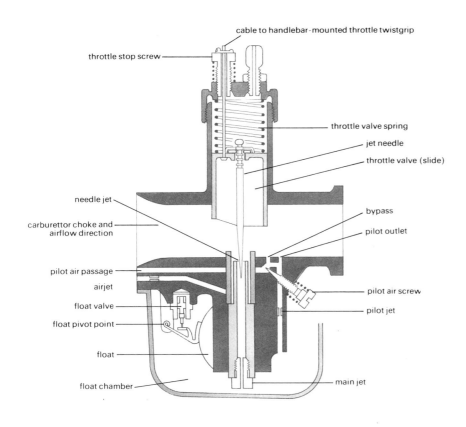

- cable to handlebar-mounted throttle twistgrip
- throttle stop screw
- throttle valve spring
- jet needle
- throttle valve (slide)
- needle jet
- carburettor choke and airflow direction
- bypass
- pilot outlet
- pilot air passage
- airjet
- pilot air screw
- float valve
- pilot jet
- float pivot point
- float
- main jet
- float chamber

having to be drawn up by the air passing over it.

Connected to the engine's inlet manifold is the carburettor's main choke tube. This has the petrol supply tube meeting it at 90 degrees and at a point where the air speed, on its way to the engine, is at its highest. If the bore, or choke, of the carburettor were of a constant diameter the air speed would be constant throughout the length of the carburettor. However, a restriction in the form of a 'venturi' is added.

The carburettor venturi, or choke, is simply a tapered restriction in the main carburettor bore. When air is drawn down the carburettor by the piston descending, it speeds up as it meets the venturi section. In doing so it passes over the petrol tube, or jet, and draws off fuel. To control the amount of petrol and air drawn into the engine a throttle valve is fitted into the choke. This can take the form of a simple 'butterfly' valve mounted on a spindle, or a slide which is lowered across the choke area. Turning the twistgrip on the handlebar lifts the slide, or opens the butterfly, allowing the engine to draw in more mixture.

By altering the restriction in the jet tube the main jet can be matched to the amount of air passing over the tube, but only with the throttle wide open. When the throttle is only partly open the amount of air drawn into the engine is reduced. This in turn means that the petrol supplied to the air stream also has to be reduced. On motorcycle carburettors this is normally achieved by fitting a tapered needle into the centre of the main jet tube, and connecting it to the carburettor slide.

As the throttle slide is lowered, cutting off part of the air supply, the tapered needle is also lowered into the jet, reducing the area of the tube. This maintains the mixture at the correct ratio. Fine tuning of this system can be carried out by raising or lowering the needle in relation to its position in the throttle slide.

For cold starting a much richer mixture is required. This can be obtained quite simply by closing off the carburettor's supply of fresh air, thus 'choking' it. Now when the throttle is lifted the air supply will be restricted but the needle will still allow more petrol to find its way into the engine.

Another method of providing a rich mixture for starting is to bypass the main system altogether. When the choke lever is operated a needle is lifted from its seat allowing petrol to be drawn into a secondary drilling in the body of the carburettor. This acts like a small carburettor, and provides a rich mixture which is fed into the main choke system. When the choke is in the 'off' position this secondary carburettor is inoperative.

In order to obtain a smooth tickover, a separate idle system is necessary with the throttle slide controlled carburettor. When the engine is running at very slow speed the air flow over the main jet tube is so slow that a steady stream of fuel cannot be drawn off. To overcome this another drilling, similar to the secondary choke set-up, is used. However, this time an accurate mixture is required, rather than just a rich one for starting. This means that some form of adjustment is necessary.

When air is drawn into the idle drilling it mixes with a supply of petrol from the main float bowl, the amount of which is controlled by an idle jet. Just before this mixture is fed into the main choke stream a tapered needle is introduced across the drilling. This is the 'idle screw'. Adjusting it from outside the carburettor body alters the size of the drilling aperture, thus letting more, or less, petrol and air mixture out into the main air stream. This type of idle control is known as a 'quantity' control.

On some carburettors the idle screw is fitted into the airstream part of the drilling before the petrol is introduced. Moving this tapered screw in or out alters the amount of air mixed with the fixed amount of petrol. This system is known as 'quality' control.

With the engine ticking over on the idle system, opening the throttle will allow the air speed over the main jet tube to increase until the engine can draw its fuel from here. However, the transition from running on the idle drilling to running off the main jet tube may not be smooth. The idle drilling is very small and as the throttle is opened the engine may stop drawing air through it before the main, or needle, jet can take over. The answer is a progression drilling. This is a drilling similar to the idle system, though not adjustable, which takes over when the throttle is first opened. As the air speed reaches the point where the needle jet can supply the engine, the progression drilling ceases to function.

With legislation tightening the control of exhaust emissions, much better control of mixture ratios has become necessary. This in turn has led many manufacturers to adopt the 'constant vacuum' type of carburettor. Although this type is very similar in operation to the 'static' carburettor previously described, it does differ in one important area. With the CV system a butterfly is used for throttle control, but this operates in conjunction with a throttle slide. With this type of carburettor the throttle slide is not controlled from the twistgrip. Instead a

'chamber' is arranged above the slide, and this is linked with the main carburettor choke. When the throttle opens the butterfly valve, air is drawn from above the slide which because of the resulting air depression moves up, taking the needle with it. When the throttle closes the vacuum is reduced and the slide comes down. By linking the slide in this way it controls the choke area according to the engine's needs, rather than just lifting as the twistgrip is operated.

All motorcycles need electrical power in one form or another if only for ignition. Most machines draw this electricity from a battery mounted on the bike, which in turn is charged from an engine-driven generator. No matter how complicated this generator may appear it is based on very simple principles of electricity: if a conductor, i.e. a piece of wire, is passed through a magnetic field it will cause a flow of electrons, an electric current, in that wire. When the wire is passed through the south pole of a magnet the flow will be in one direction, but if it is then passed through the north pole the flow will be in the other. Thus the electricity will alternate its direction with each full revolution. With a trail bike or a simple moped this type of electricity can

A SUZUKI GS 1000 CLUTCH

1. Primary driven gear assy
2. Washer
3. Spacer
4. Bearing
5. Sleeve hub
6. Nut
7. Washer
8. Washer
9. Drive plate
10. Driven plate
11. Pressure disk
12. Spring
13. Bolt
14. Washer

15. Oil pump drive gear
16. Spacer
17. Bearing
18. Clutch release rack
19. Thrust bearing
20. Washer
21. Clutch release pinion
22. Oil seal
23. Washer
24. Bearing (1)
25. Bearing (2)
26. Clutch release arm
27. Bolt
28. Cushion

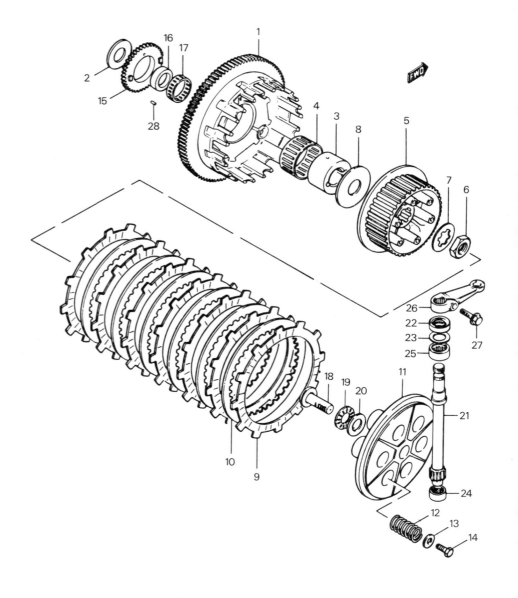

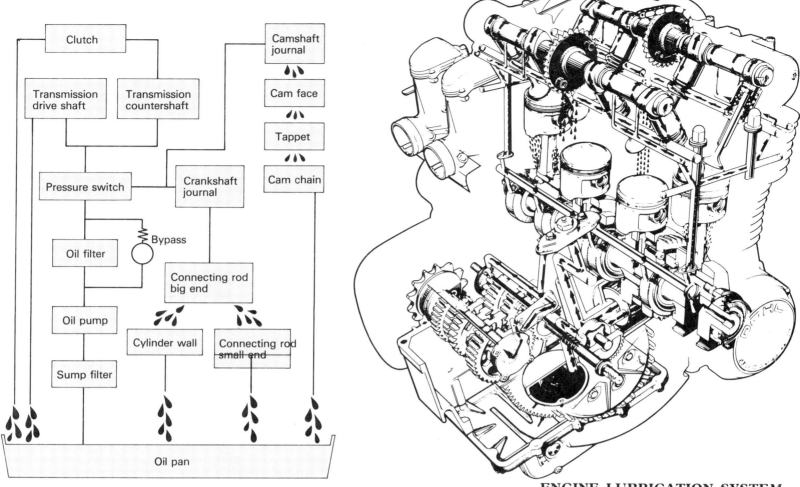

ENGINE LUBRICATION SYSTEM

be used directly to power the lights, but this means that the lights only work when the engine is running, because there is no battery acting as a source of power.

The main use of alternating current is, in fact, for lighting. An electric light bulb produces light by heating an element. Alternating current can be passed back and forth through the bulb so quickly that the element does not have time to cool down between each 'wave'. The naked eye certainly cannot detect any alternate heating and cooling of the element, so the stream of light from the lamp appears constant.

However, this type of electricity cannot be used to charge a battery since a battery is a device for storing electricity and the alternating current would just be flowing into it and then out again! The battery might become quite hot, but it would not charge.

To charge a battery there must be some form of direct current, that is, a flow of electricity in one direction only. Until the introduction of electronics, ensuring this was a fairly cumbersome business. A generator had to be fitted with two pick-up points, one collecting all the pulses from the north pole, the other collecting those from the south. This system involved slip rings or commutators, brushes and mechanical contacts all of which tended to go wrong or wear out. This 'dynamo', as it was known, has all but been replaced with the electronically 'rectified' alternator, that is an alternator with its current

converted to DC (direct current).

The simple alternator is a single coil of wire spinning in the field of a permanent magnet. By putting a diode, or semiconductor, into the output circuit, direct current for charging a small battery is obtained. The diode is a device which allows electricity to flow in one direction but not in the other. This means that every other pulse, or 'wave' as it is known, is allowed to pass through, while the other one is not. This is known as 'simple half wave' rectification. An improvement on this is to arrange a 'bridge' of four diodes which allow both halves of the wave to flow in the same direction. This is known as 'full wave' rectification. (In practice, rather than try to turn the coils of wire through the magnetic field, the field magnets are rotated around the fixed coils of wire.) With this simple set-up the output of the generator is dependent on the speed at which the magnets are spun, thus lights go dim when the engine is running at low speed. It is therefore necessary to try and control the output.

To do this the strength of the magnetic fields needs to be controlled. This is achieved by replacing the heavy permanent magnets with electro-magnets, that is, coils of wire with an electric current passing through them. Because the current being fed back into the field coils is very small only light brushes are required, in contrast to the brushes of the dynamo which had to pass all the current generated by the unit.

To control the output of the generator it is only necessary to increase or decrease the flow of electricity to the field coils. Another electronic device is used to sense the needs of the battery. When a heavier charge is needed it takes some of the electricity from the generator and feeds it back into itself, to increase the output. This means that the unit is effectively feeding on itself. However, current must be fed into the field coils before it can start producing any charge of its own; a classic case of the chicken and the egg. To overcome this, small permanent magnets are sometimes retained to provide a charge for initial excitement, or a feed can be taken from the battery, to get things started.

That is basically how all alternators work. Larger units, for very big machines with many accessories, work in exactly the same way, it is just that there are several sets of coils providing the current, instead of the one in a simple alternator.

Cycle parts

Some people would argue that the frame and suspension of motorcycles has hardly changed since the early days when people started bolting small engines into bicycle frames. However, while things may not appear to have changed much, a lot more is known today about suspension and frames and already some manufacturers are breaking with convention on their production machines.

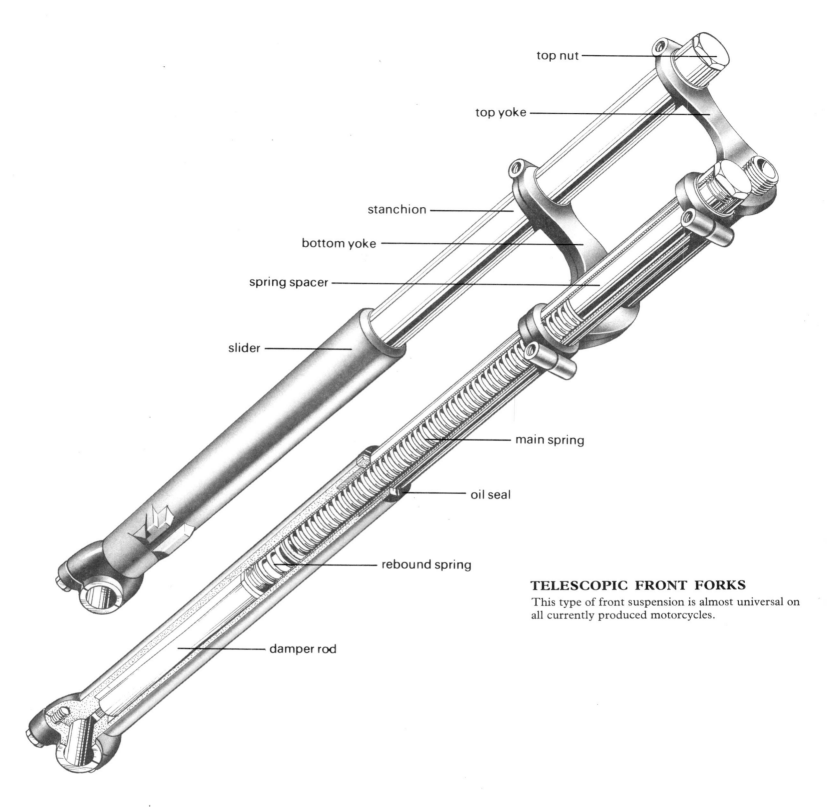

top nut

top yoke

stanchion

bottom yoke

spring spacer

slider

main spring

oil seal

rebound spring

damper rod

TELESCOPIC FRONT FORKS
This type of front suspension is almost universal on all currently produced motorcycles.

Basically the main frame should be stiff. Any flexing of the frame will alter the steering angles built into the forks. Recently the trend has been to follow the example of the car world and make the engine a part of the main structure.

At the front of the machine telescopic front forks reign supreme. For many years now they have been decried as

inadequate in many respects, but they still seem to do a more than passable job and most machines are fitted with them.

Telescopic forks are simply two tubes clamped in position just forward of their pivot point which is at the steering head. When the wheel is clamped to the bottom of the forks its centre is also forward of the pivot point and this gives the steering geometry 'castor' and 'trail'. A line drawn through the centre of the steering axis meets the ground in front of the wheel's

point of contact with the road. The distance between these two points is the trail. The front wheel's castor action is like that of a wheel on a tea trolley. It tries to turn round on itself. Trail has a self-centring action which damps this tendency out. A combination of the two allows the front wheel to turn and remain stable and controlled.

A common steering angle is 62 degrees, and most machines will have a steering angle quite close to this. Fitted to the bottom of the fork's main tubes are the sliders. These carry the wheel and they support the weight of the machine and rider by having a coil spring acting on

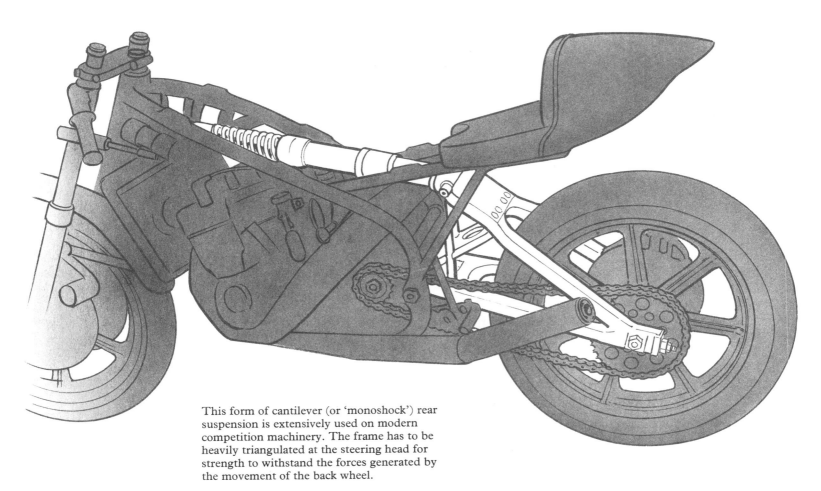

This form of cantilever (or 'monoshock') rear suspension is extensively used on modern competition machinery. The frame has to be heavily triangulated at the steering head for strength to withstand the forces generated by the movement of the back wheel.

them. The spring is normally fitted inside the fork's main tube, or stanchion.

When the forks encounter a bump in the road the wheel and sliders compress the spring. This allows the front wheel to remain in contact with the road. The spring also absorbs the 'shock' instead of transmitting it to the main frame. However, once compressed the spring will rebound and force the wheel back down the forks. The momentum will carry the spring past its original resting place and when it reaches its limit, depending on the force of the original bump, it will compress once more. This means that the bike would continue to bounce up and down long after the obstacle has been passed. To overcome this a damping system has to be used. If the front forks are filled with a quantity of oil in the lower slider this will be under pressure when the forks move up the stanchions. Since it is impossible to compress oil the only answer for it is to move up the forks with the sliders. A small hole, or valve, is fitted between the oil reservoir and the space it wants to occupy. As the wheel hits a bump the spring absorbs the shock but the oil limits the rate of movement. The amount of movement is determined by the size of the valve hole, and the viscosity of the oil.

If the valves are arranged so that the forks have no damping on the compression stroke, but encounter damping resistance on the rebound, the system is known as 'single damped'. This simple system allows the wheel to absorb shocks freely but stops

the oscillations from continuing after that because the fork spring returns to its normal length under the controlled resistance of the oil being squeezed through its valve orifices. The system with bump and rebound damping is known as 'double' or 'two way' damping.

At the rear of the machine the same system of hydraulic damping is applied but, of course, steering does not have to be taken into account. It does, however, have to take drive and if this is done by chain other problems are encountered.

The system used on most bikes is a simple pivoted fork which carries the wheel. A suspension unit is fitted either side and connected to a subframe. The top and bottom run of the final drive chain from the gearbox pass either side of the arm's pivot point and this simple fact gives rise to several problems. Firstly, the suspension's travel is limited because the chain will make contact with the pivot point beyond a certain distance. This problem can be reduced by moving the arm's pivot point closer to the gearbox sprocket but this is not always a practical proposition.

Chain tension is another problem. As the arm moves up and down its distance from the gearbox sprocket will alter, which in turn alters the tension in the chain. Another headache for the frame designer, which has only really come to light with the introduction of very powerful engines, is the torque reaction of the chain on the suspension movement.

If a straight line is drawn through the centre of the gearbox and rear wheel sprockets, it will probably pass the swinging arm pivot point either just above, or below it. When a lot of power is applied to the chain it moves the rear wheel sprocket by pulling on it. If the imaginary centre line passes above the suspension pivot point the chain will try to compress the rear suspension. If the line is below the centre, the back of the bike will 'sit up' as the power is applied.

Another weakness of the swinging arm, or pivoted fork, is the lack of lateral stiffness. In the vertical plane the dampers have the main job of stopping one side of the arm deflecting more than the other. To help combat this problem the cantilever suspension system was designed.

With this set-up the rear arm pivots from the normal position but the forks are triangulated. The top points of both triangles are joined together and a single damper unit is fitted from there to the frame, sometimes reaching up under the fuel tank to the steering head.

Another variation of the cantilever system is to triangulate the frame underneath the main backbone. Instead of linking the two triangles directly to a damper unit they operate a bell crank. This transfers the movement of the arm to a damper which is mounted upright in the centre of the frame. By altering the ratio of the bell crank full damper rod movement can be obtained for any given amount of suspension movement.

Apart from the triangulated arm being much stiffer in the vertical plane, the 'monoshock' system also eliminates the problem of matching two damper units. An attempt to overcome this matching problem has been made by using a suspension arm similar to the bell crank suspension but fitting a single damper in the conventional position. However, due to the loads only being transmitted through one side of the arm, it has to be very stiff for the design to work. This in turn usually means an extra weight penalty.

Although all these systems offer advantages over the conventional swinging arm, they are complicated, and therefore expensive to make. Like the telescopic front fork, the swinging arm is likely to remain on standard production motorcycles for some time because it is simple and effective.

Basically only two types of brake are used on production motorcycles: the drum and the disc. The drum brake is a circular drum, as its name suggests, with a hub built into its centre. This hub carries the wheel bearings about which the wheel revolves. On one side of the drum the hub and the outer section are joined together forming a rigid unit. This unit is usually cast in alloy and the braking surface is

provided by a steel ring, set into the drum's inner circumference.

The heart of the drum brake is the backplate assembly. This carries two shoes which fit inside the drum and have the same outside radius as the inside of the drum. In the simple drum brake these shoes are fixed at one end and the other end rests on a simple cam. A cable from the handlebar operates the cam, which rotates and spreads the two brake-shoes bringing them into contact with the brake-drum.

Since the drum forms the centre of the wheel it revolves with it, but the brake-plate is fixed, usually to the fork leg. When contact is made between the friction material on the brake-shoes and the brake-drum, the wheel is slowed down.

With this arrangement one of the shoes has its operating end facing the direction of the drum's rotation, while the other has it trailing. This is known as a single leading shoe brake. When the trailing shoe makes contact, the action of the drum tries to force the shoe away from the drum's face. When the leading shoe makes contact it is pulled on to the drum, and this action is known as a 'self-servo effect'. Obviously the shoe which is pulled on to the drum is going to do most of the work in slowing the bike down.

To improve the working of the drum brake the twin leading shoe unit was developed. This has a cam at the leading edge of both brake-shoes, therefore when the brake is operated both brake linings are self-servo assisted.

To improve the power of the drum brake its diameter and width can be increased so that the mechanical advantage is improved. The problem here is one of weight and heat. A large drum can be very heavy, especially as it must be rigid if it is not going to distort due to the heat generated during braking. Any distortion of the drum can interrupt contact with the shoes, resulting in reduced braking efficiency. Also if the drum were to go oval, an intermittent braking effect would result, causing the brake to judder. Some of these problems can be overcome by keeping the diameter down to a reasonable size, and more advantage gained by doubling up on the number of brake-shoes.

With the advent of multiple brake-shoes the drum brake reached the limit of its development. The now widely used disc brake has many advantages over the drum and has almost totally replaced the drum on high performance motorcycles. With the disc unit the hub of the wheel does not form part of the brake. The steel

KAWASAKI FRAME
(not showing swinging arm)

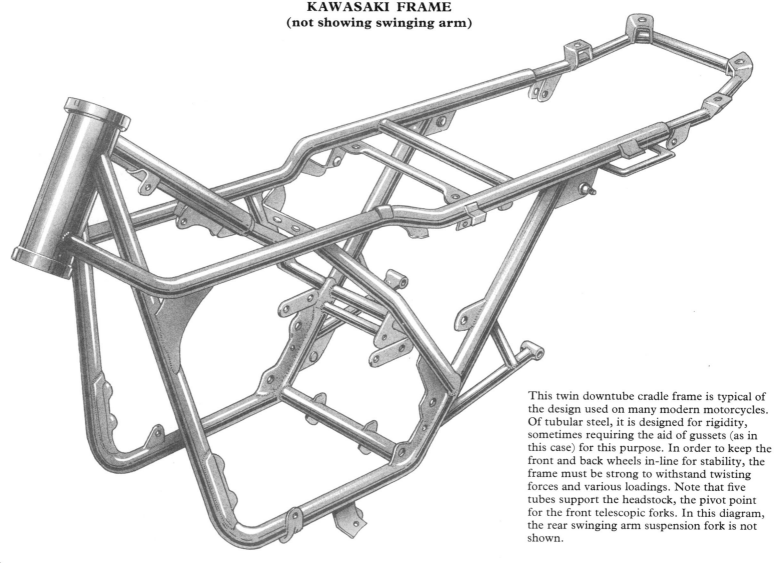

This twin downtube cradle frame is typical of the design used on many modern motorcycles. Of tubular steel, it is designed for rigidity, sometimes requiring the aid of gussets (as in this case) for this purpose. In order to keep the front and back wheels in-line for stability, the frame must be strong to withstand twisting forces and various loadings. Note that five tubes support the headstock, the pivot point for the front telescopic forks. In this diagram, the rear swinging arm suspension fork is not shown.

DOUBLE-ACTING PISTON DISC BRAKE

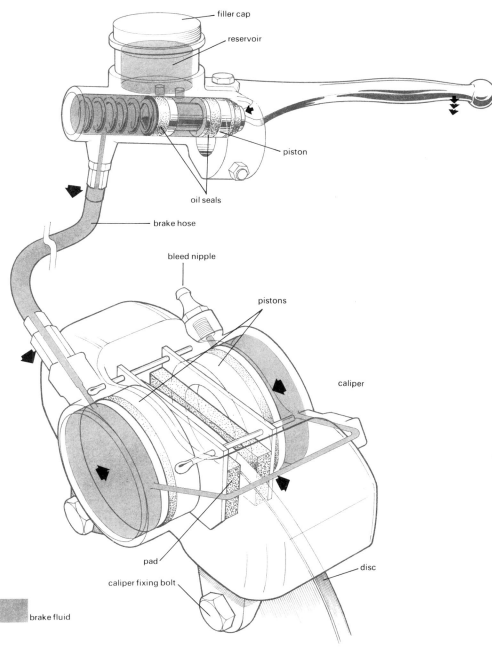

Lighter and more efficient than the drum brake, the hydraulic disc brake is now the more commonly used of the two designs. In addition to the type illustrated, there is a sliding caliper type and a cable-operated disc (see text). Since hydraulic fluid cannot be compressed, pulling on the handlebar lever forces the fluid to the pistons in the caliper which in turn force the pads to press against the disc. The high pressure required at the disc is gained by the mechanical advantage of the handlebar lever moving approximately four times the distance of the pistons.

INTERNAL EXPANDING DRUM BRAKE

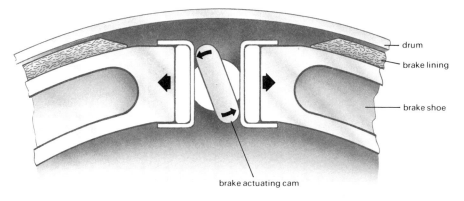

Operating the brake lever forces the brake shoes apart via the brake cam. This in turn forces the brake linings, which are bonded to the shoes, against the internal face of the brake drum.

or alloy disc is simply bolted straight onto the side of the hub. The actual braking is done by a caliper which clamps two friction pads onto the side of the disc. The caliper is mounted on the fork leg and it is usually operated by hydraulic pistons.

When the brake lever is pulled in, the arm operates a master piston which forces fluid down the brake lines and into the caliper. From here the fluid comes up against two pistons with brake material, or pads, resting against them. As the pistons are forced along their respective bores, the pads are forced out on to the sides of the disc. Because the two pistons are opposite each other the disc cannot be pushed to one side or the other.

This type of hydraulic caliper works very well but is expensive to manufacture as there are two sets of bores and pistons and both must be sealed.

The less expensive sliding caliper has only one hydraulic piston. This operates a brake-pad in the normal way, while the second pad on the other side of the disc is fixed rigidly to the caliper. When the piston moves out towards the disc only one pad comes into contact. More pressure on the lever causes the piston to move further, but as the disc is fixed the sliding caliper is drawn across it. This causes the second, fixed, pad to come into contact with the brake-disc.

This system works well provided the caliper is always free on its pivot point. To reduce the possibility of the pads remaining in contact with the disc, a spring is sometimes fitted which pulls the caliper back into its neutral position. With the double piston caliper there are no springs to pull the pistons away from the disc. The rubber seals that seal in the hydraulic fluid simply distort as the piston moves out. When the pressure is released the seals regain their shape, pulling the pistons back.

While a drum brake can be operated by hydraulic pressure, most production motorcycles have always had cable-operated drums. However, some lightweight machines are fitted with cable-operated disc brakes. The caliper is then of the sliding type, and the moving piston is activated by a cable-operated mechanism. Lever pressures are comparable with the hydraulic disc and the only disadvantage with cable operation is the need to adjust the brake periodically, but otherwise cable operation is very simple.

The reason hydraulic brakes are self adjusting is that after each brake operation the caliper only moves back just enough to clear the disc. As the brake-pad wears the piston is automatically forced further out along the cylinder to compensate for this. The main danger with this system is that the brake-pad can still give good performance although worn to the point of failure.

How a Bike is Built

A fine example of the lack of a recognizable production line is illustrated by this picture of three assembly workers putting together wiring harnesses for BMW machines. Each worker is supplied with all the necessary parts to build a headlamp unit, complete with all its attached wires and switchgear. The finished unit, complete with its mounting brackets, is then passed on to other production workers for installation into the motorcycle. The woman in the foreground is manufacturing speedometer and rev counter drives, and brake master-cylinders.

The background

Unlike motorcars, whose rapid progress has resulted largely from the demands of a buying public which requires reliability, shape, comfort and economy more than anything else, motorcycles are, by comparison, sophisticated antiques. The average modern motorcyclist rides for pleasure, he wants to feel he is riding a motorcycle, and he wants to be seen to be riding a motorcycle. The fact that his misplaced traditional loyalties are costing him dear in terms of performance, quality and hard cash are, seemingly, of little interest, and the world's makers know it.

The truth of this is best illustrated in the sad fate of all machines showing contempt for the average rider's inflexible demands for stereotyped orthodoxy. Not one of them has proved commercially successful and, whatever their merit, none has influenced later design. The most successful—that is, profitable—makers have always been those who have obstinately refused to stray from the hackneyed route of traditional conformity.

Until the Japanese entered the world market in the mid-1950s virtually all manufacturers conformed to the same production principles. Whether British, Italian, or German, every motorcycle was designed to be assembled by craftsmen, and production lines were, in effect, little more than series of assembly benches staffed by skilled fitters with a deep understanding of motorcycle engineering. Most were intensely loyal to their factory and prided themselves on contributing positively to the good name of their employer by ensuring that their own work was second to none. The majority underwent apprenticeships within the company finally employing them.

This dependence on craftsmanship was to prove the undoing of the big European companies. By relying almost wholly on the skill of their production workers to ensure quality, rather than on the original design, they left themselves open to attack from Japan, a nation founding its motorcycle manufacturing techniques on designs requiring neither high-grade materials nor assembly by craftsmen. Most European motorcycle makers regarded every model that left the factory as an advertisement of their engineering skill. This was as true for BSA, who produced 60 per cent of the entire British industry's output and whose range included some plainly utilitarian machines, as for Moto Guzzi in Italy who filled a similar role to BSA in Britain, or BMW who, in Germany, built motorcycles designed to be prestigious. Even plebeian little machines like the BSA Bantam boasted frame construction methods which would not have disgraced a Brough Superior and which, arguably,

were as good as anything built today. Most engines and transmissions required a certain amount of selected component assembly if they were to operate reliably for very long, and owners were required to contribute to the good order of their machine by conforming to some very protracted maintenance demands.

Even though the quality of materials used in the construction of European machines was high, this still could not make up for the advantages of absolute reliability and freedom from continual maintenance that the Japanese designs offered. It was plain that, at some point, the Japanese dedication to profit had bypassed the normal European fascination with craftsmanship for its own sake. This probably occurred because, in building up a brand new motorcycle industry under modern conditions with none of the strong traditions of Europe to influence them, the Japanese had no hesitation about building machines with, for instance, weld spatter surrounding wrinkled gussets at frame joints subject to high stress. If the motorcycle worked efficiently and reliably it was, surely, to the buyer's financial advantage if the cheap frame joints performed, at least as far as the buyer was concerned, as well as the beautifully made European brazed lug, or hand-welded and ground joints. The money thus saved, the Japanese reasoned, could well be spent on areas they regarded as more important, such as engine development, and it was.

It is therefore obvious that there are two distinct motorcycling philosophies, although increasingly over the past few years they have begun to move significantly towards one another. This is best illustrated by BMW's investment in purely commercial machines of undoubted high volume sale, and Honda's move towards the production of smaller quantities of special machines for Europe incorporating features of a type not wanted in America. It follows, therefore, that the methods of actually making the two types of machine are completely different.

An example of the problems associated with the change from craftsman-built systems to mass production assembly is well exemplified by BMW's difficulties when they left Munich for Berlin in 1968. Courageously, they broke with the old ways, realizing their commercial impracticability, but not entirely aware of the pitfalls ahead. Helmut Bonsch, then head of the motorcycle division, recalls: 'We learned more about building motorcycles in our first two years in Berlin than we did in our entire previous history.'

Without their old craftsmen who so lovingly built the R69S and its Earles fork relatives, BMW found themselves at the mercy of guest workers from outside Germany who were interested only in

earning a good wage and who cared little for the product. 'We thought we knew all about tele-forks, but when the people at Berlin began to assemble them they leaked oil, misaligned, became stiff in action, and generally proved quite impossible. We had to completely redesign our tele-forks so workers could not damage them during the building process. This we did, but even then we found bikes with bad faults! An investigation proved another group of employees were overtightening the front mudguard bridge-piece, and it was eventually causing the sliders to warp.'

This seemingly minor problem perfectly illustrates the present hazards of designing and manufacturing motorcycles.

The European system

Of all the European producers none is more typical of the old school than Ducati. Untypically, they are state owned, although this is only because, rather than allow the company to drift into bankruptcy during the lean 1960s when America went almost wholly Japanese, the Italian government bought the falling Ducati shares for themselves. It was done to maintain the engineering group's valuable experience under its own roof, rather than allow it to dissipate and be lost.

Right at the top of the management is Ducati's engineer, Fabio Taglioni. In Britain he would be referred to as the chief designer, and would be relegated to a middle management role, subservient to the dictates of the board. In Italy, however, the motorcycle designer reigns, if not actually supreme, then with the most enormous influence on all company policies. Under him are a few young qualified designers, each one expected to prove his worth by exceeding the abilities of his contemporaries, rather than by displaying any team co-operation. In this manner the Italians manage to achieve greatness through a few designers quite deliberately nurtured to a degree of talent far above the ordinary, and from which pinnacle their craft is accorded the status of an art, or is at least accepted as such by worshipping Italians.

Taglioni, then, would design the complete basic motorcycle, but would leave certain areas in a sort of no-man's-land. This has long proved to be the undoing of the Italian industry, particularly Ducati. Lately, with the advent of the Darmah model, the traditional neglect of the ancillary parts, once the fundamentals have had their excellence proved, has gone. Ducati now take notice of the rest of the world's demand for correctness of detail. Lack of it is one of the principal weaknesses of an engineer-dominated manufacturing process. For the engineer at the pinnacle of the pyramid of power, there can be little appreciation of the appalling, almost impossible frustrations of selling, buying, and owning a motorcycle which, while admirable as an engineering exercise, is downright awful as a practical road vehicle because of poor switchgear, unreliable ignition, an uncomfortable seat, thin paint, peeling chromium plating and so on.

To give an example of the power of the traditional Italian engineer: Ducati decided they wanted to enter the 500cc market with a transverse parallel twin equipped with Taglioni's desmodromic valve gear. Taglioni refused to agree with the board about the correctness of such a design and stubbornly refused to have anything to do with the project. It was an unwise board decision to press on, as they would later discover.

One of the subordinate young designers drew up the plans for the machine. It vibrated badly once it had been built. It was a conventionally built overhead camshaft machine and not a desmodromic one, and twin balance cranks were installed into the crankcase. They smoothed the engine well enough, but absorbed power and raised engine temperature unduly. One was removed as a compromise, and then the other. Still the performance was low. Ducati, desperate by now, engaged Leopoldo Tartarini of Italjet to complete the project that they were unable to finalize themselves.

Presumably Tartarini managed to persuade Taglioni to help him out, because the desmodromic valve drive they were relying on was finally installed. Much more of the 500 twin was manufactured outside the Ducati factory than usual, most of it at Italjet. But the project had been delayed too long and the public was offered a whole range of brand new Japanese middleweights to choose instead, apart from which the reliability and finish of the 500 was so bad that the first few buyers quickly spread word around and the trade lost faith.

Ducati manufacture approximately 10,000 motorcycles annually, the greater proportion being the large capacity V-twins for which they have become so justifiably renowned. These are all turned out on a single production line using the 'batch' system popular with all smaller manufacturers. It is quite simple really, and enables manufacturers of this size to develop and make a whole range of different motorcycles on a single production line, thus keeping assembly costs to a minimum. One week the production workers will concentrate on, say, 100 Desmo Darmah models; the following week they will turn their hands to making 100 500cc vee-twin Pantahs; the week after that 100 900cc SS machines will

leave the line, and so on.

Ducati are renowned for their purist approach to motorcycle engineering. To this end they probably stand supreme in the commercial world. To maintain their status, however, Ducati rely implicitly on the highly specialized skills of production workers with a great sympathy for motorcycles, just as the old fashioned factories of the past did, and to which the majority of European factories, even now, pay tribute in some way. This approach to motorcycle manufacturing, however admirable in idealistic terms, creates problems of industrial and commercial inflexibility, as so aptly proved by an inability to build a sound 500cc machine. Because they lack experience with alternative engine layouts, Ducati find themselves beset with all the problems associated with the development of new models from a completely blank drawing board. Therefore the gestation period is longer and more fraught with difficulties and the production models more likely to prove unsatisfactory. The advantage of the system can only be recognized after a five year period, by which time the model in question will have fully undergone that most demanding of all road tests—the public one by machine owners. During the same period warranty claims will have been numerous enough to have reduced company profitability to near zero, and the faith of the retail trade distributing the models will have been severely strained, and, in many cases, ruptured. This is not peculiar to Ducati, but is common among almost all smaller European companies.

Once the five year period is over the faults of the machine in question will have been eradicated, its good qualities improved, and the result will be a motorcycle of quite brilliant performance. By then, however, the company, in this case Ducati, will have almost exhausted its meagre resources, with insufficient capital left to spend on properly developing the new model they will need in another five years to replace the one in hand.

The advantages of motorcycles of this type are many, despite their shortcomings. Their material quality is high—it has to be to provide the type of performance the makers demand which, in many respects, is superior to that of Japanese motorcycles. The engine is simple to keep production cost and weight to a minimum and, therefore, pleases the cost-conscious owner with an eye on maintenance bills. Their production life is necessarily long, for the sake of profitability, and so simplifies spare parts distribution. Because they are products of motorcyclists' brains, rather than the contrived instruments of marketing experts, they provide a singular quality of performance that frequently appeals to the dedicated, older motorcyclist.

Because of the small production quantities involved and the labour intensive methods employed, probably the biggest bonus enjoyed by Ducati and their kin is the ability to create limited numbers of prestige models. Laverda, for instance, once offered their endurance racing 750cc SFC on the market. It was built in the competition shop by race mechanics from either specially made or hand-selected components, and was sold at cost price as a publicity vehicle. Ducati did much the same thing with their original 750cc SS. This was their prestige super sports production racer.

All these Ducatis were fitted with desmodromic valve gear. As this method of valve operation required approximately four hours' work by an expert on each cylinder head to achieve operational efficiency, the high labour cost can be easily imagined. To accompany this hand assembly, all other working components of the 750 SS models were of the hand-selected type, which does not mean that the rest of the normal production motorcycles were assembled from left-over parts of inferior quality, as some people think, but that all the chosen machines were utterly faithful to the original design. A few private individuals vastly improve the performance of their ordinary machines of whatever make by following a similar practice, popularly known as 'blueprinting'.

Of the 10,000 motorcycles built annually by Ducati, no more than a few hundred were ever built to this standard before the whole production system was revised six years after the V-twins first made an appearance. In a final effort to save the factory from government threat of closure, new machining operations and quality control systems were installed. It cost a lot of money, but it proved worthwhile as Ducati motorcycle reliability improved. It also guaranteed the end of the specially built 750 SS. With the advent of new production improvements the desmodromic mechanism was adapted to accept more orthodox production line installation. Much stricter quality control ensured that all components, whether bought in or made by Ducati, conformed more closely to the design requirements, and so all Ducatis were improved, leaving the need for hand-built specials from selected components unnecessary, at least in Ducati's opinion. (This may sound like so much publicity material believed credulously, but a detailed inspection of a Ducati Darmah compared to an early 1970s twin will quickly prove otherwise.)

During the actual assembly of a Darmah, 15 quality control stations maintain vigilance, and two roving quality control inspectors patrol the operation. Each worker has to sign his particular contribution to the assembly process, and the

A completed BMW engine, without its covers, ready for installation into the motorcycle frame.

completed motorcycle is then subjected to rolling road and track test procedures. To ensure that the desmodromic valve gear on which Ducati now rely so heavily retains its quality, every 25th set machined by the factory is returned to the inspection engineers for complete measurement. In common with most smaller manufacturers Ducati buy in a large proportion of their machined parts, including the rough forgings of the gears used in the desmodromic valve drive.

Ducati have no foundry of their own, and this is quite common among motorcycle factories. The two exceptions are Laverda, who own the huge FAMM foundry and who manufacture for various firms including Puch, a company which is almost unique in the motorcycle world in manufacturing almost everything required to build a motorcycle except for the tyres. In fact Puch are a major component supplier to other motorcycle, cycle and car makers. But Ducati keeps the work in the

Italian motorcycle industry by obtaining their engine castings from the nearby Moto Morini company. They then machine the castings to their requirements.

There is no single production line recognizable as such at Ducati until just before the motorcycle is completed. Instead there are a series of sub-production areas in which various major component units are assembled, and which converge towards a final assembly area.

To any spectator at Ducati the primary

impression is one of the immense skill and confidence displayed by the workers, rather than admiration for the advanced production methods employed. The place looks like a motorcycle factory should, with men in oily overalls operating lathes and gear cutting machines, and others using familiar tools like ring spanners and feeler gauges during the various production operations. Concrete floors are stained with oil; the bitter smell of freshly machined steel mixes with the sweet one of the cooling lubricant from lathes; the occasional whine of a power tool interrupts the murmur of conversation and the rattle and clink of hand-held spanners.

The Japanese system

Honda's approach to motorcycle production is quite different. Instead of Ducati's 600 employees devoting their skills towards an end product that could not exist without them, the Japanese company employs around 12,000 people to assemble motorcycles under a system designed to minimize the human contribution. This should not be taken to mean that Honda deliberately dehumanize their workers, but simply that they long ago recognized the disadvantages of relying on highly skilled engineers and mechanics to assemble motorcycles sold principally to wage-earners in the middle and lower income range.

Over a period of time Suzuki, Yamaha and Kawasaki and, in particular, Honda, have continually modernized their assembly systems until they match the most advanced car production lines anywhere in the world. There are no oil-stained floors at Honda. Production workers closely resemble medical orderlies, they and their environment are so clean; all tools are power operated, and every stage of assembly is designed in such a way as to avoid the necessity of relying upon true engineering skills, although obviously dexterity and experience play their part. Instead of a multitude of individuals at work benches, there are long moving assembly lines of motorcycles attended by white-coated workers. It is all very different from the traditional European system, although even in Europe two companies at least are making serious attempts to break with tradition.

Apart from the obvious differences in manufacturing operations, the great disparity between the Japanese and European motorcycle industries lies in their marketing approach. The Japanese rely on teams of marketing experts of enormous skill to research into every aspect of sales potential and possibility. By finding a market gap, a public desire, or weakness in a competitor's range, Honda, for instance, will exploit it

by designing a motorcycle to fill the gap. There is no single designer to whom they pay tribute, but a whole team made up of design, marketing and production people, of which marketing is probably the most influential department, with production coming second. In the drawing up of every new machine hundreds of people are involved, ranging from raw material buyers who cost the project in material terms, salesmen who project sales analyses, production engineers who arrange new production lines and manufacturing operations, to stylists who shape the future machine, and the design engineers who have continually to modify the design to suit the requirements of everyone else involved.

Even the latter are further divided into specialist groups. One section will concentrate on the engine, another on transmission, a third on the frame and another on braking, while a fifth works in co-operation with the electrical system makers' design team, and another with the carburettor supplier and government agencies to ensure adequate emission control and silencing. Split even further, smaller groups of engineers within, say, the engine development team, will specialize in valve gear or crankshaft systems, while some among those in the team of frame engineers will liase closely with the tyre suppliers to ensure high speed stability.

In Japan it takes approximately two years to get a simple utility motorcycle into production from the start, and four years for a big multi-cylinder machine. This is very different from the European operation, where the responsibility for the concept, design and production of a new model so frequently rests on the shoulders of no more than a handful of individuals, or even one man alone. To quote Massimo Laverda, managing director and chairman of the entire Laverda group, 'We think marketing is rubbish. We know whether or not a new model will succeed. Marketing costs far too much money and anyway, it is just as frequently wrong in its predictions as we [the engineers and accountants] are.' The truth is that, with a few exceptions, European companies are much smaller and therefore more adaptable to change, mistakes cost much less to rectify, and few of them can afford a special marketing division. Of greater importance is the fact that the managers are closer to the hard realities of everyday motorcycling, and are frequently enthusiastic riders themselves. They feel, therefore, confident that their intuitive flair, their 'nose' for the market, will match the studied marketing exercises of their Japanese counterparts. With luck it does, as proved by the phenomenal success of Moto Guzzi's transverse V-twin variations. Equally, the

Japanese system can fail, as the unsuccessful Honda CB360 demonstrated. But such failures are rare; most new Japanese machines are guaranteed a healthy future before they even leave the boardroom, yet many motorcycles from European countries are either withdrawn after their showroom introduction or become borderline cases forced to exist on small sales to dedicated marque buffs willing to accept the disadvantages attendant on all rare models. Benelli's 650cc twin, and Laverda's race-bred 500 Montjuich are both examples of borderline cases.

The group system

The group system is one shared by many motorcycle concerns. Puch build trucks and small arms; Laverda have interests in combine harvesters and foundry work; Yamaha make musical instruments; Kawasaki are part of a giant engineering and construction consortium; MV-Agusta only built bikes as a hobby while the parent company built Bell helicopters under licence on a vast scale, and so the list could continue. These days almost every motorcycle manufacturer is forced to have major interests in another manufacturing industry simply to spread invested capital more wisely over a wider range of interests. The old days of ultra-specialization have gone for good. There are two reasons for this. The first lies with the impossibility of survival in a constantly fluctuating market: motorcycles, having become almost exclusively leisure vehicles, are one of the first things to suffer a sales recession during a general economic depression, and they are in the forefront of any recovery. No specialist motorcycle maker could hope to survive alone in such a transient and fickle sales arena. Secondly, new models require proportionately greater amounts of development capital each year because of escalating costs all round. As part of an industrial complex, a motorcycle division is able to rely on financial support from the entire group, which it needs to design and launch the new machine.

Honda build cars, outboard engines, light agricultural machinery and stationary plant under the Honda brand name. What is not generally realized, however, is that Honda, like their three home contempories, also own, or have a major shareholding in, all their ancillary component suppliers such as electrical and suspension systems. Showa, the Japanese suspension maker, for instance, is almost entirely Honda-owned, yet Suzuki use Showa equipment. The philosophy behind this lies in the sensible assumption that Suzuki will survive, with or without Honda, so

Honda might just as well profit by their existence and, by so doing, simultaneously insure themselves against a depression in Honda sales.

With all this in mind it would probably come as a surprise to any European visitor to notice the lack of actual manufacturing processes in any of the Honda motorcycle plants. With only rare exceptions, all components are brought into the factory ready for assembly. This goes on continually because the factory holds no more than a couple of days' stock of supplies.

Under the European method of operation this would prove impossible, because the reliance on outside manufacturers for finished gears, for instance, would be too great. In Honda's case, however, the engineering company manufacturing the gear teeth is Honda-owned and control is therefore excellent.

Quality control operations are probably the foundation of Honda's success. Although the company manufactured 2.5 million two wheelers in 1978, and anticipated the production of close to three million in 1982, the consistency of quality displayed by the machined parts of their motorcycles is equal to the finest made anywhere in the world. In this manner the performance and reliability of all Hondas are virtually standardized. All of the 1,000 engineering companies owned by Honda are subject to the most stringent quality control systems during all their manufacturing operations. Once the finished articles arrive at the main assembly plant further inspections take place—at reception and during the assembly process.

Where the company considers quality is not required then it is not incorporated, as best illustrated by the low-grade outer engine covers of most Hondas, which require varnishing to resist oxidization, and the frames. The latter are fabricated in the cheapest possible manner from the cheapest possible steel, occasionally including so many impurities that accident repair, either by welding or bending, is impossible. The structure of the metal is such that it cracks when bent and, in some cases, actually vapourizes during the re-welding process. Whether Honda should

The assembled power unit is carefully positioned into the frame. The powered hoist is controlled by the production worker (foreground) who has the switchboard in his right hand. The chromium-plated tube under his left hand is an engine protection bar bolted to the frame prior to engine installation, to facilitate its fitting.

be chastised any more than, say, Ducati for their electrics, is a matter open to discussion among motorcycle buffs. The hard fact of the matter is that, like them or not, Honda frames perform consistently and Ducati electrics do not.

One company is an exception to this rule of motorcycle production and its vehicles bear a name that many an otherwise intelligent motorcyclist holds in misdirected contempt. That company is Piaggo, who build Vespa scooters. In 1945 Piaggo, Italian aircraft makers, decided that some form of cheap two-wheeled transport was required by an impoverished Italian public. Fortunately they had never previously built motorcycles, so they employed aircraft and car manufacturing techniques to build their two-wheeler.

Even Piaggo would admit to some very serious flaws in their little machines, these being principally concerned with tiny wheels and mismatched suspension, but these are performance, not production, inadequacies. As far as the suitability of the Vespas for assembly purposes is concerned no other two wheeler holds a candle to them: their box section pressed steel construction and compact power units are marvels of ingenuity that lend themselves perfectly to simple production methods. Not even Honda, for all their sophistication and money, can match Piaggo's advanced methods of manufacturing.

The assembly line

In point of fact there is no such piece of equipment as an assembly line. Even the most advanced factories consist of various stores, manufacturing and assembly systems, all of which overlap and are subdivided further into operations contributing to the assembly of the final product. Towards the completion of a motorcycle it might appear that it has undergone a simple building process on a single moving assembly line, but this impression hides the truth. To clarify a typical operation let us follow the process at an entirely hypothetical manufacturer.

As so few factories have their own foundry our typical manufacturer would, in all probability, receive regular deliveries of all engine cases, cylinder heads, cylinder barrels, wheel hubs and other parts in raw cast form. These would be taken to the machine shop stores and the various machinists would draw on them as necessary for cutting and grinding into the finished shape. In most cases highly qualified machine tool setters will have set the lathes and turning machines, either by computerized or automatically controlled machining systems. Machine operators will attend the machining process, during which time finished items will be selected by quality control inspectors to ensure that they comply with the required standards.

The other major cast items to come into the factory would be wheels, but in all probability these would arrive finished because of the ultra-specialized manufacturing techniques necessary to make a flawless, well balanced, safe wheel. They might even arrive fitted with tyres to simplify and speed up motorcycle production, and to minimize storage space. It is equally likely that brake discs would already be fitted.

Castings should not be confused with forgings. The difference between the two lies in the extreme pressure used during the manufacturing process of the forging. Forgings brought in by motorcycle makers comprise crankshafts or crankshaft parts,

gears and gear shafts, camshafts and rockers, connecting rods and, in most cases, pistons which, like castings, would undergo machining in the motorcycle factory machine shops. As shown by the list of forgings these are the highly stressed components requiring greater strength than casting alone could provide.

Once the quality control inspectors are satisfied with the finished parts they are placed in another store to await collection from the engine assembly section.

All electrical components would be bought in, including starter motors, generators, current control systems, wiring looms, switchgear and lights. So would carburettors and allied parts such as filters and induction hoses. This is because the design and manufacturing skills associated with such highly specialized equipment is beyond the economic scope of most, indeed all, motorcycle factories. Buying parts from a few specialists ensures that the development and manufacturing costs of these expensive items are shared by the entire industry, thus keeping costs down. In our case the electrical system would probably come from Stanley, the Japanese maker, switchgear from Nippon Denso, also Japanese, the wiring loom from a small specialist contractor and a headlamp from Bosch in Germany.

The same rule applies to suspension units, especially rear ones, although a few factories, such as Triumph, BMW and Puch manufacture their own front forks. Our maker buys his in, probably from Marzzochi, the Italian suspension specialist.

In all probability our factory would make its own frames from bought-in tubing. The tubing would be drawn from factory stores as required by the frame shop, then it would be cut into set lengths and heated for bending, all in the same machine. At this point the bent frame tubes would be placed in a jig, which in effect is nothing more than a strong frame capable of clamping separate tubes into their correct position for welding. Once correctly set up each frame joint would be electrically machine welded, and all the brackets and tabs required for component support also welded into place.

After it had cooled the frame would be measured for accuracy by light beam, probably at the steering head and pivoted fork bearing housings. Any deviation would be rectified by a man with a flame torch, a long length of solid bar used as a lever, and strong arms. This may be a crude method, but it is effective.

Once the frame had been welded, it would be hung from a slowly moving chain in line with the other frames, and cleaned, probably chemically but possibly sand-blasted, before being swung into a drying room, and then along to the spray

room where a single coat of primer would be applied. It would be baked dry, still hanging from the moving chain as it passed through a long electrically heated oven. After that the top coat, perhaps two for a prestige model, is applied in another fully automated spray chamber.

Quality control inspectors using a simple jig would ensure that the frame still measured up to the correct dimensions, and would simultaneously inspect it for welding and painting flaws. If found, these would be attended to by a small team, again using hand equipment.

Probably the first item to be fastened to the frame during its journey down the first recognizable assembly line would be the swinging fork, which would have undergone a similar building operation in

Final testing is carried out in a sound-proofed room, complete with 'plug-in' exhaust gas extractors. The motorcycle, in this instance a BMW R100RS without its top fairing assembly, is placed on free-running, connected rollers, and ridden by a test rider. Brakes can be applied to the rollers to simulate hills and headwinds, in order to gauge engine efficiency under load. Under test conditions the machine is now anchored to the floor for safety reasons, after the rollers once seized, causing the machine to catapult forward through the doors into the production area.

the factory as the frame itself. The frame would be hand bolted to the slowly moving production line and the fork's bearings would be fitted by a compressed air machine tool operator. A couple of clicks and those impossible-to-remove bearings would be firmly housed. The same man might slide the fork spindle through the frame and fork bearings, and then tighten them to a predetermined load with another compressed air torque spanner. Compressed air tools are safer and cheaper to use than electrical ones.

As the frame moves along the assembly line items would be added, seemingly arbitrarily, but in fact in a carefully planned order that precludes the likelihood of one restricting the fitting of another: the wiring loom, ignition coils and horn, battery, seat, rear mudguard and so on.

Then the front forks would be bolted into place, again by one man using compressed air power tools set to predetermined torque ratings, but he would simply insert the complete fork assembly comprising fork legs, disc brake calipers, yokes, mudguard top bridge piece, headlamp bracket, and perhaps the handlebars and control levers. These, in turn, would have been assembled on another sub-assembly line elsewhere.

With the forks in place wheels would be fitted. Wheel spoking, even on the jigs used by most European manufacturers who find it impossible to justify the cost of a Japanese-type automatic wheel lacing machine, is a skilled job, and one most frequently carried out by women.

Few motorcycle factories make their own wheel rims; these are most usually supplied by the tyre maker. Before lacing, however, wheel hubs have to be fitted with bearings, another job carried out by power tool operators. The hubs are heated within an electrical coil to facilitate the fitting of the bearings. These would be checked for accuracy, and then the spoke lacing would be done and after that the tyre fitting, again a semi-automated task.

Depending on the type used, most machines would have their brakes assembled before the wheels were put in position. In the case of cast wheels this means discs bolted in place, and in the case of drum brakes, having the shoe-equipped brake-plate installed. Once again, and especially now that hydraulic disc brakes have become popular, few motorcycle manufacturers make their own. In this instance they would come from Girling, who, with Brembo, supply most of the world's motorcycle manufacturers. In another part of the factory the engine and transmission system would be moving slowly along its own assembly line, one quite as long, complex and time consuming as that for the cycle parts. Which of the two should be called *the* assembly line is

impossible to determine.

Crankcases would usually be drawn from stores as required. They are always machined in pairs in order to ensure perfect bearing alignment, whether of the vertically or horizontally split type. Inside would be fitted the crankshaft, drilled with oilways and complete with connecting rods. Then the transmission gears would be fitted, probably followed by the primary transmission system. At this stage quality control inspectors would measure every power unit for accuracy, rejecting those which failed to conform, marking the failed parts and returning them for correction before they can be reused on the assembly line.

The cylinder barrels would then be fitted over the pistons, probably by a machine in a manner similar to the whole engine assembly procedure. European makers, however, still favour labour-intensive engine assembly operations because it is uneconomic to install fully automated systems for production runs of less than hundreds of thousands.

In most cases the engine line would be of the constantly moving type, with restricted space free-wheeling areas which allow the line workers space and time to complete their tasks without undue waste, wherever they are employed along the line. In every case, the power units would hang from the line and be clamped securely into place for a few minutes at a time during the fitting procedures.

All valve and ignition timing would be carried out automatically during assembly, and only checked by hand in the last stages of machine completion. Once the cylinder head is fastened on and the cam boxes fitted, the power unit is fitted with carburettors and electrical systems and is ready for frame installation.

All factories still employ people to fasten the power unit into the frame. This provides an excellent chance for an inspection of all major parts, as well as ensuring that any overlooked faults are corrected. This meeting point of power unit and cycle part assembly lines generally involves quite a number of people.

The next stage seems somewhat strange: since most motorcycles are now exported, they have to undergo what is known in the trade as 'knock-down', ready for crating. Therefore most of the carefully assembled machines coming off the production line now have to be partly dismantled. This generally entails seat and handlebar removal at minimum but, depending on the market for which it is intended, can involve as much as draining the engine oil and removing battery, wheels, fuel tank and footrests. These are all packed into the crate, nowadays of form-fitting, shock-absorbent plastic, although still occasionally wood, and are ready for fitting by

either concessionnaire or retailer in the sales area.

The cylinder head manufacturing processes deserve a chapter to themselves, for in them can be found the manufacturer's true craftsmanship. This only applies to four-strokes: the two-stroke engine's quality lies in its induction and exhaust harmonics which entail design, rather than production, engineering abilities.

A cylinder head has to support camshafts or rocker gear, dissipate heat, form at least part of the combustion chamber, retain oil, absorb the relentless hammering of valves, silence mechanical noise, guide high speed gas movements, and look good. It is the foundation and the cap of every four-stroke's success, so the wide range of skills required to perfect it can probably be imagined.

After the designer has worked out the dimensions of the head, both internally and externally, a craftsman is used by the manufacturing foundry to give the blueprint material form. He is the pattern maker, and his art—for that is what it is—is required for all castings and forgings. He works in wood, generally beech or some other fine-grained hardwood, and carves a bare wooden cylinder head (or some other part when necessary) to the satisfaction of the designer. Then a hard plaster female mould is made of the wooden pattern, and from it an alloy head is cast. This is used to form the actual casting moulds used in production, although the task of translating the original blueprint to final production casting is a long, complicated, expensive and frequently worrying affair.

Once the bare head shape has been resolved, it is no great problem to machine it to take the exhaust pipes and valve guides, turn out the correctly shaped combustion chamber and gas passages, drill its oilways, fit its location studs and grind its faces. These jobs are all performed entirely by automated machine operations from start to finish, principally because machines do not deviate from the design dimensions, while even the most skilled men do. Nevertheless, most European factories employ highly skilled machinists of long experience to finish off all heads and make sure they are free of casting 'flash' and machining ridges, a job generally unnecessary in Japanese factories because of the different grade of materials and casting methods employed.

So it can be seen that the idea of the single production line is unworkable. There are many of them, as exemplified by the description of the cylinder head's production—another being that of the exhaust system with all its tube bending, electric welding, baffle insertion, chromium plating and final bolting together. Each one contributes to the assembly of the final product.

ENTHUSIAST'S TOOLKIT

The motorcyclist who has absolutely no interest in the mechanics of his machine is a rare phenomenon. Even though modern motorcycles are becoming more complex, and owners have more and more pressure placed on them to allow only dealers to service and repair them, the desire to know about the workings of their machine is still very strong in most owners.

This wish for mechanical knowledge may vary in intensity: some people desire only to be able to do simple routine service adjustments, while others will not be satisfied until they can do complete engine and cycle part overhauls. But whatever level of competence the home mechanic wishes to reach, it is essential to have the right tools for the job.

The most important piece of advice to give anyone who is planning to buy tools for the first time is: buy the best you can afford. Obviously you will have to use your judgement when deciding whether price always indicates quality. For example, you can time your machine's ignition stroboscopically as accurately with a strobe light costing £5 as with a light costing £25. The difference is that the more expensive one will provide a beam powerful enough to do the job in daylight, whereas the cheaper one would probably mean that you would have to wait until dusk or find a well-shaded spot before the beam could be seen sufficiently well to carry out the job. You have to decide whether it is worth spending five times as much as you really need in order to have this advantage.

It is worth buying more expensive items, however, in the case of spanners and screwdrivers. A cheap set of these may appear to be good value, but is often shown to be a false economy, for example when the spanner loses its jaw shape as soon as it is used, and probably also burrs the nut to which it is being applied. Today, most motorcycles are produced in Japan with light alloy and sometimes even expensive magnesium castings making up engine parts. When dealing with such engines the utmost care has to be taken, and that means using good-quality tools. In fact the engine screws on some Japanese engines have been made from such soft alloys that their cross-head pattern is easily gouged out. Often the only successful way to remove them without ruining their shape is with an impact driver.

Happily the situation is improving with the wider use of Allen (hexagon-head) screws as original equipment. In general, European and American engines have better-quality castings and engine screws which can withstand a little more abuse, but they should be treated with as much respect as their more fragile counterparts.

Another advantage of using good-quality tools is that the job may be done much more easily and quickly: they may be applied to the intricacies of a job with confidence and their reliability enables you to concentrate on the job rather than on the tools, and this also makes learning a much more straightforward process. First-class tools are also very satisfying to handle, and it is possible to feel as much pride of ownership in them as in the bike itself.

Most riders operate a 'two tier' system when it comes to toolkits: one on the bike for minor and emergency work, and the other more comprehensive kit at home for more major surgery. The problem of duplicating arises, however, and this could be expensive. If you own a new bike such as a BMW with a very good standard toolkit it would be unnecessary to duplicate, but on the other hand some lightweights have spartan toolkits of such poor quality they should be used as a last resort only. You can build up your bike and home kits to complement each other or as completely separate items. In the latter case it would

make sense to start a quality home kit from scratch.

The following discussion of motorcycling tools aims to help you select the most useful ones in their correct order of importance, for progressively building up a comprehensive kit which will eventually enable you to tackle jobs previously outside your scope.

Basic tools and equipment

The following items comprise the basic toolkit and other equipment needed for carrying out routine servicing and minor repair jobs.

A handbook, or workshop manual, or better still both, is the first requirement. You cannot adjust a spark plug gap or set valve clearances accurately unless you know the manufacturer's recommendations. In fact, the more reference material you can find about your particular machine, the more likely you are to be able to carry out an efficient job. Magazine articles often give useful tips not mentioned in 'official' manuals, and these can save both time and money. Advice in official literature can often be unintelligible, leaving the reader puzzled and unsure of his plan of action. Many completely omit certain procedures, such as fitting a new tyre. So start your toolkit

A standard toolkit to be proud of. This high-quality kit, which includes comprehensive instructions and a first-aid box, is a feature of the BMW R65.

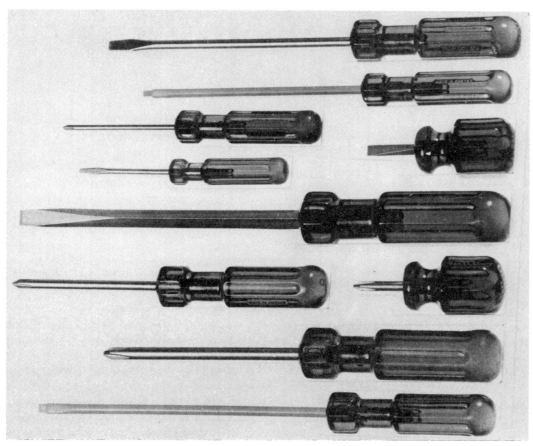

An enthusiast with this type of screwdriver kit should be ready to tackle most jobs.

with plenty of written advice and reference material.

A tyre pressure gauge is the next item to buy. Choose one you can carry at all times and which has both kilogrammes per square centimetre (kg/cm^2) and pounds per square inch (psi) scales. Garage forecourt pressure gauges are notorious for being out of order, and for being grossly inaccurate when they are working. Buy a good-quality gauge you can rely on, preferably a dial type. For convenience, make sure it retains its reading until it is reset, and that it can be used easily on the valve stem.

Schraeder caps, which are valve dust cups with mandrel-type ends for unscrewing valve cores, are easily stolen, so it is worth carrying a spare one in your machine's tool compartment at all times, in case of theft.

A spark plug spanner is a vital piece of equipment: if the engine breaks down, the first thing to check is the spark plug and whether or not it is working. This is done with a plug spanner. Buy one which is readily accessible to all the plugs your engine may have. The majority of spark plugs require 14mm spanners, but some are 12mm and others 10mm.

Having bought a plug spanner which also fits readily into the bike's toolkit, you are likely to duplicate it when you buy a socket set (see page 109). To avoid this, and reduce overall costs, buy sockets one by one or a set without a plug socket.

Screwdrivers Look over your bike carefully before choosing screwdrivers. Stub drivers, angled drivers, drivers with T-bar ends for extra leverage, spiral ratchet and pistol grip drivers are among the many types available. The important thing is always to buy screwdrivers which fit snugly into the straight slot, Phillips, or crosshead screws you have on the bike. A small screwdriver set for electrical components and other small items, a stub driver for tight clearance situations, and a large driver for major work where leverage is required should be regarded as minimum requirements. The large driver should have a hexagon or square shank to allow extra force to be applied with a spanner.

Pump ratchet systems are justified for professional mechanics who have to work at speed; for the home enthusiast they are a luxury. Many people think that Phillips, crosshead and Pozidriv screws are the same, but this is not the case: Phillips screws are more deeply recessed and are less common on motorcycle engines than crosshead screws; Pozidriv screws are very similar to Phillips screws and were designed as an improved version to be used with power-driven tools, with less chance of the power tool jumping out of the star-shaped slot.

An impact driver is designed to shift stubborn and corroded screws and bolts. An impact driver handle converts a hammer blow into a powerful twisting action, and is remarkably effective. It can be used for both undoing and doing up screws and bolts, depending on the bits included in the kit. An impact driver can often loosen a screw with a hopelessly

chewed head. Depending on its design, it can be fitted with all types of screwdriver, Allen key and socket attachments.

Allen keys Allen (hexagon-head) screws are becoming more commonplace on motorcycle engines because they are more efficient than conventional screws, in that the key-to-screw working surface area is greater and the deeply recessed hexagonal screw-heads allow the key to fit deeply, thus almost eliminating the possibility of the key slipping out. Available as straightforward L-shaped keys with screwdriver-type handles, T-handles or in the form of sockets, they are sold in both metric and Imperial sets. For the owner of a machine with Allen screws, a key, or keys, in the bike toolkit and socket keys in the home toolkit would probably be the best combination.

Open-ended spanners Having determined whether your machine is fitted with metric, AF or Whitworth nuts and bolts, a suitable sturdy open-ended spanner set is the next item to buy. Though it only has two working surfaces, this very fact is part of its purpose: it can be used in the most awkward spaces where a socket or ring spanner would not have access.

Instead of buying this type of spanner as a set, it may be a better plan to buy one at a time. An inspection of the bike's engine and frame may reveal a nut and bolt to which only an open-ended spanner would have access at both ends, in which case two of the same size would be required. Since open-ended spanners can also be obtained with a ring spanner combination half, the enthusiast can avoid the purchase of two identical spanners and also make his toolkit more versatile. For example, if the nut and bolt in question required two 17mm open-ended spanners, one could be bought with a 15 mm open-ended opposite half, and the other with a 19mm ring spanner opposite half.

Ring spanners are less versatile than open-ended spanners in terms of access to awkward places, but have the advantage of spreading the force applied to the nut or bolt to all faces rather than to just two. A ring spanner can also tackle nuts and bolts hidden in slight recesses, depending on the offset of the ring from the shaft; and for the enthusiast working alone it can be left attached to a bolt, leaving both hands free if required for the opposite end of the bolt. An open-ended spanner would more easily come off a bolt being loosened unless it could be firmly wedged in place. In a situation where either an open-ended or ring spanner could be used, the latter is a better choice because of its extra working surface area.

A feeler gauge, which is an instrument for measuring minute gaps and tolerances, is a necessary item in all motorcyclists' toolkits to set spark plug gaps, valve

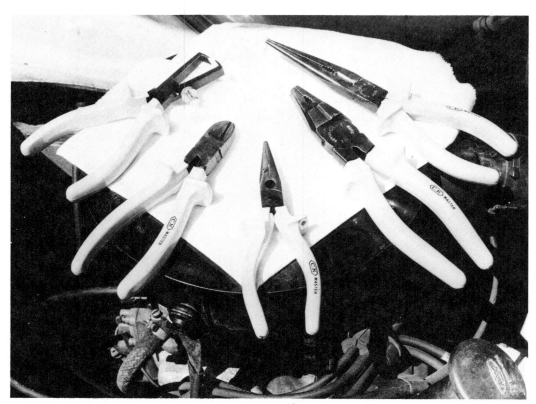

A comprehensive range of pliers, which will be useful for a variety of jobs which a spanner cannot tackle, as well as for their intended function.

clearances, and where applicable contact breaker gaps. Made up of blades of varying thicknesses which open out individually like the blades of a penknife, feeler gauges are sold giving measurements in hundredths of a millimetre, or thousandths of an inch. If you own a bike whose handbook gives one sort of measurement, then it would make life easier to buy the appropriate type.

Pliers fill a multi-purpose role: they are often used beyond their intended scope for such jobs as holding a bolt while the operator is busy elsewhere with a spanner. Pliers are good for undoing the spring link on a chain, removing the split pin from a wheel spindle, crimping, and for a variety of other jobs where a spanner cannot be used. Most have the added facility of wire-cutting edges. Long-nose pliers are also useful, for probing into corners where fingers will not reach. Circlip pliers should be the third pair completing the set. These have points at the end of each nose for inserting into the eyes of a circlip so that the circlip diameter can be contracted or expanded and the circlip withdrawn. Circlip pliers are used when front-fork oil seals are renewed, piston gudgeon pins removed and clutches and centrifugal oil filters examined.

Files If your machine includes a contact breaker in its ignition system, the faces of the contacts should be kept free of pitting, and they should meet square on. A magneto file, which is rather like an engineer's stone, will aid in this aspect of maintenance and keep costs down by reducing the frequency that new contact breaker sets have

to be fitted. This is the only essential file to have, although in practice many home mechanics have a variety including triangular, half-round, flat and special 'Riffler' files for modifying the porting in a two-stroke engine. Always fit handles to the file tang.

An oil can A small can of general-purpose oil for penetrating rusted nuts and bolts, lubricating the contact breaker cam, and a host of other uses, is inexpensive and essential. A small can with a long nose and thumb-operated pump is also necessary, to squirt oil into various parts of the engine to prime it after it has been rebuilt or left standing for a time. A can with a flexible nose is better still for squirting oil round corners. For engine oil changes a funnel will be needed.

As well as lubricants, the orderly mechanic should have a drip tray. This is not only useful should the engine develop a slight weep, but it can also be placed under the drive chain while the chain is being lubricated (this can be done with old engine oil and an old paintbrush, which is a far less expensive method of rear chain lubrication than using spray cans, and just as efficient).

A grease bath is obviously not strictly part of the toolbox, but belongs on the workshop shelf, as an indispensable item used for warming up grease over a kitchen or camping stove, for periodic, thorough applications to the rollers of the drive chain.

A grease gun For clutch mechanism and swinging arm spindle lubrication, grease nipples are usually provided, and a high-

pressure grease gun is required, with flexible extension if necessary, to pump grease into the grease nipple. High melting-point grease is often the best to use. It is ideal for greasing headstock bearings. In addition, to prevent them from rusting or corroding into place, exposed threads, brake-arm pivot points and wheel spindles are other grease points.

A puncture repair kit Unless your machine is one of the latest models with tubeless tyres, a puncture repair kit specifically for motorcycles is essential. So too is a set of at least two good-quality tyre levers. A foot pump or bicycle-type pump with motorcycle valve adaptor should also be considered.

A hydrometer, a glass or plastic vessel containing a float which indicates specific gravity of a liquid according to its buoyancy, will tell you what state of charge each of the cells in the battery is maintaining. A low reading indicates that recharging is required. For complete battery maintenance, the enthusiast will also need a battery charger and distilled water to top up the battery electrolyte level, plus petroleum jelly or some other type of proprietary anti-corrosion jelly to smear on to the battery terminals.

When buying a hydrometer and battery charger the purchaser should in general opt for small versions of both. Motorcycle batteries contain less electrolyte than car batteries, and consequently there may not be sufficient in each cell to lift the float off the bottom of its container. The general rule for recharging a battery is to pass a current of no more than a tenth of the battery's amp hour rating. Ideally, therefore, a 12Ah battery would require a trickle charge of only 1.2 amps. If a charger which reduces current to such a low level cannot be found, the home mechanic should try to locate an 'ampere damper' to reduce the current from the charger.

Cleaning materials which you will require will obviously include a number of rags and polishes. A suitable degreaser, several brands of which are available, will also be required for cleaning external and internal engine components. You may choose between a spray-type degreaser or a less expensive type, to be applied with a paint brush. Access to a hosepipe is useful when degreasing, for providing a jet of water to enable you to rinse off the degreaser thoroughly.

A hand cleaner is also an essential part of the home mechanic's equipment. Before you start work, it is also a good idea to rub a barrier cream which protects against dermatitis into the hands. It makes the hands easier to clean afterwards because it stops grease and grime becoming too ingrained in the pores. Nevertheless, a good hand degreasant such as Swarfega will still be necessary for cleaning off the grease which will inevitably cover your hands.

Clothing Appropriate clothing is an integral part of good motorcycle maintenance. While working on a motorcycle, whether out of doors or in a workshop, the mechanic will have to spend some time on his knees, undoing engine cases and so on, and is bound to come into contact with grease and petrol. Overalls or other clothes which you do not mind getting dirty are therefore essential, since the wrong clothes will affect the quality of the work you do on your bike. (If you are wearing decent clothes and do not want to dirty them, you will be more concerned about them than anything else. You will probably find yourself using a 'fingertip' approach instead of getting to grips with a job.) A good pair of overalls will have fairly large pockets, useful for carrying rags and sometimes tools, though as a general rule carrying tools in pockets is not a good idea unless the pockets are on the legs and therefore do not stop free body movement.

A pair of stout, comfortable boots should also be worn. If possible, follow the example of many workers in engineering workshops and wear boots with steel toecaps to protect the feet from injury.

A pair of close-fitting cotton gloves should be available for use if necessary. They are useful for several reasons: apart from keeping the hands clean, they help to prevent cuts and take some of the pain out of maintenance. Some professional motorcycle mechanics wear them all the time: because they absorb oil and grease, the chances of an oily tool slipping out of your hands are reduced. Undoing a nut which requires a great deal of pressure in a confined space may result in skinned knuckles unless gloves are worn. Hands are also more prone to cuts on a cold day because the skin is 'brittle'. Furthermore, with numbed hands it is more difficult to feel a cut: the first evidence of it is more likely to be the sight of blood than the sensation of pain. You will then have to stop work in order to clean the cut and put on a plaster, and this can be avoided if you wear gloves.

Workshop equipment

Some of the most expensive articles available to the home mechanic need to be housed in a workshop or garage, so if you wish to acquire any or all of the following items, you will first have to have a proper workshop. This should have good light available during the daytime and powerful strip lighting for night working, a sturdy bench with vice, tool rack and store racks for neatness and efficiency, and a safe method of heating with adequate ventilation and a fire extinguisher.

ABOVE Using a hydrometer to check the battery condition of a 1,000cc Moto Guzzi

BELOW A compression tester in action.

Welders/brazers Usually jobs left to professionals, welding and brazing can now be undertaken by the home mechanic. Electric welders on the market allow you to weld heavy items such as frame tubes and footrests. Brazing kits may be used for lighter work such as repairing snapped rear carriers, accessory stays and soldering cables. Such lightweight gas kits can be used to braze or solder iron, steel, copper, brass and aluminium. Eye protection should always be worn when using this type of equipment.

Paint sprayer As a rule, the more expensive the spray equipment, the better the finish will be. Nevertheless, quite professional finishes can be obtained with relatively inexpensive equipment. A separate air compressor is highly desirable to keep the spray at a constant pressure. Adequate ventilation must be considered if you are spraying indoors. A sprayer's mask to prevent paint inhalation should also be worn.

A hydraulic workstand is, of course, a luxury for the home mechanic; even some small motorcycle dealers do not have one. A hydraulic stand raises the motorcycle to any convenient work height. Less expensive models worked by a crank instead of hydraulics are available.

Lathe With this type of machine tool an enthusiast joins an engineer's level, in that he can turn cylinders and tapers, cut threads, and carry out numerous other functions. Lathes have a rotating workpiece and fixed cutter.

Power washer If a bucket and brush is not good enough for cleaning your bike, expensive industrial-type pressure washers powered by electric motors will shift mud and grease, and some even strip paint.

The equipment discussed in the very first part of this chapter is of course more than

This motorcycle stand is pneumatically operated.

adequate for most maintenance jobs. However, if you are rich and enthusiastic enough, you can buy trade equipment such as that listed in this section, although you would probably have to enrol on a course in how to use it. Sophisticated diagnostic equipment which enables you to read off HT voltage, impedance, contact-breaker points condition, amperage, rpm, dwell, and so on is also a possibility. This type of equipment is beyond the range of all but very few enthusiasts, but is included to give the beginner buying his first spanner the chance to dream of extending his skill and facilities towards this level.

The items listed in the next section are more likely to be within financial reach of most enthusiasts.

Specialized toolkit items

Socket sets vary from pocket to giant-size sets. It is a good idea to buy two sets, one fairly large and one small for precision work. The larger one should have, for example, socket sizes starting from 10mm or the equivalent in other sizes, and should include a reversible ratchet handle, speed brace, long and short extension, tommy bar, knuckle joint, and plug spanner socket. This set will be ideal for big jobs such as removing and stripping the engine. The smaller set, in order to complement the main set, should ideally include all the facilities of the larger version to aid versatility when you tackle small precision jobs such as carburettor dismantling. As already mentioned, sockets in various drive sizes can be bought individually, allowing you to either make up your own socket set or to add to a set you have already bought.
Torque wrench If you have decided upon, say, a 0.5in drive socket set as your main system, a torque wrench of the same drive size should be chosen if engine strips are to be undertaken. Good workshop manuals list torque settings for major nuts and bolts. Most torque wrenches have metric and imperial scales. Over-stressing bolts (easily done by the home mechanic) can stretch them and even crack expensive alloy engine cases, but using a torque wrench prevents this: if for example a bolt has to be tightened to 27 joules (20ft/lb) the mechanism inside the wrench can be adjusted to this setting and once the force of 27 joules (20ft/lb) has been reached the mechanism overrides and so warns the operator against further pressure. Though fairly expensive, a torque wrench should be considered essential, particularly if alloy barrels and cylinder heads are being tightened, to prevent uneven pressure and consequent warping.
Timing tools Setting the points gap on ignition systems has already been mentioned, but this is not the only aspect of the

subject. The 'dwell' time when the points are closed and primary current is allowed to build up inside the ignition coil is of great significance, as is the actual point the spark plug fires. Owners of machines whose ignition systems are completely transistorized are spared these worries, although they may have to check that timing marks align. These checks, if necessary, will be outlined in the workshop manual.

Static timing. With conventional battery and coil ignition on a two-stroke engine, first set the contact breaker gap with the feeler gauge, then time the point at which the contact breaker first opens to coincide exactly with the recommended piston position. The most accurate method is to use a dial gauge. This measures the minutest distances with great accuracy and can be bought with an adaptor to screw into the spark plug hole to measure piston movement. If, for example, the engine is designed to fire with the piston 2mm (0.08in) from the top of its stroke, the dial gauge enables the piston to be set exactly at this position while the contact breaker is adjusted so that it begins to break contact at exactly this instant.

As a less expensive alternative, the position of the piston may be measured in terms of crankshaft rotation in degrees rather than linear motion. A timing wheel is attached to the crankshaft so that the piston at the top of its stroke corresponds with zero degrees on the timing wheel. If the timing point is expressed as five

degrees before the piston is at 'top dead centre' this can now be measured easily by turning the crankshaft accordingly and setting the contact breaker back-plate. This method is necessary on all two-stroke engines where the spark plug is not directly in line with the crown of the piston. With a dial gauge any such offset would upset the direct relationship required between the dial gauge rod which bears against the piston crown and the amount it moves the dial pointer.

Stroboscopic timing. It is also possible to check engine ignition timing with the engine running by means of a strobe. As well as checking the timing, the strobe also verifies whether or not the advance mechanism is working. The combustion mixture requires time to burn, so the ignition timing has to be progressively advanced as the engine revolutions increase.

The well-equipped two-stroke enthusiast should therefore have a *dial gauge* to set the ignition statically, and a *strobe light* for double checking and for verifying the all-important advance.

Four-stroke engines rarely have their spark plug holes diametrically opposite the straight-line motion of the piston; they are usually offset to allow space for inlet and exhaust valves. A dial gauge would therefore not be appropriate; the most accurate method would be with the use of a strobe light.

Multi-tester. As the name implies, this type of instrument has many uses, one of

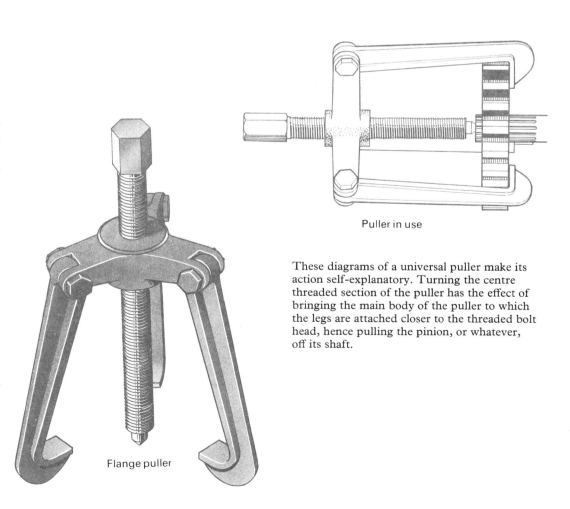

Puller in use

These diagrams of a universal puller make its action self-explanatory. Turning the centre threaded section of the puller has the effect of bringing the main body of the puller to which the legs are attached closer to the threaded bolt head, hence pulling the pinion, or whatever, off its shaft.

Flange puller

which is ignition timing. For the enthusiast who wishes to keep costs to the minimum, however, setting the ignition statically with the aid of a simple battery and bulb is an alternative to using a dial gauge, strobe or multi-tester. The bulb is connected to the contact breaker so that it goes out the instant the contact faces part. If you do buy a multi-tester, you can use it not only instead of making up a bulb and battery system but also for circuit checking and current measurements. The electronics market abounds with such devices.

Dwell metres are not commonly used by motorcyclists, but are mostly used in the automotive industry where car engines have a minimum of four cylinders. Obviously a dwell meter can be used on four-cylinder motorcycles and several makes are sold in combination with an electronic tachometer and points condition indicator. The electronic tachometer accurately monitors engine revs while the mechanic can check the ignition timing advance with a strobe light to make sure full advance is reached at the maker's specified engine rpm.

Spark plug sand blaster Sand blasters are now on the do-it-yourself market and, while they probably would not justify their keep for a single-cylinder owner, they could well save the multi-cylinder machine owner money in the long run. Home sand blasters usually include a proper spark plug gapping tool and feeler gauge blades. A much less expensive alternative, however, is a small stiff wire brush. Although not as effective as a sand blaster, a brush is usually the only choice for the owner of a six-volt motorcycle since most home sand blasters require 12 volts.

Pullers Engine dismantling invariably demands the use of a puller to separate two items, such as a flywheel from a crankshaft. Generally, a puller is regarded as a special tool if made for a specific job on a specific engine: for example, Triumph twin-cylinder engine clutch pullers are special tools which cannot be bought from an accessory shop. To decide whether or not a universal puller would be of any use for your engine or cycle parts, you would have to study the workshop manual. If there is any doubt, try to obtain the correct

special tool through your dealer. It may be more expensive but is preferable to struggling with an all-purpose puller which does not quite fit your machine.

Special tools The motorcycle owner who wants to keep his machine for a long time and wishes to carry out all his own maintenance will definitely require a set of special tools, the kind usually used only by dealers. They are not always available to the general public, since some importers limit them to dealers only, and if you have a problem obtaining them you either have to let your dealer do the work or visit an engineering workshop to see if a set could be made specially for you. Sometimes it is possible to make your own. For example, the special tool peg spanner to free the centrifugal oil filter outer casing on some Honda engines can be made from a piece of steel tube of the appropriate diameter.

Compression tester Workshop manuals should give a compression figure for your engine. The instructions on how to use a compression tester should be followed exactly, as with all tools. If the cylinder you are testing is well below the tolerance

A top-quality stroboscopic timing light for accurate ignition timing.

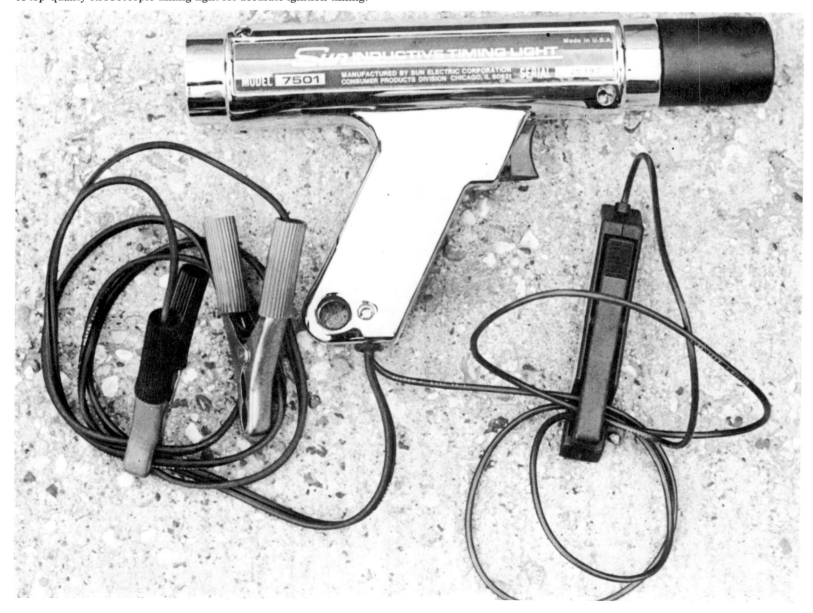

The budget-conscious enthusiast could consider a small socket set such as this.

stated you can suspect a torn head gasket, a sticking valve in the case of a four-stroke, or gummed-in or broken piston rings. A compression tester can help the owners of a multi-cylinder motorcycle to pinpoint quickly which cylinder is giving trouble, should only one not be working properly. The owner about to tune his engine for more power would also benefit from a compression tester, which enables you to verify if the engine is in top condition to start with.

Vacuum gauges are necessary for quick servicing by dealers, to synchronize carburettors on popular multi-cylinder machines. Vacuum gauges are very expensive, particularly for the four-cylinder owner. This is because a full set is essential, and buying one or two will not provide satisfactory results on a four-cylinder engine: an adjustment on one carburettor may affect engine speed and hence involve a difference in vacuum in all the inlet tracts which cannot be seen, unless all four carburettor vacuums can be examined at the same time. Less expensive than the dial-type vacuum gauges is a system of mercury columns. A resourceful person could make his own kit, using mercury columns in glass tubes to measure the depression in each inlet tract.

A cable oiler is used for lubricating cables under pressure without the need to remove the cable from the motorcycle, and reflects the growing tendency to want clean-fingered, swift servicing where possible.

A chain breaker A drive chain which breaks but is not worn out can be re-claimed by removing the broken links with an inexpensive chain breaker which forces out link pins. With a chain breaker, the mechanic can make his chain any length he wants.

A Mole wrench, or Mole grip, is like a large pair of pliers with a locking device. Because Mole grips are adjustable and easy to use people often tend to over-employ

them, for example for holding nuts which would be better served by a spanner. Their vice-like grip makes them useful in many situations : they can often undo a nut which has worn edges; they can act as a gear lever if the original has fallen off; and they can bend twisted mudguards back into something like their original shape.

An adjustable spanner Only the very best quality adjustable spanners seem to be able to maintain a firm grip on a nut. Their use is to be avoided, however, if you have a spanner of the correct size for the job in question, but they are still justified in anybody's toolkit because they are adaptable to any size of nut.

A Vernier caliper gauge, which looks like a slide rule, accurately measures internal and external diameters. The Vernier can determine where bearings have worn beyond their useful tolerance, and measure the bore of a cylinder, the choke size of a carburettor, and so on.

A micrometer, of which there are two types, one for measuring external diameters and the other internal, is an alternative to the Vernier. Though it does not look like a Vernier it does the same job but with greater accuracy, measuring to less than 0.02mm (0.001in). Not surprisingly, they are considerably more expensive than a Vernier.

A valve-spring compressor People usually like to decarbonize, or 'decoke' their engines from time to time. Two-stroke owners have a comparatively easy job because there are no valves in the cylinder heads. Four-stroke engines have, however, and if you wish to renew valve springs while doing a decoke, a compressor tool is necessary. Once the valve spring is free the Vernier can be used to measure its free length and determine if indeed it has 'shrunk' under the strain.

Valve lappers The other usual accompaniment to the decoke is lapping in the valves. Here coarse and fine compound is required and a piece of wood with a sticker

at the end, rather like a child's rubber suction-tipped arrow, to rotate the valve first one way and then the other so that it forms a gas-tight seal over the cylinder head. Valve lappers which take the tedium out of this operation are on the market.

A soldering iron Broken wires can be made good by using a terminal kit (see below) or by soldering. Soldering irons can also be used for heavier jobs such as soldering light cable nipples, though achieving a good joint, needed for this type of duty, requires the right technique. Another use of a soldering iron is burning holes through plastic. If plastic parts such as new mudguards are being fitted to the bike, burning a hole through the plastic for the bolt is simpler than drilling. (The plastic blob left at the side of the freshly made hole can simply be sliced off with a razor blade.)

A terminal kit While a soldering iron is necessary for the jobs a terminal kit cannot handle, such as directly soldering a wire to a switch, a joint made with two connectors from a terminal kit can be readily undone and reconnected again. A comprehensive kit should include all types of connectors and insulators, plus a crimping tool with wire cutters and strippers of different diameters. Particularly useful for wiring up electrical accessories, a terminal kit eliminates the old, clumsy method of twisting the ends of two wires together and wrapping insulating tape round them.

An electric drill with more than one speed is the main powered tool required by the home mechanic as well as the do-it-yourself enthusiast. Various attachments in addition to drill bits may be acquired separately. Buy a well-known and respected make with a good accessory range which includes a drill stand, flexible drive, wire brushes and polishing mop.

A screw extractor kit When even the impact driver (see page 105) has failed to remove a screw with a ruined head, a drill has to be used to make a hole large enough for a screw extractor to grip and drag out the screw, by counter-screwing it (because of its opposite thread pattern).

A tap and die set is used for making good ruined threads in, for example, an engine casing. The tap is used to cut a new thread of slightly larger diameter than the old one, and a new screw of the appropriate size is then fitted. The die in the set is used to cut a thread on the shaft of an uncut or ruined screw.

A portable gas burner of aerosol size with a burner nozzle is very useful for applying heat to metal in order to expand it and allow either its removal or fitment. For example, a bearing on a shaft which has to come off but is stuck can be 'sweated' off by applying heat locally with a concentrated flame.

A pop rivet is used when a more permanent way of holding two components together than a nut and bolt is needed. The pop rivet tool, which is inexpensive, allows two components to be assembled when access to only one side is available. If they have to be removed later the rivets can easily be drilled out.

Adhesives on the market today are good enough to cope with fairly major work such as repairing engine casings, re-attaching broken cooling fins and so on. An epoxy resin adhesive is ideal for emergency repairs, and may also be suitable for a permanent modification. You may also require an impact adhesive, when for example you are recovering a seat. This adhesive is spread on both the surfaces to be joined, allowed to become tacky and then the surfaces are pressed together in exactly the right position, whereupon they adhere immediately. For small tacking jobs, however, an ordinary multi-purpose glue should suffice.

Gasket If the motorcyclist does not want to buy a proper gasket set until he has to do an engine overhaul, he could buy a 'tube of gasket'. This type of gasket is of silicone rubber which is squeezed out of a tube like toothpaste. It can be used on any shape of engine casing, though it cannot be substituted for a head gasket. When the engine is subsequently overhauled, this type of gasket is removed easily. It can also be used to make O-rings, repair seals leaks and splits, and work as a general-purpose adhesive. Where horizontally split crankcase halves have to be joined without a gasket, a 'jointing' compound is required.

Locking compounds Where a nut and bolt have to be 'locked' in order to prevent them coming apart through vibration, the enthusiast can use locking compounds such as Hermetite Torqseal instead of locking tabs, anti-vibration washers, or nyloc nuts, all of which should be included in his general assortment of nuts and bolts. The company which produces Torqseal also makes a similar compound to prevent the outer half of a bearing from rotating within its housing. The use of this 'bearing fit' compound can sometimes save the owner a great deal of expense. For example, a main bearing whose outer surface starts rotating in its housing could wear the housing to the point when new crankcases would be needed. Bearing compound applied in time could avoid this.

Hammers For tapping engine casings apart a soft-face hammer is necessary to avoid damaging the casing. Usually a rubber hammer is best for this type of job. Heavier jobs such as knocking out a rusted wheel spindle would require an engineer's ball-pein hammer with a forged steel head. A hammer with a copper face on one side and a hide face on the other can tackle jobs between the two extremes. Also available are hammers with replaceable plastic inserts to cope with varying types of work.

Hacksaw Well-equipped toolkits usually contain at least two hacksaws, a small 'junior' model for fine cutting and a larger model for heavier work. For engine and cycle part services and overhauls a hacksaw should not be necessary, but for making and fitting accessories and carrying out modifications the hacksaw is a useful item.

A stillson is similar in appearance to an adjustable spanner but with serrated teeth on its contact faces. It is very useful for biting into a nut whose edges have been rounded off through wear or abuse. However, it should not be used for general duty in place of a spanner. Also on the market for shifting seized nuts is a nut splitter, which breaks off a nut without damaging the thread of the bolt to which it is fixed.

A toolbox provides a convenient method of tool storage, particularly if you do not have a workshop. If you want a toolbox which will act as a sort of portable tool display unit with several compartments, then the cantilever type is the best choice. If the place where you work is more than walking distance from home, a canvas tool bag should be used to transport tools, strapped across the back seat of your bike: a large steel cantilever box would be cumbersome to carry on a motorcycle. Many other types of steel and plastic toolboxes are on the market, some of them with provision for a padlock.

Other items for the tool collection could include an inspection lamp or torch, a spoke key for setting spoke tension, a C-spanner for adjusting rear-suspension unit preload (where applicable), a proprietary idle mixture setting device, a measuring cylinder with cc gradations for measuring fork oil and the like accurately, and a tyre depth gauge. They could also include a steel rule, magnet, and centre punch, a sturdy wire brush for general-purpose cleaning, a scriber for marking metal components for easy identification, a piston ring clamp for allowing easy insertion of piston into cylinder bore, tin snips for cutting light-gauge metal, touch-up paint, an emery cloth, and a general-purpose dewatering aerosol for protecting ignition systems against damp and for lubricating parts generally.

A chain breaker about to push a link pin out.

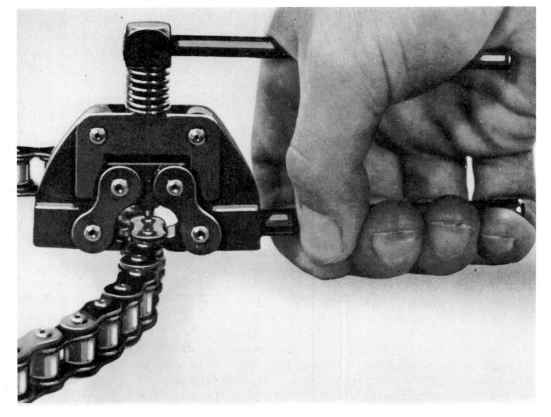

TT&GRANDS PRIX

ALTHOUGH many consider the Isle of Man to be the birthplace of road racing, motorcycle and motor-tricycle races began on the Continent, where De Dion, Bouton and Werner machines competed in races staged between Paris and such distant points as Bordeaux, Marseilles, and even Vienna.

The speed limit on all British roads made it impossible for the newborn motorcycle industry to race or test its products to the full. Some British manufacturers took their motorcycles to the established cycle-racing tracks at Crystal Palace and Canning Town in London, or to Aston Villa in Birmingham, but the short, paved tracks did not provide the answer to their problems.

In 1904 the Royal Automobile Club approached the Isle of Man authorities for permission to stage trials on the island, where there were no speed restrictions, for the European motorcar races sponsored by the American newspaper magnate James Gordon Bennett. The Manx Government agreed. At once the Auto-Cycle Club, the forerunner of the Auto-Cycle Union, requested similar facilities for the motorcycle industry so that it might run eliminating trials to select a team for the 1905 Coupe Internationale, an annual endurance race organized by the Fédération Internationale des Clubs. The Governor of the Island, Lord Raglan, gave his consent and, in spite of sparse support, the A-CC ran its International Cup eliminating trials in 1905 on the Isle of Man with reasonable success. The winner was J. S. Campbell on a 6 hp Ariel-JAP, second was Harry Collier on a 6 hp Matchless-JAP, and third was Charlie Franklin, also on a JAP-powered machine.

The British team competed in the International Cup races, which were run near Paris, but was hopelessly outclassed by the Austrian and French motorcycles. However, the following year was to prove a turning point in the fortunes of the British motorcycle industry. When the Austrian Puch motorcycle company won the International Cup races at Putzau, Austria, and it was discovered that they had been cheating by giving impermissible assistance to the winning two machines, there was an uproar. The races were abandoned and the FIM was dissolved.

On the long train journey back from Austria to Britain, the Collier brothers, Freddie Straight, secretary of the A-CC, and the international jury representative, the Marquis de Mouzilly St Mars, began discussing the future of road racing. They wanted to stage an event similar to the International Cup races on the roads of Britain, but with the refusal by Parliament to allow the closure of public roads for racing, the situation seemed hopeless.

However, the marquis promised that, if a venue could be found, he would provide a trophy for the winner of the race.

Discussions continued but the problem of venue remained unresolved until finally it dawned on the A-CC that, as they had held their International Cup race trials on the Isle of Man, the obvious solution would be to organize a full-scale closed-roads motorcycle race there. To their joy, the Manx Government agreed.

The A-CC wasted no time in formulating the regulations needed to specify precisely the types of motorcycle that would be permitted to race in the Isle of Man event. First, they had to be touring motorcycles as sold to the general public. They could be twin- or single-cylinder machines, as it was planned to have two race classes, and there was to be no engine-capacity or machine-weight limit.

The First Manx Circuit

The next stage was to plan a suitable course for the races. It was no good following the RAC car-trials route over the Snaefell mountain track because none of the single-speed, belt-driven motorcycles of that period would have had any chance of completing the climb. Instead, the A-CC plotted a circuit which ran from the ancient Tynwald mound at St John's along the Peel Road towards Douglas to join up with the present-day TT circuit at Ballacraine. The course then struck northwards through Laurel Bank and Glen Helen, uphill past Sarah's Cottage, along the Cronk-y-Voddy straight, through Barregarrow and Rhencullen, and into Kirkmichael. Here it turned sharp left at the entrance to the village to head southwards along the coast road to Peel, where it turned eastwards on to the home straight.

The plan of campaign for that first TT race was five laps of the St John's circuit, a compulsory 10-minute rest to refuel and fettle machines and refresh the riders, then a further five laps to the finish: a total of 253 km (158 miles) of sheer torture for riders on unsprung machines that were little more than motor-assisted pedal cycles. The circuit consisted of unmetalled, flint-strewn, rutted tracks with steep hills.

Only 10 men completed the arduous race; but as the exhausted riders were helped from their machines, all were exalted by their achievements. In spite of punctures, broken belt drives, hair-raising slides, and numerous other hazards, such as straying animals and spectators wandering onto the circuit, the meeting was considered a tremendous success.

Winner of the single-cylinder class was Charlie Collier on his JAP-engined Matchless at an average speed of 61.15 km/h (38.22 mph). He took 4 hours, 8 minutes, 8 seconds to complete the course,

LEFT Indian continued to compete in European road races until the end of the 1920s. Here one of the finest riders of his day, 'Flying Freddie' Dixon, negotiates a corner aboard a 3½ hp Indian in the 1923 Belgian Grand Prix. The condition of the circuit, with ruts and sharp pebbles littering its unpaved surface, explains why Dixon (like most other riders of the time) has spare inner tubes wrapped around his waist.

ABOVE A 1926 Scott two-speed, water-cooled two-stroke twin. Alfred Scott designed the first successful two-stroke racers, and his twin-cylinder, rotary-valve two-strokes won the Senior TT in 1912 and 1913.

PREVIOUS PAGE American road racer Kenny Roberts, 500 cc triple world champion.

The Mountain Circuit

In 1911 the A-CC announced a new Isle of Man racecourse, the machine-destroying Mountain Circuit. The 60.75 km (37¾ miles) course, including a long climb up the eastern flanks of Snaefell (426 m/ 1,400 ft), seemed a formidable task to set the motorcycle manufacturers and even the most skilful riders. It was obvious that single-speed, belt-driven machines would not be able to cope with the circuit. For many manufacturers it was back to the drawing board to attempt to design transmissions that would provide variable gearing—low ratios for the steeper hills, high ratios for the faster stretches. Some tried three-speed, rear-wheel-hub gears, similar to those found on present-day pedal cycles; others, such as Royal Enfield, used two-speed all-chain drive, while Douglas sought the answer by using two-speed countershafts on the primary drive from the engine.

It was the American Indian motorcycle company that solved the problem with its countershaft two-speed gears with chain drive to the rear wheel. Indian took first, second, and third places in the 1911 Senior TT race over the Mountain Circuit at an average speed for the winner, O. C.

11 minutes ahead of Jack Marshall on a single-cylinder Triumph. Rem Fowler finished third to win the twin-cylinder class on a Peugeot-powered Norton.

Surprisingly, the Triumph machines were the only ones without pedal assistance, and this became a point of discussion when plans for the 1908 TT races were drawn up. If Charlie Collier had not had the benefit of pedal assistance on his Matchless, might Jack Marshall have won instead? To avoid any dispute, Freddie Straight and the A-CC stipulated that no pedals were to be allowed in future.

With pedals abolished for the 1908 TT races, Jack Marshall proved the critics right when he won the event by almost four minutes from Charlie Collier, in spite of having to stop to repair a puncture and change an exhaust valve. He completed the race in 3 hours, 54 minutes, and 50 seconds at an average speed of 64.78 km/h (40.49 mph).

By 1910, entries for the TT races had risen to 80 machines. The motorcycle industry had realized the commercial advantages that could be gained from racing success on the Isle of Man. Competition was fierce both on the race track and in the motorcycle showrooms. In four years, the winning times on the 253 km (158 miles) St John's circuit had dropped from 4 hours 21 minutes to 3 hours 7 minutes. Average speeds were now over 80 km/h (50 mph), and when Harry Bowen lapped the St John's course on his BAT twin at 85.04 km/h (53.15 mph), the race organizers realized that a longer, more punishing circuit was needed. The St John's course had had its day.

Godfrey, of 76.21 km/h (47.63 mph).

It should be remembered that at this time the motorcycles competing in the TT races were still very much based on the roadster touring motorcycles available to the general public. There were no one-off specials, only prototype roadsters incorporating design ideas and modifications that were being tested on the race track before being built into the following year's production machines.

The 1920s and 1930s

In those pioneering days before World War I there was no start money for competitors or large prize-money purses for race winners. Competitors such as Harry and Charlie Collier, Howard Davies, and the other early masters were often the men who also designed and built the motorcycles for sale to the public. It was not until the 1920s, when the European motorcycle industry enjoyed a period of rapid post-war expansion, that the true 'works riders' came onto the scene. Norton, Velocette, AJS, Matchless, New Imperial, Rudge, Cotton, Sunbeam, HRD, and

BELOW A beautifully preserved Rudge Ulster 500 cc racer of the 1930s. Although the big Rudges won only one Senior TT (1930), the four-valve-per-cylinder 250 cc Rudges enjoyed many Lightweight success in pre-war TTs.

RIGHT Bill Ivy (Yamaha) flashes through Parliament Square, Ramsey, in 1968, en route to breaking the Lightweight 125 cc lap record at 161.52 km/h (100.32 mph) – the first rider in this class to beat the 'ton'.

other successful motorcycle companies could afford to vie for the services of professional or semi-professional road-racing aces such as Freddie Dixon, Stanley Woods, Jimmy Simpson, Walter Handley, and Jimmy Guthrie.

As the European motorcycle industry expanded, so countries such as France, Belgium, Germany, and Italy began to organize their own grands prix. This in turn tempted the British manufacturers to challenge the foreign motorcycle builders on their home grounds.

Yet still the motorcycles they chose to race were development models of roadster sports motorcycles. In fact, it was not until the 1930s that manufacturers began building road-racing specials that were designed to win road races purely for prestige. Such machines were often quite unlike roadsters that bore the same name on their petrol tanks. But this did not lessen the commercial value of successful racers. Ordinary motorcyclists still continued to prefer the products of the TT- and grand-prix-winning factories.

In mechanical and technical terms, almost every possible configuration in the design of the internal-combustion engine had been tried by the mid-1930s. Overhead valves, double overhead camshafts, four valves per cylinder, four cylinders per engine, rotary-valve two-strokes, sleeve-valve four-strokes—at some time some engine designer somewhere had built it to prove that it did or did not work.

At the end of the 1930s, with World War II imminent, national prestige became an important factor in road-racing success. To win races was paramount and, for the first time, the design of road-racing motorcycles departed radically from its original intention of improving sooner or later the stability, handling, or outright speed of the ordinary roadster. The most notable example of this in the late 1930s was the use of superchargers for extra race-winning power. BMW developed a supercharged, OHC, 500 cc twin and Gilera produced their double-OHC, water-cooled, four-cylinder Rondine, while both Velocette and AJS planned double-OHC, super-charged, twin-cylinder, 500 cc machines.

RIGHT Mike Hailwood, riding his poor-handling Honda Four, leaves Governor's Bridge on his way to winning the Senior TT of 1967, in which he established the lap record of 175.12 km/h (108.77 mph). His victory in this race is generally regarded as the greatest performance in the history of the TT races. 'Mike the Bike' won nine world championships and 12 TT races before he retired following Honda's withdrawal from 1968.

Road Racing Since 1945

World War II put an end to road racing for almost eight years. At the end of the war the motorcycle manufacturers were able to sit back and take stock of the situation. Pre-war Nortons, Velocettes, and AJS road racers were dusted off, along with a few Rudges and Excelsiors, and in 1947 road racing resumed on low-octane 'pool' petrol.

The Isle of Man TT races recommenced as though the world had stood still for eight years, with the pre-war TT aces Harold Daniell and Freddie Frith taking the honours for Norton and Velocette. However, lessons learned before the war by the Italian motorcycle industry were not forgotten. The FIM banned supercharging for post-war racing, but the memory of the high-revving, super-performance, four-cylinder Gilera Rondine lingered on in the minds of pre-war enthusiasts.

AJS de-supercharged their double-OHC, 500 cc flat parallel-twin racer to produce the sometimes successful 'Porcupine' (so called after the spiky cooling fins on the cylinder heads), while Velocette and Norton continued along pre-war lines with their established single-cylinder 350 and 500 cc OHC racers. Admittedly, both machines resembled the roadsters being produced at the time, but as competition became more fierce on the grand-prix circuits, so the race-development engineers gradually broke away from the roadster production departments. On the other hand, racebred improvements in frames and suspension systems steadily found their way onto the better-quality road machines. Among the most important of these were telescopic front forks, swinging-arm rear suspension, and improved braking.

It is probably true to say that the most decisive separation of racers and roadsters came in the early 1950s with the advent of the Gilera 500 cc four-cylinder racer, followed soon after by the MV Agusta 500-Quattro. National and factory prestige were by now paramount, and victory on the circuits was what mattered.

Unfortunately, this war of attrition on the grand-prix circuits was to have an almost disastrous effect on road racing.

RIGHT Pierpaolo Bianchi (Morbidelli) accelerates out of a corner in the Belgian Grand Prix, on his way to winning the 1977 World 125 cc Championship. The Spa circuit, near Liège, is one of the great European centres of grand-prix racing.

TOP RIGHT Giacomo Agostini, who has won more world championships than any other road-racing star. Here the great Italian takes his Yamaha 500 two-stroke four the shortest way round a corner in the 1977 French Grand Prix at the Paul Ricard circuit, where he finished second.

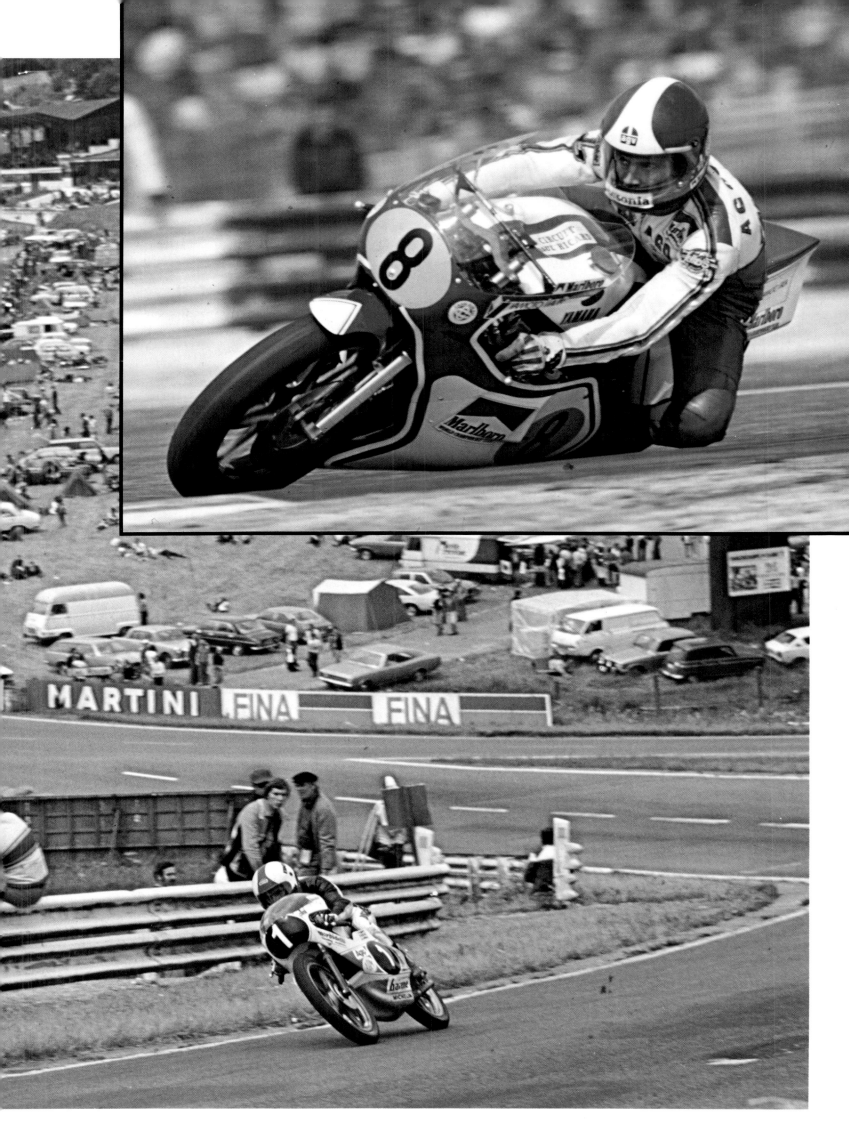

ABOVE Akimoko Kiyohara (54) before the start of the 250 cc German Grand Prix at Hockenheim, near Heidelberg, in 1977. His mount is the interesting two-cylinders-in-tandem, water-cooled, two-stroke Kawasaki. In the background, on a Harley-Davidson two-stroke twin, is Walter Villa (1), 250 and 350 cc world champion of 1976.

RIGHT Barry Sheene, wearing his lucky number 7, corners in characteristic style during the 1977 German Grand Prix aboard the Suzuki 500 cc, four-cylinder, two-stroke racer. Sheene won the World 500 cc Championship in 1976 and 1977.

The cost of developing and producing highly specialized racing motorcycles rose out of all proportion to the benefits or advantages to be gained from extra sales of roadster machines. British manufacturers were the first to feel the pinch and to withdraw factory support from works teams; they were followed in 1957 by the Italian Gilera and Moto Guzzi factories. Grand-prix road racing for a time almost faded into obscurity: the glamour, excitement, and challenge had gone out of the sport as all but MV Agusta withdrew from the scene.

Fortunately, on the other side of the world, there was the rapidly expanding motorcycle industry of Japan, with its sights firmly set on American and European motorcycle markets. When Honda arrived on the Isle of Man in 1961 it had signed many of the top British and Italian road-racing aces. The crowd watched with interest as the Japanese wheeled out a Lightweight 250 cc racer with four cylinders, and then gasped as the little machine proceeded to lap the TT circuit at 159.3 km/h (99.58 mph) – almost as fast as the 350 cc MV Agusta and only 5 km/h (3 mph) slower than the Norton 500 cc machine which won the Senior TT.

Yamaha and Suzuki were the next to enter the grand-prix racing scene and until 1967, when Honda and Suzuki withdrew, the struggle was three-sided, but entirely Japanese, in the lightweight racing classes. The machines bore little or no resemblance to the roadster models that the companies were offering in the showrooms, but with modern designs and resourceful promotion the Japanese industry succeeded both on and off the race track. The only European challenge came from MV Agusta in the 350 and 500 cc classes.

In the late 1960s designs became more and more complex, which practically killed the sport for all but the works riders, until finally the FIM, which dictates what the competing manufacturers can or cannot do, tightened up the regulations. Honda and Suzuki, having dominated the scene, then withdrew in 1967 and road racing was again in danger of losing its popularity. Yamaha, however, continued racing in the smaller 125, 250, and 350 cc classes and took over where Honda had left off, marketing over-the-counter production-racing machines developed directly from its existing roadster models. Yamaha became so dominant that Suzuki was obliged to return to the grand-prix racing scene, with Barry Sheene leading an outstandingly successful team during the 1970s. In early 1978 the road-racing fraternity confidently expected Honda to make a full-scale and very determined return to road racing in order to recoup some of the sales of roadster machines which they have lost to the other marques.

LEFT In 1981 at the British GP, Honda brought over American teenager Freddie Spencer to campaign their million-pound project NR500 which was fast becoming a costly joke. The bike, which featured a vee-four, four-stroke motor with oval pistons, eight carburettors and 32 valves, had its best ever race and for a while held on to fourth place with Spencer exploiting its light weight and fine handling. Revving to 22,000 rpm was too much for the engine, and it was retired.

BELOW Kenny Roberts demonstrating angles of lean with his square-four Yamaha at the 1981 French GP. Note the small 16 in diameter front wheel and tyre.

The Future of Road Racing

There seems little doubt, then, that road racing will survive, in spite of continuing crises of one kind or another. As we have seen, the enormous cost of preparing race machines and of supporting them with highly skilled trackside engineers and other staff from time to time discourages even the enormously prosperous Japanese manufacturers from running works teams. But even though grand-prix machinery often bears little resemblance to the ordinary roadster – or even to the superbike – success on the track remains a potent sales factor in the High Street showroom.

Nonetheless, the character of road racing is changing. One sad but significant development is the demise during the 1970s of the Manx TT as a factor in the international grand-prix championship. The Mountain Circuit – with its unique mix of steep hills, narrow and sharply curving country roads, and city-street sections – has always been by far the most challenging of the major international circuits, and many of the top riders have accepted that it is too long and too hazardous to enable the riders to familiarize themselves with its difficulties before racing begins – practice sessions being severely curtailed by the congested grand-

prix calendar. The circuit's heyday ended with the 1972 meeting when Giacomo Agostini, the last of the great masters of Manx, decided to abandon the TT for ever after a fellow Italian rider and close friend had been killed in the Lightweight 125 race. Today the grand-prix world championships have taken over from the old TT and are effectively decided on such famous continental circuits as Spa (Belgium), Paul Ricard (France), Hockenheim (West Germany), Monza (Italy), and elsewhere.

Another trend is towards races involving machines of larger engine capacity than that of the classic Senior 500 cc models. Typical are the Superbike events that are proliferating in the United States as well as in Europe. A further extension of this trend is the long-distance endurance events for what might be called racing roadsters of up to 1,000cc and more. Fast developing into a classic in this category is the annual 24-hour *Bol d'Or* run on the long and tortuous Paul Ricard circuit near Toulon. Although the prodigious power and technical sophistication of the *Bol d'Or* raceware are beyond anything the average motorcyclist can see in his local showroom, the remarkable stamina and reliability that must be built into the machines that succeed in this type of race are likely in the long run to have beneficial effects on the quality of motorbikes in general.

NEAR RIGHT Mick Grant demonstrates just how much power there is available from the works Kawasaki 750-triple, two-stroke racer. On this machine he set a new outright lap record of over 180 km/h (112 mph) at the Isle of Man in 1977.

FAR RIGHT Phil Read, ex-Yamaha, ex-MV Agusta, and a past world road-racing champion in 125, 250, and 500 cc classes won his first TT, the Junior 350, in 1961. Read won the 1977 Formula 1 World Championship TT on the Isle of Man for Honda, and is seen here at a midnight pit stop during the 1977 *Bol d'Or* 24-hour race.

MAIN PICTURE Barry Sheene and Johnny
Cecotto in the 500 cc British Grand Prix in
1978.

BELOW New Zealander Graeme Crosby gets
away first at the 1981 Austrian GP. Eventual
World Champion Marco Lucchinelli (No 5), a
wheeling Kenny Roberts (No 1) and Randy
Mamola (No 3) follow.

SPEEDWAY

LEFT Breathtaking action at close quarters, with cinders flying as the riders go into controlled slides around the oval track: the atmosphere of speedway racing has changed little since this French watercolour was painted in 1928.

SPEEDWAY racing bears little or no relationship to the motorcycling enjoyed by so many millions on or off the road. The two-wheelers ridden on the 400 m ($\frac{1}{4}$-mile) shale or ice tracks are single-speed, methanol-burning, 500 cc four-strokes that have no brakes, relatively little suspension except on the front forks, and require a unique riding style.

Four riders on equally matched machines release their clutches and hurtle flat out towards the first corner. Jostling for position, forcing other riders off line, it is the bold and skilful rider who gains the advantage. The speedway rider needs courage and superb throttle control to remain in charge of his careering, unbraked motorcycle. Too little throttle and he has dirt blasted into his face by the more daring competitors, too much throttle and he is fighting to control an unleashed beast that is trying to ride him into the safety fence on the outer edge of the track.

Normally there are 13 four-lap races during the course of a meeting, with the seven riders, plus two reserves, in each of two teams interchanging riding order so that two riders from each team compete against different riders from the opposing team in every race. The winner of each race scores three points, second two points, and third one point. The team which amasses most points through the individual scores of its members is the winner of the match.

Like football teams, the speedway clubs are organized into leagues, with first and second divisions. The competitors ride two or three times a week at home or away on specially prepared shale tracks and their fans follow them from one end of the country to the other to give their devoted support.

Speedway racing originated in the United States where, on established tracks which were used for pony trotting, dirt riders found the perfect location for a new motorcycle sport. Using the big Harley-Davidson and Indian 1,000 cc V-twins, they rode at breakneck speed around the dirt ovals to entertain the sensation-seeking American public of the 1920s.

After a number of serious accidents, including some fatalities, the capacity of the motorcycles was limited to 500 cc. This reduction in performance caused riders to experiment with riding techniques and, in order to maintain speed through the turns, it was not long before the more daring competitors were broadsiding their machines through the corners with power still turned full on.

A demonstration visit to Australia by the American riders fired the enthusiasm of the motorcycle riders 'down under', who up to that time had been riding on grass tracks, or on concrete. A cinder track, similar to the American pony-trotting tracks, was laid at Maitland and,

RIGHT Steel-plated boots scrub the shale track surface as New Zealander Ivan Mauger, 1977 World Speedway Champion, leads Valeri Gordeev, John Louis, and Edward Jancarz around the 350 m (380-yard) circuit. The sport is truly international, with top-class riders coming from western and eastern Europe, Australasia, and the United States.

BELOW Peter Collins demonstrates the skill that brought him the world title in 1976. Fragile-looking front forks and wheel, no brakes, and a powerful single-cylinder, four-valve motor with only a single gear characterize the contemporary speedway bike. The three overwhelmingly dominant power units in speedway at the moment are the Weslake, the JAWA, and the ERM.

RIGHT The almost crab-like motion of the machines on the corners of a speedway circuit is well caught here as Ole Olsen, the great Danish ex-world champion, leads the tightly bunched trio of Ian Turner, Alan Molyneux, and Jan Henningsen. Note the position of the riders' left feet–quite different from the older leg-trailing technique shown in the painting on pages 80–1.

styles, and power units were modified and developed. It was found that the 500 cc, single-cylinder, JAP four-stroke, with its steam-train power characteristics, was absolutely ideal for speedway. No gearbox was required because the big single was able to pull from a standstill to maximum revs on the short start-and-finish straight without need for a second gear. Also a short wheelbase with a solid rear-end frame and minimum-movement sprung front forks were perfect for sliding under power through the turns.

The JAP-engined machines were to reign supreme for over 30 years—until the appearance of the Czech-made ESO 500 cc four-stroke in the 1960s. The ESO (which later became JAWA) engine was simple and robust and, with a somewhat shorter stroke, produced more power with even greater flexibility than the British-made equivalent. By the mid-1960s JAP had been eclipsed and JAWA virtually took over the speedway-motorcycle market for almost a decade.

Then, in 1974, the British Weslake Engineering Company, based at Rye in Sussex, designed and built a 500 cc, four-valve, single-cylinder speedway/grass-track motor which was superior to the JAWA in all ways. Don Godden tested it at a grass-track meeting at Lydden in Kent in October 1974 and it beat all opposition hands down.

The Weslake motor rocketed to success and JAWA knew they had to do some drastic redesign work to remain competitive. Four valves appeared to be the answer and both JAWA and the Swedish ERM company now build four-valve speedway motors. However, at present, it is only Weslake who supply over-the-counter power packs with four-valve design. The JAWA unit has been reserved purely for selected riders.

Apart from national speedway meetings held in Sweden, Denmark, Poland, Russia, West Germany, the United States, Australia, New Zealand, and Britain, there are also international 'test' matches between some of these countries. Then there are the individual national championships and, the most coveted prize of all amongst speedway riders, the Solo World Speedway Championships.

Since World War II, it has been New Zealand and Sweden that have dominated the World Championships, with Antipodean Ivan Mauger winning the title no less than six times, closely followed by Ove Fundin of Sweden who has five and Mauger's compatriot Barry Briggs who has won the championship four times.

Fortunately, Britain was soon back in the running with riders of the calibre of World Champions Peters Collins and Michael Lee who took the title in 1976 and 1980 respectively.

by 1926, the sport had really caught on, with the first 400-metre track being set up in Brisbane. Here a rider by the name of Cecil Brown is credited with developing the spectacular leg-trailing, broadside riding style.

Enthusiasts in Britain heard about the exciting new speedway craze, and, in 1927, the Camberley Club in Surrey staged the first dirt-track meeting in this country. Unfortunately, the organizers seem to have been a bit slapdash in their research into the sport, and ran the event on a deep sand surface on a clockwise course—totally opposite to the established ideas. However, a month later at Droylesden, near Manchester, a proper dirt-track event was staged, and the following year, with the visit of the Australian speedway promoter Johnnie Hoskins, the foundations of the sport of speedway were truly laid in Britain.

Machines used for dirt-track riding, as it was then known, were little more than roadster motorcycles stripped of all lighting and other ancillaries and with a pair of turned-down handlebars to make them look the part. Some roadsters, notably the old in-line, horizontally opposed, twin-cylinder Douglas, were more suitable than others. The Douglas, in fact, with its very low centre of gravity and long wheelbase, was particularly suitable for the leg-trailing speedway riding technique then in vogue, and it remained one of the more popular and successful competition machines with the British riders throughout the 1930s.

However, as has happened in other forms of motorcycle sport, specialization began to creep into speedway. Machines were adapted in frame design to suit riding

Grass and Ice Racing

Two offshoots of speedway, both of which use machines of similar design, are grass-track racing and ice racing. It could be said, however, that speedway is a derivative of grass-track racing because motorcyclists rode on the rough grass tracks before they were organized to ride as teams on dirt tracks; moreover, many of the best of the present speedway stars

LEFT Probably Britain's greatest grass-track specialist, Don Godden has also had conspicuous success at long-track (800 m) speedway races on the Continent. Here, aboard his Godden-Weslake Special, he demonstrates perfect balance in a controlled slide at a grass-track meeting.

BELOW Wildly spinning rear wheels throw up a curtain of mud at the start of a grass-track race at Lydden, near Dover. Riding technique is similar to that on a dirt track—many of today's speedway stars began on grass—but the machines have two-speed gearboxes, rear suspension, and minimal brakes.

learned their trade on grass.

As for ice racing, this is a motorcycle sport like no other. The machines resemble speedway motorcycles, but the tyres are fitted with needle-sharp, 38 mm ($1\frac{1}{2}$ in) steel spikes which bite into the surface of the ice circuit. These spikes allow the riders to bank their motorcycles at unbelievable angles when cornering. In fact, the riders wear old pieces of motorcar tyres on their left knees and shins which allow them to ride around the turns resting on the knee.

The motorcycles used are single-gear, JAWA-powered, 500 cc four-strokes, which, like ordinary speedway machines, have no brakes and on which the clutch is used merely for starting and the throttle to control the speed.

Ice racing originated in those countries where the winters are hard and thick ice forms on lakes and rivers–although nowadays, of course, events are held on specially refrigerated outdoor or indoor tracks. The sport is dominated at present by the Russians and Czechs who invented it, but it is likely that this spectacular sport will eventually spread much farther afield, especially in those countries where normal speedway has proved enduringly popular.

ABOVE An eastern European development of speedway takes place at sub-zero temperatures on ice. The racing tyres are fitted with needle-sharp spikes, which dig into the ice and allow the riders to bank their machines at incredible angles. Competitors strap a section of tyre to their left knees to lean on while cornering.

RIGHT The steel spikes are fitted high up on the near-side wall, rather than on the crown, of the tyres because the machines race anti-clockwise on an almost circular course. The ice racers are powered by the single-cylinder four-strokes used in conventional speedway bikes, but conditions are often so cold that the motors have to be warmed with a blowlamp before they will start.

Drag Racing

THE fury of a supercharged, triple-engined dragster at full throttle has to be heard to be believed. The noise of 12 unsilenced exhausts is ear-shattering as the rider guns the throttle, drops the clutch, and smokes away from the start line.

The experience is over in a matter of seconds. A quarter of a mile (400 m) is covered in less than nine seconds, with machines attaining speeds in the region of 270 km/h (170 mph). Then, energy spent, they burble back to the pits to be fuelled and oiled, ready to race again.

Many motorcycle enthusiasts find a day spent watching motorcycles accelerating from point A to point B 400 metres away extremely tedious; others, particularly those with a technical knowledge, are amazed at the incredible ingenuity which goes into building a dragster.

Drag races are really won in the workshop. Each motorcycle is an individually built machine incorporating the ideas of its designer-builder, who hopes through his skill to create a winner. Far more hours are spent in the workshop building, modifying, rebuilding, and modifying yet again to improve performance by perhaps a fraction of a second, than are spent actually riding the bikes. The racing is purely a means of testing and proving theories that have been built into the machine in the workshop.

In open drag-racing events, anything goes in terms of specification. Any number of engines may be used in supercharged or unsupercharged form, coupled to single-speed or multi-speed transmissions, and slotted into equally varied frame designs.

LEFT Andy Chapman's *Mighty Mouse* regularly proves that it is not necessary to build multi-engined monsters to compete successfully in drag racing. His machine is based on a 500 cc Vincent Comet, and even in its highly modified form, complete with supercharger, its remarkably light weight has enabled Chapman to give many of his big-bike rivals a beating.

Early Days

However, the sport was not always like this. Like most other forms of motorcycle competition, drag racing had very humble beginnings, with competitors riding almost standard roadgoing machines against the clock over a measured quarter mile.

This early form of drag racing began in Britain in the early 1920s, when it was known as sprinting. There was no side-by-side racing between two competitors, and the results of these sprinting competitions were decided purely on the times of the riders. Today there still exist two separate controlling bodies for the sport: the NSA (National Sprint Association) and the BHRDA (British Hot Rod and Drag Racing Association). The motorcycles raced by members of these associations are basically the same, but in the Sprint Association results are judged against the clock whereas drag-racing results are decided in a knock-out competition of two riders actually racing against each other on the drag strip.

Drag racing as we know it today was imported from the United States, where it had become apparent that sprinting

against the clock had little spectator appeal compared with two riders engaged in a man-to-man contest.

The sport began to grow in popularity during the 1950s, when all manner of roadster engines were slotted into lightened frames. Very few competitors at that time were using special fuel, and extra acceleration was achieved by reducing the weight of the motorcycles as much as possible. Everything that could be drilled for lightness without drastically reducing strength was drilled. Items such as 50 cc motorcycle front forks were fitted to 500, 650, or even 750 cc machines, with miniaturized drum brakes being built into the front wheel to reduce weight still further.

As competition became more fierce, the sprint riders turned to supercharging and the use of the oxygen-rich methanol fuel. This vastly increased engine power but it immediately created another problem –lack of traction at the rear wheel. When the clutch was dropped on a supercharged dragster the rear wheel spun wildly on the track. There was no way in which all the extra power could be transmitted to the drag strip using the conventional round-section racing tyres.

Then the Avon tyre company solved the problem by producing a wide, flat-sectioned tyre with no tread and an outer covering of high-hysteresis rubber, a soft, tacky material that grips the road. The tyre was named 'the slick' and with it there was a drastic reduction in standing-quarter-mile times. The only problem was that on dragsters of the period there was a tendency for the tyre to grip so well that the front of the motorcycle would leap into the air and the entire machine would try to loop backwards over the rear wheel.

Frames had to be redesigned, and they became longer and longer and their centre of gravity lowered as far as possible in order to keep the front wheels on the ground. Speeds improved yet again.

As the frames grew longer, so one or

BELOW A burn-out on the drag strip at Santa Pod: competitors melt the surface rubber on their rear tyres to give them improved grip when starting. The effect is dramatic and often entails fitting a new tyre at every meeting—but every aid to speed is crucial when a hundredth of a second can make the difference between victory and defeat.

two rider-designers decided to slot another engine into the frame and build twin-engined specials. The use of fuel blends of nitro and methanol on the supercharged multi-engined specials created rear-tyre adhesion problems and it was not uncommon to see a motorcycle hurtle off the start line and its rear tyre spinning and smoking the entire length of the drag strip.

More rubber was needed on the track surface to stop this loss of power and traction. Slick-tyre widths were increased,

LEFT Another burn-out, this time without the drama of flames. The headlight, fairing, and conventional front forks identify this Kawasaki as a contender in the 'street-legal' production-machine category. The performance of such machines, however, is considerably greater than that of the ordinary roadsters on which they are based.

BELOW Many drag-racing enthusiasts take pride in beautifully decorated machines. But the attractive appearance of Anton de Vos's Kawasaki (seen here by the Santa Pod engine-starting rollers) should fool no one. With two huge 1,000 cc fours hooked in line, it is one of the fastest machines on the strip.

and as the chance of breaking the grip of the new wider tyres was reduced, so all the power had to be absorbed by transmissions. The consequence was that gearboxes and clutches failed and drive shafts snapped. New ideas had to be tried.

The grass-track champion and speedway rider Alf Hagon overcame the transmission problem by getting rid of the gearbox altogether and using a single-speed machine. By incorporating a giant 1,300 cc JAP V-twin supercharged motor in a flimsy but rigid frame, he used a spinning rear wheel almost as a variable transmission. The idea worked and the very flexible and powerful JAP motor blasted him over the standing quarter mile in under 10 seconds, with a terminal speed of around 256 km/h (160 mph).

The Eight-Second Barrier

At this time Britain was still lagging behind the United States, where a special slipper clutch had been developed. This allowed the rider to rev his power unit to the limit for maximum power on the getaway and, as soon as he released the clutch, it would slip to avoid rear-wheel spin, at the same time increasing its grip as the speed of the motorcycle increased.

Twin-engined dragsters were superseded by triple-engined monsters which, with the slipper clutch, brought the standing-quarter-mile times to below the 9-second mark. American ideas were soon to be copied by the British designers, and with engineer-riders of the calibre of John Hobbs, who built the double-Weslake-engined *Hobbit*, the 8-second barrier was broken.

The fastest recorded time is now a little over 7 seconds for the run, and British, American, and Dutch riders are vying for the prestige of being the first to

break the 7-second barrier. However, as speeds increase, it becomes more difficult to knock even one hundredth of a second off the record.

Track surfaces and tyre adhesion are all-important and for some while riders have been doing 'burn-outs'. This involves propping the front of the machine against a solid wall and spinning the rear wheel until the surface rubber begins to melt owing to friction. At the same time bleach is poured over the tyre and sometimes even petrol is set alight around the spinning rear wheel. When the tyre is hot and sticky it gives its greatest adhesion and the dragster is ready for its run.

'Burn-outs' and 'Christmas trees' are all part of drag-racing jargon. The term 'Christmas tree' refers to the starting system used in drag racing. It resembles a very large traffic light with a red light, three amber lights, and a green light for Go. This is situated between the two competing riders, who watch intently as the lights change from red through amber to green. If a rider can anticipate the green light perfectly be releasing the clutch at maximum revs, he is off to a flying start.

Drag racing has become an extremely expensive sport and most of the top riders manage to build their multi-engined specials only with the help of sponsorship from motorcycle companies. In an effort to reduce costs, racing has been split into a number of classes, including one for ordinary roadster motorcycles.

Although not as exciting to watch, the roadster-class races at least enable ordinary riders to enjoy the sport. In fact, some even ride to the events on their machines, fit the competition numbers, race the machines, and then ride home again–just as the original competitors must have done in the early years of motorcycle sport. In some ways, the history of motorcycling has turned full circle.

ABOVE LEFT The slender spaceframe seems scarcely able to accommodate the two huge supercharged, four-cylinder Honda motors of American Russ Collins' drag racer, one of the two or three fastest machines in the world in 1977.

ABOVE Although drag racing began in the United States and is still a very big-time sport there, many of the top American riders now compete regularly at Santa Pod against the British stars. One such American ace is Tom Christenson, seen here aboard his Norton-powered *Hogslayer*, which earned its name by regularly overcoming Harley-Davidson-powered monsters. The machine was one of the first to beat eight seconds.

RIGHT American star Bo O'Brochta with his turbocharged Kawasaki 'Terminal Van Lines Special' gets ready for a burn out. In recent years this simple, single-engined bike has dominated the sport in the USA with its low 7 second quarter-mile times and near 200 mph terminal speeds.

SCOOTERS
AND
MOPEDS

Mopeds

Since the time of the earliest steam-driven motorcycles of the 19th century, the moped has been an established form of motorcycle. As its name suggests, the vehicle has both pedal and engine power. Its appeal has been, and still is, universal because anyone who can ride a bicycle can ride a moped. The only difference is that riding a moped takes a great deal less effort!

The other great factor determining the success of the moped has been its relative freedom from legislation. Today, even though legislation has recently become more restrictive, 14-year-olds in some European countries can still ride mopeds with the same freedom that they ride bicycles. In developing countries it is often the case that the whole household, regardless of age, uses a moped as the only means of transport.

Over the years legislation has altered the original meaning of the word moped. In

America, the definition varies from state to state, but is roughly to the effect that: a moped has fully operational pedals, automatic transmission, does not exceed 50cc, produces no more than 1.5 brake horse-power, and is capable of no more than 40kph (25mph) on level ground. Owners of machines which comply to these regulations in many states find that they are exempt from insurance and road licensing requirements and do not even require a driver's licence. In a few states there is not even a minimum age stipulation for riders, and most can evade the compulsory helmet law for motorcycle riders which exists in many states.

Sometimes the confusion arising from such laws can work in favour of the individual. One such case in the context of mopeds is widely known by Harley-Davidson riders in America. At the famous Daytona race track in Florida, one of the American states which enforces a compulsory helmet law for all riders other than those on mopeds, a Harley rider was

stopped by the police for riding his 750cc model without a helmet. The bike happened to be a vintage model with pedals, and because it had pedals the rider managed to convince the officer that it was a moped and therefore outside the jurisdiction of the helmet law!

In Britain, riders have to wait until they are 16 before they are allowed to ride powered two-wheelers on public roads, and then they are limited to 48kph (30mph) 50cc mopeds which do not necessarily have to have pedals to assist the engine. They are also subject to all motor vehicle laws. Ironically, the same country allows car drivers with a full licence to ride this type of machine without the need for a special licence or learner plates. So today's 'mopeds' have by no means escaped legislation completely, but they are nevertheless open to a wider section of the public than any other type of powered two-wheeled transport.

The birth of this humble form of transport was the birth of motorcycling. It was

LEFT The moped has always had universal appeal, combining as it does the advantages of both powered two-wheeled transport and pedal cycling.

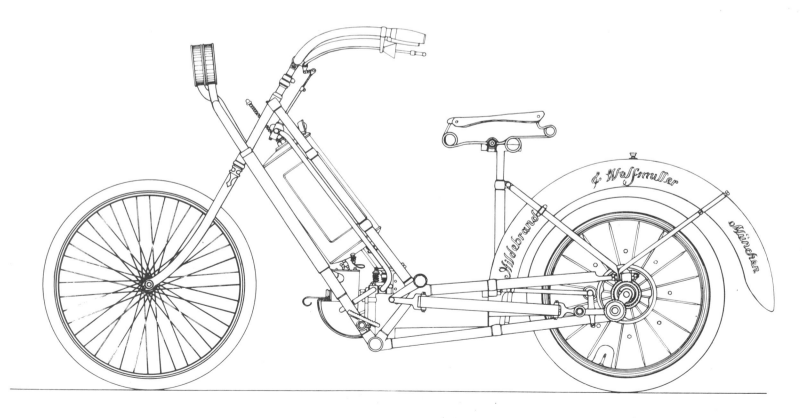

Hildebrand and Wolfmuller motorcycle, 1894

a natural progression to mate an engine with an existing bicycle frame. The earliest recognized form of powered two-wheeled transport was a 'boneshaker' bicycle without pedals, powered by a steam engine. It is thought that the first such vehicle was built in 1818. From boneshakers, steam engines were attached to penny-farthing bicycles. Inventors in America and Europe were busy attempting to make a success of the combination. The first recognized production model was the German Hildebrand of 1889, the design of which was originally conceived in France.

Meanwhile, experiments were being made with other forms of power: three years before the Hildebrand production model, the Humber Company of Britain had produced an electrically driven tandem; and the four-stroke internal combustion engine invented by German Nikolaus August Otto in 1877 was more than ten years old.

Otto's invention was to be the most significant of course and, though he was more interested in stationary engines, his colleague Gottlieb Daimler set up a separate workshop and applied the new technology to two-wheeled transport. His 0.5hp engine installed in a boneshaker frame is regarded as the first true ancestor of the motorcycle.

During these early days of motorcycling, most machines were 'mopeds', regardless of their engine size. Even the first four-cylinder motorcycle, the Holden of 1897, had pedals attached to the front wheel in order to get the machine moving and help the engine which was connected by direct drive to the rear wheel. Not only that, but early engines were unreliable and it was reassuring for the owner to know that, should the engine stop, he could at least pedal home.

Pedals were also often the only practical means of starting the engine. The machine would be lifted by its stand or some other means, so that the driving wheel was clear of the ground, and then be pedalled furiously to warm the viscous engine oil and help the petrol to vaporize. A magazine published at the time said that no motorcycle would be successful without pedals. Another reason that they were necessary was that, on hills, the angle of incline would often prevent the flow of fuel to the engine.

As more and more motorcycle factories sprang up in Europe and America, the question of where to situate the engine was answered in various ways. In 1895 the De Dion-Bouton Company in France produced a 0.5hp engine fitted behind the rear spindle of a pedal tricycle. This company was one of several which were making three-wheelers at the time.

Clip-on engines driving either the front or back wheel of a bicycle became fashionable and, as their popularity grew, so the desire for the tricycle declined.

Two Russian brothers, Michael and Eugene Werner who were living in Paris, became prominent pioneers of this new trend. They mounted a 217cc four-stroke engine in front of the handlebars of a bicycle as an aid to the cyclist. It drove the front wheel via a twisted rawhide belt. The engine weighed only 29.5kg (65lb) and established the Werner as the first practical motorcycle. When, just after the turn of the century, the brothers situated their engine in the centre of the bicycle frame, they started a trend which nearly all two-wheelers have since followed.

Singer of Coventry in 1900 marketed a 222cc engine driving a bicycle wheel which was intended to replace the front or rear wheel of a pedal cycle. The 302cc Clyde of 1901 made further use of the pedalling gear by incorporating a Chater-Lea back pedalling brake on the rear wheel. In 1902 a 2.75hp Excelsior with the engine mounted on the front downtube took what was recognized as the world speed record at the Canning Town cycle track, covering 1.6km (1 mile) in 1 minute 24 seconds from a standing start. Pedals and a chain to the rear wheel started this clutchless engine, which in turn was directly connected to the rear wheel.

A twin-cylinder air-cooled 2.5hp engine, designed by J. F. Barter in Bristol in 1905, was clipped to the frame of a pedal cycle, and was originally known as the Fee, and later the Fairy. This model featured a small counter shaft gearbox attached to the

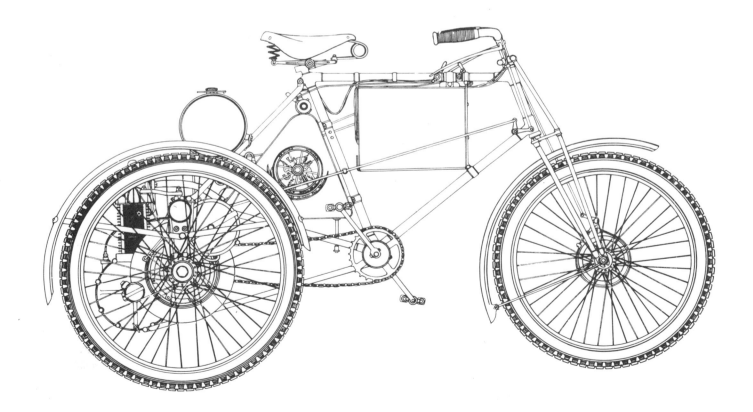

1¾hp De Dion-Bouton motor tricycle, 1896

front downtube, which then drove the rear wheel by a rawhide belt. Manufacture was later taken over by the famous Douglas brothers who produced their first motorcycle in 1907.

That same year, the Isle of Man Tourist Trophy races were introduced to promote motorcycling sport. Fuel regulations in the race were stringently enforced, and pedalling was therefore vigorously applied up all hills by the riders. Single cylinder machines were allowed 4.5 litres (1 gallon) per 114.8km (90 miles), and twin-cylinder machines the same amount of fuel for 120.7km (75 miles).

Just before the outbreak of the First World War, BSA marketed the Autowheel, which consisted of a twin-cylinder horizontally opposed two-stroke engine and wheel, which clamped to the rear section of the bicycle and drove the rear wheel by chain. By 1912 it had been refined into a single-cylinder 1hp engine and later incorporated a two-speed gear in the engine crankcase. Because it cost much less than a motorcycle to buy and it gave good economy, at more than 35 kilometres per litre (100 miles per gallon), the Autowheel became very popular. It was also used on industrial trucks, invalid carriages, and scooters.

During and after the First World War, more emphasis was given to larger, more efficient machinery with kickstarters, gearboxes and clutches. The 1920s was the 'golden era' of motorcycling. Single-speed mopeds still had their place, but the pedal as a means of starting the engine on large capacity motorcycles was almost a thing of the past, thanks to motorcycle development which was accelerated by the needs of war.

Attention was focused on sporting achievements during the golden decade, which was followed by a period of depression in Europe, and the moped as we know it today did not materialize until after the Second World War.

The depression which lasted till after the Second World War created a need for cheap transport. It was obvious to the people rebuilding the motorcycle industry that moped-type vehicles were the answer to this demand, and several factories producing such machines sprang up in several of the many nations ravaged by the war.

Many people greatly profited from the relatively unhappy circumstances of the time; and one such example is today's biggest motorcycle manufacturer, Soichiro Honda of Japan (who had made piston rings before the war). In 1948, working from a small wooden shed, he bought 500 army surplus Tohatsu generator engines and fitted them to bicycle frames, driving the rear wheel by means of a pulley. Army surplus hot water bottles were used as fuel tanks on the earliest models. They

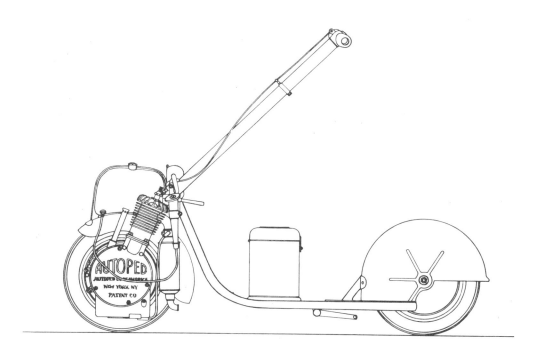

1¾hp Autoped scooter, 1916

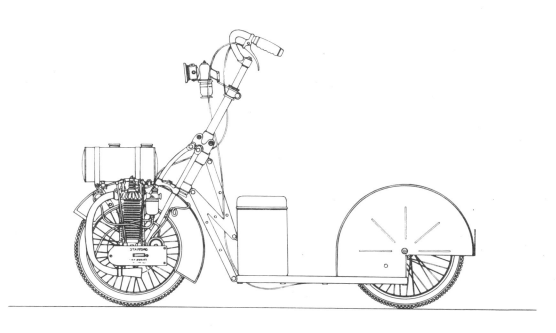

1½hp Alvis auto-scooter, 1920

sold well because petrol was still rationed in Japan and people wanted not only mobility but the chance to become independent individuals again. Owning their own means of transport gave them a chance to demonstrate this individuality.

When the supply of army surplus began to drop, Honda copied the design from a pre-war two-stroke engine and found a company to make the power units which he continued to fit to another manufacturer's bicycle frame. This was the Honda A and the pedals on it were definitely for use. Developing one horsepower at 5,000rpm, the engine was often in need of human assistance, particularly when it was asked to run on almost anything combustible because of the fuel shortage.

The A's sequel was an 89cc three wheeler. Then came Honda's first motorcycle, the Honda C. But though it had front suspension and a three horsepower engine it still had pedals. The pedals were discarded for the D model of 1950 and the same year saw the germination of a great empire, thanks to Honda's sales approach of setting up a dealer network in Japan which put many of the rival businesses out of action. Total Honda sales in 1952 were 14,000, and jumped to 30,000 in 1953, mainly because of the F Cub motor which was sold as a clip-on unit for bicycles.

It was not until 1959 that Honda looked to the overseas market. He had the effect of a Svengali when he made his move, by both creating markets and changing the image of motorcycling. The slogan 'You meet the nicest people on a Honda', introduced in 1962, caught the imagination of people who would otherwise have never considered two wheels.

Lightweight motorcycles which could be ridden by most members of the family led this Honda campaign and were an enormous hit. By 1964 the factory which had started with 13 people controlled over 60 per cent of the lucrative American market. Today, the company has 40 plants in 30 countries and employs more than 30,000 people.

In 1958 Honda introduced the C-100 'step-thru', so called because the rider could seat himself or herself as on a scooter. The fuel tank was under the seat. Its appeal was worldwide and sales of this model and similar lightweight step-thrus from 49cc upwards reached the million mark after three years. Such models were accepted as family transport and, though they did not have pedals, were treated as moped-type vehicles. Women could ride them wearing skirts and still retain their dignity, and people of meagre means could afford them. The step-thrus thus brought about a revolution in transportation.

As in Japan, manufacturers in Europe were picking up the threads of the industry after the war by fitting engines to bicycle frames. One of the most famous examples came from the Italian Garelli factory. Called the Mosquito, it was a simple 38.5cc two-stroke unit to fit bicycle frames driving the rear wheel by means of a pulley. It was at first viewed with scepticism, because it was thought that the 0.125 hp engine would not be powerful enough and that the pulley would slip when it rained. But the Mosquito quickly became popular after it proved itself. It travelled at a maximum speed of 32kph (20mph)

though it later had its compression increased from 5:5 to 6:1 in order to make it a little faster. Its most significant modification came in 1955 when Garelli designed an automatic centrifugal clutch, which meant in theory that pedals were no longer necessary to get the vehicle moving. The rider merely had to open the throttle and let the ingenious transmission engage itself. In practice, pedal assistance was necessary for a quicker getaway, but the moped had nevertheless achieved new esteem and was no longer considered to be just a glorified bicycle.

The French have no qualms about riding 'glorified bicycles'; in France the moped is regarded in the same way as a bicycle and the populace buys mopeds in great numbers. One design particular to France was the Velo Vap, introduced in 1958. The 48cc two-stroke engine was situated above the front wheel and could be lowered by means of a lever on to the wheel to drive it via a roller. This type of engine is still made today.

History repeated itself when the Cyclemaster was introduced in Britain after the war: this machine drove the rear wheel in almost an identical manner to the Singer of half a century earlier. Even Honda produced an engine-driven wheel on the P50 moped which was introduced during the 1960s.

Some attention was devoted to battery powered mopeds such as the German Solo Electra, introduced in the early 1970s. It ran for 40km (25 miles) before a recharge was necessary, and it was capable of about 25kph (16mph); but this type of moped never caught on, though it did find an application as an indoor vehicle in factories and warehouses.

The folding moped, which fits into a car boot, has been more successful. It was designed as city transport to obviate

parking problems by allowing the driver to park his car out of town. Probably the best known example is the French Motobecane. Introduced in 1973, it had scooter size wheels, a collapsible seat and handlebars and, by means of a hand-grip midway along its frame, could be lifted and carried like a suitcase.

Today's range of mopeds is as diverse as ever, from the humble Velo Vap type to tuned six-speed models like the Italian Fantic. The majority are two-strokes because this type of unit has less moving parts and is lighter and easier to produce than four-stroke equivalents. The most socially acceptable of all two-wheelers, however much its definition varies from country to country, the endearingly economical 'moped' started the motorcycle movement and, perish the thought, may one day be its sole survivor.

The first scooters

The motor scooter, which may be described as an open-framed motorcycle, began its history at the turn of the century, when it was first made. It did not become really popular, however, until after the First World War, when sales rose dramatically (though they were low compared with its later success after the Second World War.

If we imagine a child's scooter with an engine attached to it, we can visualize the early attempts to make this type of vehicle. In 1916 the Autoped Company of New York introduced a 1.75hp scooter which was also made in Britain by Imperial Motor Industries. Powered by a 162cc four-stroke engine, the single-speed drive to the front wheel was engaged simply by raising the handlebar column. An alternative model with an electric motor driving the front wheel was also produced. Its batteries were carried in a box on the platform where the rider stood.

After the First World War, the growth of the scooter industry occurred mainly in Britain, then also the world's centre of production for other two-wheeled vehicles. Most designs retained small wheels which allowed the rider's feet to be situated on floorboards within the wheelbase, with enough space to carry some luggage or an additional passenger.

The 1hp Skootamota of 1919 gave the rider a seat above the overhead valve 125cc engine which was situated above the rear wheel. Designed by Granville Bradshaw, this model had brakes on both wheels operated by hand and foot levers like the scooters of today. The brakes were external contracting units and the model also featured 38cm (15in) diameter wheels.

Another popular model during the short-lived scooter boom of the 1920s was

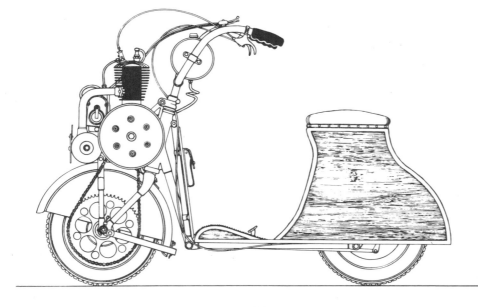

2½hp Autoglider, 1920

the 2.5hp Autoglider, built in Birmingham. It had laminated spring suspension and luggage carrying space in the box section under the seat. Powered by a Union 292cc engine located above the front wheel which it drove by chain, the Autoglider carried its fuel tank between the handlebars and went approximately 32 kilometres to a litre of fuel (90mpg). An alternative model was available without a seat so that the rider could carry a standing passenger as well as himself.

A hybrid of motorcycling and scooter design emerged in the shape of the 1920 350cc Pullin Groome, a lightweight model with a frame consisting of pressed steel plates welded together and incorporating the fuel and oil tanks. The horizontal two-stroke engine was fully enclosed. Partition panels were incorporated in the frame design to allow access to the engine for maintenance. Both wheels had knock-out spindles for easy removal, and the design featured telescopic suspension. Drive from the single-cylinder unit to the rear wheel was by chain for the two-speed epicycle gear. The rear wheel featured two brakes, one operated by hand and the other by a foot pedal. This innovative vehicle was hampered by the company's financial problems and production was halted in 1925, but designer Cyril Pullin, a former TT rider, tried again on similar lines with his 496cc Ascot Pullin. Weather protection was improved for his new model with a

windshield and wiper. It cost £75 at the time but its advanced specification failed to win enough sales to maintain production and it was on the market for only two years.

Alvis, famous for its cars, introduced a scooter in the early 1920s. Standing on the footboards, the rider was propelled by a 142cc single-cylinder overhead valve engine situated on the left side of the front wheel, with the fuel tank above the wheel and the engine flywheel on the right side of the wheel. The Grigg 1.75hp scooter of 1922 carried its two-stroke engine at the right side of the rear wheel. Again the rider had to stand up at the controls.

One of the most interesting developments of the decade was the 2.75hp Ner-a-Car of 1925. It was referred to as a 'two-wheeled car'. Originally designed in America by C. A. Neracher, it was manufactured in England by Sheffield Simplex and had a long, low-slung, pressed steel frame with a large front mudguard for weather protection. The long-wheelbased Ner-a-Car soon gained a reputation for excellent handling and stability. It had a three-speed Sturmey-Archer gearbox with a clutch and a kick starter.

By the late 1920s scooter sales were falling rapidly, because of the increase in popularity of lightweight cars and large displacement motorcycles. Though scooters were produced spasmodically,

they went through a dark age of 20 years, until the advent of the Vespa.

The scooter renaissance

In Italian, *vespa* means 'wasp'; in motor scooter language it means 'success', for the story of the Italian Vespa parallels the story of the heyday of the scooter movement. The story began in 1945 when Europe was recovering from war. Just as these hard times saw a mushrooming market for moped sales, so too did they spell a renaissance for the scooter, led by the Vespa. Designed in August of that year by Corradino d'Ascanio of the Piaggio aircraft company in Pontedera, the Vespa was built along aircraft principles.

D'Ascanio was a designer of aircraft engines and frames and was put on to the project after the factory had been razed by American war bombs. Attacking the challenge entirely from an engineering standpoint, he had his first machine ready and approved by the end of the year. By April the following year it was in production and within a decade reached the million sales mark, doubling that figure over the next five years after factories were set up in Belgium, France, Spain, England and Germany.

This fantastic success story reflects the genius of d'Ascanio. The similarity of modern Vespas to the 1945 design further

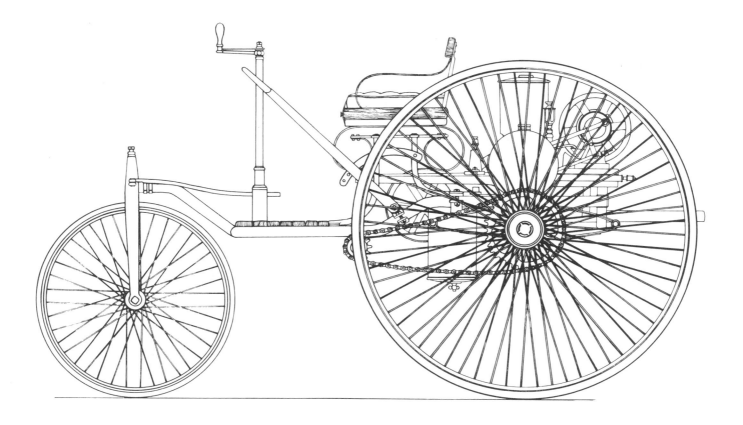

¾hp Benz motor tricycle, 1885

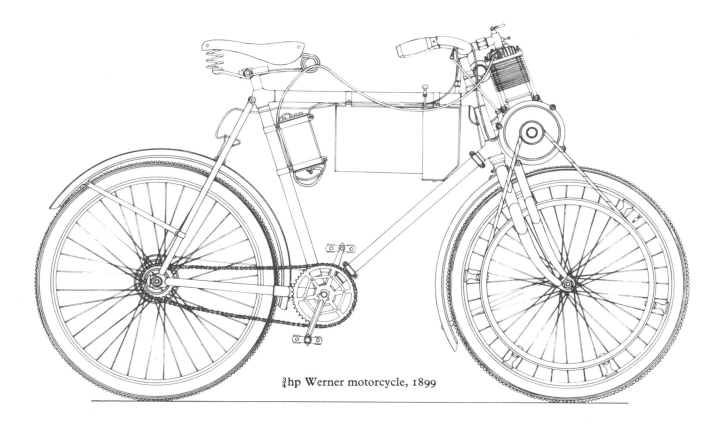

¾hp Werner motorcycle, 1899

bears out the vision and viability of the original concept. One of the neatest aspects of the Vespa was, and still is, the fact that the stub axle mounted wheels could be removed swiftly like car wheels, without the need to disturb the drive system. They were also interchangeable like car wheels. In addition, the engine was extremely compact and featured direct drive to the rear wheel.

The Vespa not only filled a need for inexpensive transport immediately after the war, but also created a new market, in the same way that hosts of glittering new motorcycles emerging from Japan inspire the desire for ownership today. The Vespa's jet set shape was so different from everything which had appeared before it that sheer novelty was as important a factor in its enormous appeal as its sound design. More than that, it was a means of two-wheel transport for the non-enthusiast: anyone could ride it. It did not demand the uncompromising devotion expected of a pre-war motorcyclist, because it did not require its owner to know about engines or enjoy diagnosing problems. In a way it was like a two-wheeled car with its simple, fan-cooled, two-stroke engine hidden by a panel on the right side of the rear wheel, just as a car's engine is hidden under the bonnet.

Because of its monocoque design and lack of motorcycle-style crossbar and fuel tank, the Vespa appealed to women, who could ride it wearing a skirt. The front apron section afforded some weather protection and it was clean, not only in appearance, but also when compared with many of the motorcycles of the day which tended to throw spots of oil on their rider's clothes.

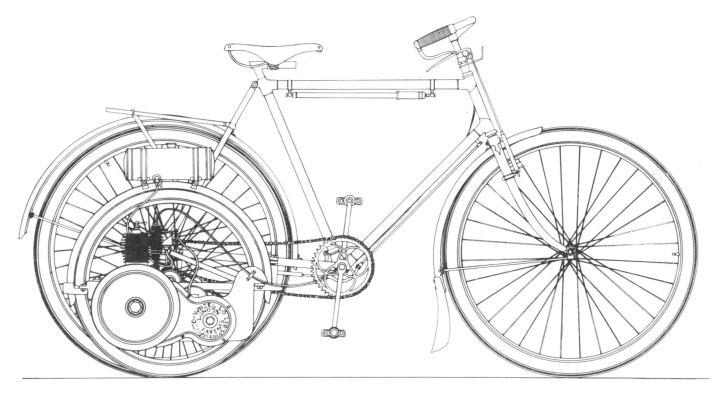

1hp Wall Autowheel, 1914

The Vespa was a new image for a new generation. It embraced and inspired a new market, and broke new ground for other manufacturers to cultivate with similar ideas.

Within three years of the birth of the Vespa, Innocenti of Milan introduced the Lambretta, the world's next most successful scooter, which won immediate acclaim. Its success was so great that it soon led to factories being set up in France and Germany.

From a styling point of view, the Lambretta differed from the Vespa in many ways: its two-stroke engine unit was not offset like the Vespa design, nor was it enclosed; the frame was steel tubes rather than pressings welded together; the front apron was much smaller; and the front wheel had the more conventional suspension system of forks on both sides, rather than the single fork leg of the Vespa. A refinement on the Lambretta, to delight the rider, was a gear indicator linked to the foot-change system.

The scooter boom

The popularity of the Vespa and the Lambretta was thus established at the beginning of the scooter boom. German designers followed Italy's lead and the popularity of scooters spread across Europe. Even Britain, steeped in motorcycle tradition, joined in after a hesitant start, and the trend spread to America where the Harley-Davidson factory, famous since 1903 for its large displacement four-stroke motorcycles, surprised many people by breaking with tradition and introducing a lightweight scooter called the Bobcat.

The strength of the new movement was such that, in Britain in 1957, scooters outsold motorcycles by 25 per cent, and this situation was repeated in other European countries. Scooter manufacturers sprang up everywhere to take advantage of the craze. Scooters even influenced motorcycles, new models of which were introduced with panels enclosing the engine and rear wheel.

Scooter sports, discussed in more detail later on, became extremely popular during this period of the late 1950s and early 1960s. Scooters were also at the centre of cults, notably in the 1960s in Britain during the 'mods and rockers' era (faithfully documented by the national press at the time), when gangs of scooter-orientated 'mods' would clash with motorcycle-orientated 'rockers'.

While the majority of scooter sales were from the Vespa and Lambretta factories with their two-stroke single-cylinder models, various other factories, including some who produced scooter sidecars, also contributed machines to the scooter market. For example, in 1958 the British BSA factory introduced the Sunbeam B2S, a 250cc four-stroke twin with its light alloy cylinder block integral with the crankcase. An identical model, the Triumph Tigress, was introduced at the same time. Another British company, Dayton, produced a powerful 250cc twin-cylinder touring scooter, and a lighter single-cylinder two-stroke model with

Puch's GP 50cc, 5-speed 'sports moped', introduced in 1975, is now illegal as a moped in the UK because of changes in legislation which class it as a motorcycle.

ABOVE Although this vintage Harley-Davidson has pedals, it is hardly a 'moped' in the truest sense, but apparently it is enough for some Daytona police officers!

electric start, called the Flamenco. Also in Britain, DKR produced a scooter which featured the fuel tank as part of the front mudguard. All four of the models in the DKR range at the time had this feature and, in addition, the top three sported electric starters. Fastest was the 250cc Manx, powered by a new two-stroke twin-cylinder engine from Villiers, whose engines were used by several other companies.

Carrying fuel over the front wheel was not a peculiarity of DKR, however; in the late 1950s Jawa CZ of Czechoslovakia produced the 172cc two-stroke Cezeta with such a feature. The Cezeta also had a warning light to indicate neutral gear, an automatic clutch, and a dual exhaust system. The appearance of the whole machine was ahead of its time.

The smallest four-stroke scooter for sale at the time was another Dayton model, the Dunkley Popular. With a 50cc over-head engine the Dunkley looked like a cross between a moped and a scooter. It had a slightly larger brother, the S65, with a 65cc four-stroke engine.

The German Heinkel factory, well known for its bubble cars, made an impression on the scooter world with a 175cc four-stroke model called the Tourist. The largest touring mounts of the day were made by another West German factory, Maico. Three models, one 200cc, the others 250cc, were considered luxury machines with their streamlined bodies.

One machine which stepped over the 250cc 'norm' for the time was the 324cc Phoenix produced by H. E. Engineering of London. This four-speed two-stroke carried 11.4 litres (2.5 gal) of fuel, weighed 127kg (280lb) and was powered by a Villiers unit. All models in the Phoenix range were driven by Villiers engines. The special feature of the marque was that the rear body section could be completely

removed by undoing three spring clips.

Some of the best designed scooters were made in Japan, where production started immediately after the war with excellent home sales and a fair trade to America. One of the first Japanese scooters with auto-matic transmission was the Silver Pigeon: its 125cc overhead valve four-stroke engine drove through expanding pulleys and V-belt. Fuji Heavy Industries manufactured a luxury 250cc side valve model, the Rabbit Superflow, automatically driven through a torque converter. It also had an electric starter and indicators as standard equip-ment.

Scooter sport

Though the lifespan of many of the world's scooter factories was short, they helped to stimulate a growing interest in scooter sport. The famous French Bol d'Or endurance road race included a class for scooters. This was later abandoned, how-ever, after scooters were modified so much along motorcycle lines that the class lost its original identity.

At first, most scooter events were social rallies. From them developed scooter road races, hill climbs, sprints, road trials, display teams and endurance races. Clubs for one make and clubs for all makes grew up in many parts of the world, and were often fostered by scooter manufacturers, dealers, and importers. Some clubs in New Zealand and South Africa even made special uniforms for members to wear on parade days.

One of the most famous scooter events, the Isle of Man rally, drew scooter enthusi-asts by the thousand each year, for a week of fun which included a 24-hour run over the TT course, racing on sand and scooter sidecar racing. In Italy the Three Seas race for Vespa riders covered 1800km

(1125 miles) over five days, on twisting roads.

Even trials riding was not beyond the scope of the scooter. In the arduous Scottish Six Days Trial, three Lambrettas were entered in 1959 and all three won awards. It was the Lambretta engine which tuners found the most suitable for road racing, and these make up the majority of the grids when occasional scooter racing takes place today.

Scooters today

Sporting activities continued unabated during the 1960s, even though scooter sales were already beginning to drop. Growing prosperity in Europe towards the end of the 1950s saw overall sales in both scooters and motorcycles reduced as more and more people turned to small cars. Germany took the lead in this, and France (where moped sales were a million a year) introduced restrictive legislation which also severely cut scooter sales. Many factories, trying hard to compete with the highly successful and numerous Vespa and Lambretta plants, had to close, particu-larly when they were also hit by the growing penetration of Japanese motor-cycles during the 1960s. Today only Vespa and Lambretta models survive.

Reviewing the present situation, reports indicate that Vespa sales have never been better in Britain. In the rest of Europe there is also renewed interest, and in Italy, as always, Vespa sales are still high. And in Malaysia and other developing countries, a new boom is taking place, to such an extent that the Piaggio factory which makes Gilera motor cycles and mopeds as well as the Vespa is the fourth largest manufacturer of two-wheelers in the world. With factories in Spain, Taiwan and Malaysia as well as Italy, the Piaggio factory is now producing 300,000 units a year. In addition, the Bejaj factory in India, originally set up by Piaggio, also manufactures Vespa copies.

Lambretta, the only other surviving scooter manufacturer, now exists only in Spain and India. The original Italian factory was converted to the production of BMC cars early in the 1970s. Current pro-duction in Spain is primarily for the home market, but the Indian factory is produc-ing for a flourishing export market.

Now that the Japanese Yen is becoming a harder currency in international finance, the prices of motorcycles from this, the world's largest motorcycle producing country, look certain to rise, and it seems likely that scooter sales will benefit as a result. The humble Vespa started a revolu-tion once; perhaps, with Lambretta's help, it will do so again.

Under 16s

For every child who rides a bicycle, joining the ranks of motorcyclists is only one step away. Indeed, some children now begin with the powered sort, because there has never been a better time for young people below the age of 16 to enjoy motorcycling: youth motorcycling is in fact the fastest growing section of the whole motorcycle movement. Whereas 20 years ago parents themselves had to build the machine if their child wanted a motorcycle, there is now a wide variety of suitable machines (called minibikes or minicycles) on the market, for children from toddlers to teenagers, and these range from play bikes to competition bikes. The minibikes are as sophisticated as the adult bikes, and just as smart.

The underlying reasons for this increase in the number of young people with motorcycles are the affluence of modern western societies today, the increase in the amount of leisure time families have, and the availability of enormous numbers of relatively inexpensive, well-made models (mainly from Japan). All these factors have led to greater parental tolerance towards motorcycling; after all, it is parents who control the family finances and determine whether or not their sons and daughters will ride motorcycles before they are allowed legally to go on public roads. Other factors contributing to the recent growth of youth motorcycling include the increased adult interest in off-road riding, made possible by purpose-built machinery being widely available. In America, particularly, families can ride together on many park lands and in certain forested areas, and it is in that country that youth motorcycling takes place on the biggest scale.

Sporting competitions

Much of youth motorcycling revolves around organized sport. In the USA motorcycling competitions involving all types of powered two-wheelers for young riders take place with major championship series across the continent, and a branch of the motorcycle industry has grown up to help create and cater for this new interest. In Europe young riders take part in racing events, display teams and gymkhana-type events, and travel abroad to show their skills. Many schools on both sides of the Atlantic teach children motorcycling, whether for fun as a sport, or in preparation for the time the pupils come of age for public road riding. Some American high schools have their own moto-cross teams.

While young Americans have made

Schoolboy scrambling—50cc junior class—is a sport in which children as young as six or seven years old take part.

Schoolboy scrambling in the 125cc senior class is a tough training ground for those aiming for the adult classes and future GP events.

youth motorcycling big business, particularly in the sport of moto-cross, the world's leading moto-cross nation, Belgium, surprisingly banned motorcycling competitions for riders under 16. Before the ban, Danielle Picard was a well-known young rider there. She won her country's 50cc moto-cross title on a Negrini in 1972, when she was 11 years old. The daughter of a transport contractor, she graduated to a 125 CZ and, when the ban in Belgium frustrated her sporting activities, looked to other countries for competition rides. Her father appealed to French and British organizers who agreed to provide her with racing opportunities to further her talent, and continue her family's tradition of motorcycling.

There are many riders who have emerged from the ranks of youth riders to achieve international acclaim as adults, for example American world trials expert Bernie Schreiber, who started with the American Trials Association at the age of ten. However, while it is the ambition of

many to become world motorcycling stars, many are quite happy to be able to compete with their youthful contemporaries. One such notable case is that of Christopher Quant from Somerset, who has artificial legs as the result of a farm accident when he was nine years old. At the age of 14, in 1976, he took up the sport of scrambling, and his first racing bike was a Rickman Zundapp. His courage and determination overcame his physical handicaps and he has set a standard of sportsmanship by which all riders may be measured.

Although most youth competitions take place off-road, there are some places where road racing is possible for riders under the age of 16. For example, at an international event in South Africa in January 1979, where double world champion Kork Ballington (himself a South African) thrilled the 25,000 spectators at the Hesketh circuit near Pietermaritzburg, not even Ballington could overshadow 12-year-old Warren Bristol, who won the 50cc race. In some states of America, where under-16s are allowed to drive cars on public

roads, talented motorcyclists of this age group may also get into road racing. Freddie Spencer, who includes road racing a Yamaha in his motorcycle competition repertoire, recorded 28 wins during the 1977 season (when he was 15), to become a young American champion.

Perhaps the most famous modern instance of a schoolboy making world headlines in road racing was when 15-year-old Ivan Palazes become the youngest ever rider to score world championship points. Ivan, from Caracas, Venezuela, rode a Morbidelli in the 125cc race at the 1977 Venezuelan grand prix and finished third, behind former 125cc world champion Angel Nieto and regular GP rider Anton Mang from Germany. Ivan's excellent riding at the San Carlos circuit merited the points, but there was some controversy over whether or not he was entitled to them. Under FIM rules grand prix competitors have to be at least 18 years old. So Ivan should not have been allowed to ride in the first place.

In southern California, riders from eight

to 12 are seen nearly every week in full face helmets and brightly coloured leathers, competing in junior speedway races. Their bikes are usually powered by engines like Honda's 125cc four-stroke single, but they look just like smaller versions of the 500cc adult speedway bikes, right down to the sponsors' decals on the fuel tanks.

In Finland, moto-cross and trials are the favourite motorcycle sports of the young population. The success of trials world champion Yrjo Vesterinen and moto-cross world champion Heikki Mikkola, both from Finland, has led to an increase in popularity of these two sports. The young moto-cross riders gain even more encouragement from the fact that they can ride on the same bill as their world class heroes. Recent moto-cross grands prix in Finland have featured youth races on the same day, using part of the world championship course. In national and club events for adults there are support races for under 16-year olds. Mainly because of Finland's small population of five million, everyone who wants to ride has the chance. Youth competitions, for the age group 12 to 16, are all limited to 50cc machines. The power units are all imported but Finland does make a few frames, such as the Solifer.

In neighbouring Sweden, the home of many moto-cross world champions, moto-cross competitions for younger riders were introduced in 1968. The Swedish Monark factory backed the venture by producing lightweight two-strokes for the young enthusiasts, and this helped the sport to gain popularity very quickly. It still retains its appeal for Swedish youngsters today.

Moto-cross and trials schools are becoming commonplace in several countries. Following the success of English schools, Ulster held its first residential moto-cross school for 13- to 15-year-olds in December 1978. Irish moto-cross grand prix rider Bob Wilkinson was the main tutor.

In England, grass track, sand racing, sidecar cross and sprints on grass are all popular, as well as those already mentioned. It is 20 years since organized competition started there, and by 1978 more than 100 clubs running youth competitions were in existence, catering for an estimated 10,000 competitors. Riders in Britain can start in competition from the age of six, and the skill and natural ability with which these small riders handle their 50cc machines is astonishing.

Australia has a thriving minibike scene, both for leisure and sporting activities. Youngsters compete against adults and, with extensive television coverage of these sports, stars are born at a very early age. Annual sales of such machines in Australia have been estimated at around 12,000, and about 20 marques making 100 different models reflect the wide interest in the hobby.

Other activities

The minibike era began in the late 1950s, when this type of motorcycle was introduced as a town vehicle, able to be carried in a car boot. Sales to young people soared after Honda of Japan presented 10,000 of them to YMCA homes in America. It was the YMCA's idea and the bikes were used to persuade disobedient youngsters to mend their ways, or lose riding privileges. (The scheme worked so well that it has been extended in America to help the rehabilitation of drug addicts by giving them a new interest in life.)

Following the initial liaison between the YMCA and Honda, in 1975 the Association requested 2,500 70cc models for a scheme called the National Youth Project Using Minibikes. Under this scheme 18 riders aged between 12 and 16 earned their way on to a desert trail ride of 1,950km (1,220 miles). The major part of the route was from Tijuana in Mexico to the southern tip of the Baja desert in California, and to avoid the heat they had to ride much of the time at night. In order to be chosen for the trip, the riders had to show significant improvements at their studies and go on crash courses in motorcycle maintenance and first aid. Each of them also had to raise £500 to finance the journey.

Some countries or companies run national schemes for motorcycles and young people. One of these was the BP oil company's 'Buildabike' and 'Motorcycle clothes' competitions, announced in 1977 in Britain. Sixty schools entered the Buildabike competition and 45 the clothing project. Both competitions were over a period of two years, and the judging took place in May 1979. The idea of the scheme was to construct motorcycles and clothing for the 1980s, thus cultivating the designers and engineers of the future as well as the riders. The winning entry for the Buildabike contest stood to gain a £4,500 minibus, two mopeds and a trophy, and there was £250 for the winners of the clothing project.

Youngsters whose parents will not allow them to own a motorcycle until they 'come of age', can nevertheless become involved in sporting events in some countries by acting as marshals.

Types of bike

American youngsters probably have the widest selection of machinery from which to choose. In 1973 a magazine market survey listed 48 minibikes and 28 of the slightly larger, more competition-orientated minicycles. When the American National Minicycle Association held its 1978 Grand National Championship at Ponca City, Oklahoma, nearly 60 races had to be run to cater for the great number of boys and girls taking part.

In European schools where motorcycle and roadcraft tuition is given, mostly mopeds are used because it is this type of two-wheel vehicle which the new licence holder is most likely to have at first. Britain operates a schools scheme called STEP, the Schools Traffic Education Programme, and mopeds are used for this. In France, the land of the moped, and Holland, laws governing mopeds are almost non-existent and riders as young as 13 or so are allowed to ride them. In Guernsey in the Channel Islands, people between the ages of 14 and 16 can ride machines up to 100cc, and are the envy of their mainland contemporaries.

Those whose parents cannot afford to buy a reasonable bike usually turn to a 'field bike', that is, an old road bike or similar, no longer fit for its original purpose but still in working order. Such 'bangers' can give hours of fun and teach their owners about motorcycle maintenance as well.

Even though dealers' showrooms are full of brand-new models, many parents still prefer the challenge of making a 'special' for their son or daughter. Some are extremely well constructed. Probably the best place to see such machines is in paddocks at race meetings. Scaled-down replicas of father's bike can be seen at road races, drag meetings, trials events and at other gatherings of motorcyclists. One such special attracted attention at the 1976 Isle of Man TT. Carl Webb, from Surrey, England, then ten years old, was piloting a mini road-race sidecar outfit with his seven-year old sister Kelly as the passenger. A 50cc Honda engine in a monocoque chassis powered the three-wheeler, which even had a steering damper. The racing screen was from a fairing once belonging to British international solo road-race star Steve Parrish. The children wore extra small full-face helmets and road-race style leathers. A similar type of mini road-race outfit was actually tried out on a road-race track, when six-year-old Gary Crane forsook a passenger to ride round Carnaby in Yorkshire, England, and was reported to have lapped at 96kph (60mph).

In examining the interest in present-day youth motorcycling, it is worth remembering that the passion for motorcycling has existed in young people ever since the first powered two-wheeler was seen on the road. One of Britain's best-known motorcycle dealers, Len Vale-Onslow, could not wait to become mobile, and in 1908, when he was eight years old, he took to the highway on his father's motorcycle. Of course, it was his father who had to pay the fine for letting him loose on the public road when the law caught up with him!

Motorcycles of the two World Wars

Motorcycles played an important rôle in both world wars, but more through improvisation than planning. On neither occasion were there sufficient motorcycles available when war was declared, and ordinary civilian machines had to be pressed into service.

In 1914 motorcycling had not yet become an activity of the masses; it was still the preserve of professional men such as doctors and solicitors, and self-employed artisans. It was fortunate that, in Britain, such men were among the first to volunteer for military service. Many were already members of Territorial Army volunteer units, and the forces could accept them and their machines as well. This was the way in which the army acquired enough motorcyclists for scouting and despatch riding duties in the early days of the First World War, for there were no special military motorcycles at all at first.

It is doubtful if the cavalry-minded senior officers of the day had really thought about employing motorcyclists in an important rôle, but with radio in its infancy and too bulky and fragile for field work, and telephone lines vulnerable to shelling, the soldiers at the front soon came to rely on runners, pigeons, and motorcycle despatch riders for communication purposes.

Not all the motorcycles of the day were suitable for war work and contemporary two-stroke lightweights were certainly not up to the rigours of the front. This may be the reason for the War Office's later distaste for two-strokes. However, two makes of machine quite dissimilar in design soon demonstrated an outstanding capability for such work. One, the medium sized horizontally-opposed twin Douglas, was the product of the vision of an engineer named Barter and the manufacturing know-how of a Bristol producer of boot-making machinery named Douglas. The other was a simple, rather conservative type of single-cylinder machine from Coventry, bearing the somewhat suitable name of Triumph. Both machines had been in production for about five years and so were well tried. Fortunately, they both came from manufacturers with the production capacity needed as well as determination to win the war (even though the two heads of the Triumph concern were of German origin; the founder of the company, Siegfried Bettman, who had

come to Britain to seek his fortune as a young man, was Mayor of Coventry at the time).

The production Triumph of 1914 had belt drive like most machines of the day and relied for clutch and gears on a mechanism built into the rear hub, as is still featured on pedal cycles. However, an improved model, with a countershaft gear box and clutch, though still with belt drive, was on the way. This model, which bore the type mark 'H', came into use in 1915. The Douglas changed little during the war, apart from the enforced substitution of British or American magnetos for the then unobtainable German Bosch magneto.

It is said that First World War despatch riders arranged No Man's Land swaps of British tyres, which were considered the best, for the prized Bosch magnetos. Some 30,000 Triumph singles and 25,000 Douglas twins went into service between 1914 and 1918. They were virtually the only solos used, although the Royal Flying Corps chose the rather sophisticated P & M machine with chain drive for solo and sidecar use on and around airfields. The spirit of adventure and the desire to be 'lone wolf', which prompted men to volunteer

as motorcyclists, also persuaded many to change over to the Royal Flying Corps, and the first pilots were nearly all ex-motorcyclists.

It was inevitable that, with its reliability demonstrated, the motorcycle should, with sidecar attached, be tried in a combat rôle. Other manufacturers therefore came on the scene with sidecar outfits adapted to carry a machine-gun and crew. One such machine was the Clyno, a V-twin, and another was the much more unlikely twin-cylinder, water-cooled two-stroke Scott, which performed particularly well in the Middle East.

Following this success, its designer Alfred Scott, perhaps the most originative of all motorcycle designers, produced a more scientific machine-gun carriage with the wheel layout of a sidecar, but a mechanical layout more like that of a motor-car. Unfortunately, the British War Office thought it too revolutionary.

Crude though the motorcycle was at that time, it performed extremely well during the First World War, and the skill and bravery of the riders became legendary. It is therefore all the more remarkable that little was done to develop the motorcycle for military use between the wars.

This restored Douglas machine is the type which was used by despatch riders in the First World War.

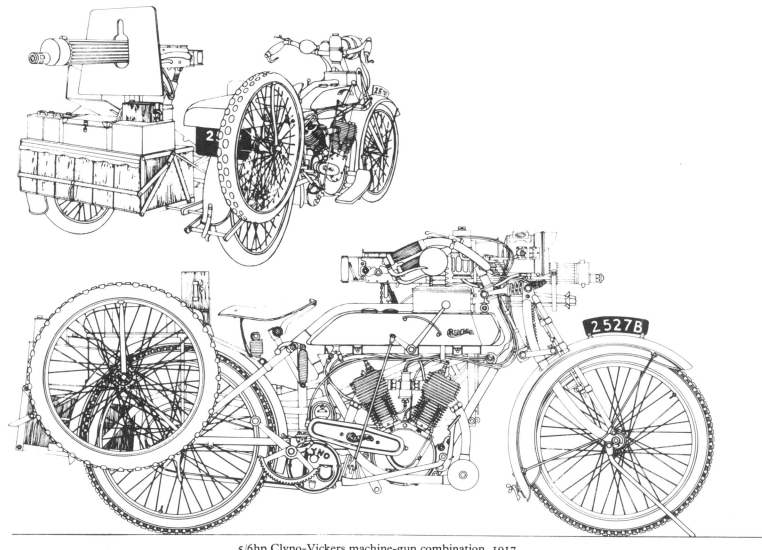

5/6hp Clyno-Vickers machine-gun combination, 1917.

Once hostilities were over, the motorcycle was no longer considered important. Money of course was short in this period of slump and depression, and the desire for disarmament was strong. A few Douglas and Triumph machines of later type (now with all chain transmission) were purchased in the late 1920s but, with plenty of time for the mock battles of Aldershot, the rôle of the despatch rider declined. Telephone lines could now be laid and pigeons of course were still available, and were cheaper. A few experiments were made, sometimes at the suggestion of motorcycle manufacturers, and sometimes as the result of a War Department idea, usually with a view to improving the cross-country ability of a single-track machine (but the caterpillar-track model that was tried out could hardly have been called a motorcycle). Curiously enough, the German Army developed a cross-country machine along similar lines for the Second World War, but it had two rear tracks and a single front wheel of motorcycle type.

In the early 1930s the British War Department did begin to approach the problem of what an army motorcycle should be like, and the resulting machine, a 500cc overhead-valve V-twin, was de-signed and built by BSA (the Birmingham Small Arms Company) which, in the absence of many orders for guns, was expanding its motorcycle production. As one might expect from a machine designed by a committee, the official WD model was too heavy, too complicated and too expensive to appeal to people wanting a machine for general use, and did not sell well when offered to the public.

By 1937, however, it had become apparent that war with Germany was highly likely, and British War Office officials had secret discussions with the larger manufacturers about the possibilities of producing a large number of motorcycles at short notice. The manufacturers made it clear that the only way to do this would be to base military machines on well-tried civilian models already in production. Thus, all the insubstantial ideas about ideal military machines were abandoned and two tried and trusted heavy-duty bikes, both with long histories going back to before the First World War, were chosen, the 500cc BSA M20 and the 500cc Norton 16H. Norton Motors therefore received an order for a considerable number of machines. (The final decision by the War Office was made, Norton say, after some of the Army 'top brass' had been on the Isle of Man to see yet another sweeping victory by Norton machines in the TT races.) BSA, being in the gun business as well, were asked if they could make War Office machines and stock-pile them until the WO could afford them. (As it happened of course, it was not long before they were wanted and the War Office could buy them.)

In the 1930s there were a few men in authority who believed in motorcycles and, when Germany began to demonstrate its muscle by entering motor and motorcycle competitions with highly trained army teams, British army teams also began to be entered for such events. For the prestigious International Six Days Trials they were coached by competition experts from the motorcycle factories, and issued with more suitable machines. In 1938 a British Army team on BSA machines won the award for the best British team. Coincidence or not, the substantial order for WO BSA machines was received soon after this success.

At Plumstead in South London the old Matchless Company, now renamed Associated Motorcycles (having absorbed the companies of AJS and Sunbeam) was

The Royal Flying Corps, later to become the RAF, chose P & M motorcycles. Many, like this one, had sidecars for local transport duties. At this time the P & M (made in Cleckheaton, Yorkshire, until the late '60s) was one of the few machines with a chain drive.

prepared to make khaki-finish, slightly detuned versions of their popular 350cc overhead-valve machine and did so with speed when the order was received. This Matchless machine was a light and lively sports model and therefore hardly the type the War Office would have chosen, but it was this or nothing as AMC had no 500cc side-valve in large production. In the event the OHV engine proved more reliable in service than the side-valves which had overheating problems. In fact the Matchless was extremely popular with war-time motorcyclists, particularly when, a year after the beginning of the Second World War, it was refined and improved to make it even more like a competition machine. It was fitted with the then revolutionary telescopic forks, which had only been seen before on the supercharged BMW machines which, in the TT of June 1939, had relegated the once invincible Nortons to third place.

The German army had been demonstrating its interest in motorcycles for several years, both in exercises and in competitions which were used as a training ground. It was clear that for communication purposes they would rely on despatch riders. They favoured small two-strokes but had also developed some very sophisticated and powerful sidecar machines with a drive to the sidecar wheel, twin-cylinder engines, and special gears for cross-country work. These were most suitable for a fighting rôle when equipped with machine guns and, as was soon demonstrated in the thrust through Belgium and France, were the cavalry of the new warfare. The significance of these adaptable machines was not lost on British military observers, and in the late 1930s manufacturers were asked to submit prototypes of sidecar-wheel drive machines. Norton was in a good position to do this,

because Dennis Mansell, son of the managing director, had already been demonstrating a sidecar-wheel drive Norton in reliability trials for several years. A military model with a jumbo version of the 16H engine was soon available, tested, and approved. Again this type of fighting outfit proved its worth in the Middle East, though its position in the invasion of the European continent was usurped by the introduction of the American Jeep. It was not that the Jeep performed much better over the rough terrain (despite its four-wheel drive) but it was easy to drive; anyone who could drive a car could handle it. Only with considerable training could a solo motorcyclist manage a sidecar outfit and some riders never mastered the art. The German army came to the same conclusion and gradually replaced their BMW and Zundapp outfits with modified 'people cars', forerunners of the Volkswagen 'Beetle'.

Despite all the preparations for war, Britain still went into battle with a scratch collection of motorcycles. There were a few WO Nortons that had been issued to regular and territorial reserve units before hostilities began but not enough for an expanding army, and once again the War Office had to fall back on volunteer riders and compulsory purchase civilian machines. Medium-weight machines of many makes and colours were seized by War Office buyers at factories and dealers' shops, and prepared for military service by being sprayed khaki all over, tyres and all. This time volunteer motorcyclists could not take their machines into the army with them (but their preparation for service was in many cases no less summary than that of the machines). 'No two-strokes' was the rule, which was only relaxed later when paratroopers required ultra-light machines for drop trans-

port and there were no four-strokes small enough in production. The impressed machines were used as a stop-gap until WO machine production caught up with demand. Great numbers of the pre-war machines had to be abandoned in the flight from Dunkirk, many civilian models among them.

A significant contribution to the motor-cycle scene during the Second World War was made by the two British weekly motorcycle magazines. Between them they had tremendous influence over civilian motorcycles and motorcycle manufacturers, and together they offered to organize the recruitment of experienced motorcyclists. These were mostly clubmen who already possessed most of the skills an army motorcyclist would require. The War Office were only too pleased to accept the offer, and tens of thousands of motorcyclists were recruited in this way. Sometimes the scheme worked too well; despatch riders would often arrive before units knew anything about the scheme.

The editors of the weeklies then established a training system based on civilian trials techniques and technical articles on the maintenance of WO machines, saving the War Office a great deal of work. But their greatest achievement was to shame the War Office into finally buying new civilian-type waterproof motorcycle coats, leather knee boots and safety helmets. Second World War motorcyclists had been sent into action wearing First World War clothing, which consisted of a short coat and slip-over leggings which were about as waterproof as brown paper, which they resembled in colour.

Once motorcycle production caught up with demand the combat units were issued with Matchless, Norton or BSA machines, but support and supply formations were still provided with various makes from the smaller manufacturers. These machines were all slightly modified, utility-finished

This Harley-Davidson rider was the first American in Germany in the First World War.

Carrier pigeons were used for carrying messages during the Second World War. Here a Royal Signals Despatch Rider, distinguished by his blue and white arm band, is handing over a message to be carried by the pigeon. The motorcycle is the M20 model BSA, of which more than 120,000 were supplied to the Forces.

versions of civilian machines. Royal Enfield, whose sales slogan was 'Made like a Gun', made side and overhead-valve models, the first usually issued to women in the ATS, WRNS or WRAF. Velocette made a few greatly sought-after 350cc overhead-valve models before they were put on precision work for the Navy, on one hand, and enamelling tin hits on the other.

The RAF acquired some of these Velocettes but still had in use some of the V-twin BSAs made in the early 1930s. Another sought-after 350cc machine was the overhead-valve Ariel which was virtually a pre-war trials model in disguise; and considerable quantities were produced. The flat-twin Douglas entered the war again but not as a motorcycle this time: only the engine was used, to power generators.

The most unfortunate motorcycle story of the war was that of Triumph. Though the War Office ideal of a machine weighing no more than 113kg (250lb) but with a maximum speed of 105kph (65mph) had been abandoned when it became clear that it would have to be production machines or nothing, Edward Turner of Triumph

had not forgotten. If there had been a motorcycle show in the autumn of 1939, he would have surprised everyone by showing a neat overhead-valve 350cc twin, a smaller version of his successful Speed Twin. Using its almost silent engine as a base, he produced the neatest, nippiest, lightest 350 there has ever been. If you imagine a post-war 350 twin Triumph engine in the rolling chassis of the single-cylinder Tiger Cub 199cc machine, you will have some idea of what the Triumph WO model was to have been. The War Office people were delighted and gave Triumph the go-ahead. But, as the first batch was ready for delivery, the factory was completely destroyed in the Luftwaffe blitz on Coventry. When Triumph struggled back into production in a temporary factory, the only jigs left were for the pre-war 350 side and overhead-valve models.

Total production of British military motorcycles for the Second World War is estimated at 400,000 machines, of which BSA manufactured more than 120,000 and Norton more than 100,000. Motorcycles played a much greater part in this war than in the First World War: between 1914–18 most riders were despatch riders, where-

as between 1940–44 the motorcyclist was widely employed to assist in escorting convoys. For every Royal Signals despatch rider, distinguished by his blue and white armband, there might be half a dozen motorcyclists from other units doing the wide range of other jobs essential to the maintenance and movement of the enormous number of men and machines involved in a campaign. Military policemen were now using motorcycles, as were infantry officers and chaplains.

One of the toughest jobs for a motorcyclist was escorting a convoy of heavy vehicles. Two or three riders would have to take turns to squeeze past a line of tanks or lorries on roads lined with ruts and holes (or no road at all), to get to a crossroads or a hazard ahead, see the convoy through safely, and then catch up and take turns in going ahead again. This was extremely dangerous work, where only long experience of rough riding could offer a chance of survival.

By contrast, the life of a Royal Signals DR was a lonely one: he worked entirely on his own. From the moment the despatch rider set off from the Signal Office with a map reference for a destination (which was often wrong), the question of when, if ever, the message would get through was up to his skill, determination and courage. During the Second World War, the dangers ahead of a DR were not so much the chance of a sniper or a wire stretched across the road—though these things could happen—but the danger of being run down or run into by one of the thousands of other vehicles on the overcrowded roads and tracks. Despite the tremendous advances that had been made in signals techniques, radio, teleprinter and underground and overhead telephone lines, in certain circumstances a DR was indispensable as the only means by which a message could get through.

The DR was probably someone who had volunteered for the job because he was a motorcycle enthusiast and felt that there was one job in the army that he could do and enjoy doing. And the bike he was on, though not perhaps the ideal bike for wartime riding, was at least a type he was used to and not unlike the bike he had left behind. In the field the DR had to be a capable and resourceful mechanic who could cope with a breakdown on his own. In both wars elaborate workshop systems were established in base areas, but their function was to rebuild seriously damaged machines so as to keep up the supply of replacements. Punctures and other minor ailments which beset the motorcycle invariably occurred far away from workshops.

It is difficult to compare the lives of military motorcyclists in the two wars, but self-reliance was a characteristic common

During the Second World War, 100,000 Norton 16H (shown here) were made. The Norton, which was chief rival to the BSA, could withstand tremendous punishment. A heavier model, with the engine capacity increased from 490cc to 633cc, was built in small numbers for use with sidecars.

to both. An advantage enjoyed by a rider during the First World War was that if the terrain became very bad he could pick up his machine and carry it. The Douglas was often preferred for this reason: it was so docile that it could be 'walked' through deep mud with its engine just ticking over and the rider walking alongside. This would have been difficult, if not impossible, with a machine of the Second World War, which weighed twice as much, and was much more powerful. In the first War the despatch rider was operating over smaller distances and was mostly at risk from shot and shell, whereas in the second War the greater risk was from fast-moving heavy transport. In the later stages of the advance to the Rhine, the danger from such vehicles was so acute and the mass of 'postal' traffic so great that the majority of Signals DRs were switched from motorcycles to Jeeps.

The German army's preference for small two-strokes and large sidecar models has already been mentioned. As expected the Americans used their traditional V-twin Harley Davidsons and Indians, slightly modified versions of civilian machines. The 500cc Indian was a particularly pleasant machine for main roads and was often issued to British Civil Defence riders, firemen and police under lease-lend arrangements. The 750cc Harley looked ungainly with its footboards and windscreen, but had good cross-country performance in the hands of an experienced rider. The Italian army opted for special heavyweight versions of their native Moto Guzzi and Gilera machines, as well as many small civilian machines impressed for the duration of the war. The Guzzi and Gilera military models both had elaborate arrangements for carrying pillion riders, who were normally officers, and a

ready means of seat adjustment for their weight was provided. The result was an exceedingly ungainly, top-heavy machine.

In Britain, the War Office ideal of a standardized military machine, instead of a variety of models and makes, persisted despite the desperate situation. By 1942 specifications had been altered slightly to permit a weight of 136kg (300lb) for a performance of 96–113kph (60–70mph) and 30km per litre (80mpg) at 48kph (30mph), to be inaudible at a 1km (0.6 mile) range. Both BSA and Triumph made prototype 500cc side-valve twins, the Triumph having the most sensible feature of a totally enclosed rear chain. Douglas and Royal Enfield also made prototypes, the former mounting a horizontally-opposed twin across the frame, like the German BMW.

Purchase of British war equipment eventually became the responsibility of the Ministry of Supply which persisted with the idea of a standard machine till as late as 1946. Triumph had updated its wartime prototype but the MOS now found it was too costly, so Triumph compromised by producing a machine using the WO-type engine but with cycle parts taken from their production civilian range, with a considerable reduction in cost. Even so, only a handful were purchased for the army, which had more old-style machines than it could use, but considerable quantities were sold to other countries, (although some were bought for the RAF and Marines).

When the war ended, the vast stocks of British military motorcycles, both in Britain and overseas, posed a problem. Many lay in open-air dumps until the public, starved of personal transport, protested. The MOS then sold them by auction but, in view of the quantities, it was inevitable that they were sold in lots and bought by motorcycle dealers who resold the good ones and rebuilt the less good. Royal Enfield rebuilt some of its own military models in civilian colours, but most ex-WO machines were given a quick respray in black or maroon and sold cheaply. With few new machines available they filled a long-felt need.

Today, the British Ministry of Defence is in no position to initiate the design and production of special machines. The last all-British military model was a 350cc BSA evolved from a civilian machine, and with the collapse of the BSA company in 1973 that supply came to an end. The latest machine supplied to the British forces is a composite machine of Canadian origin with an Austrian engine—and a two-stroke at that!

Sub-machine guns at the ready, these motorcycle scouts on their Harley-Davidson WLAs were a part of the Army Armoured Division during the Second World War.

Trials
and
Enduros

BEING in the right gear, at the right place, at the right moment, with ultra-sensitive use of the throttle to control engine speed, is probably the secret of successful motorcycling. Add a cat-like sixth sense of balance, and it is possible to understand the finesse required to become a champion trials rider.

Observed-trials riding is the slowest and therefore the safest of all motorcycle sports. Speed is not the deciding factor in these events: total machine control and concentration are the skills required to climb slippery slopes, to traverse rocks, boulders, and tree roots, and to negotiate rushing streams.

A typical one-day observed trial is run over a course approximately 48 km (30 miles) long, divided into 12 or more sections. Each section will usually have three or more 'observed' sub-sections where marshals keep a close watch on each competitor as he passes through a marked-out course. Should the rider have to put a steadying foot to the ground, he is penalized one mark. If he has to 'foot' or assist the motorcycle through the section by using feet and legs while still in the saddle, he is penalized three marks. The maximum penalty is five marks, and this is scored if the motorcycle ceases forward motion, or goes off course and fails to complete the section.

At the end of the trial, all the marshals' cards are collected and the scores of each competitor totted up. The rider who has lost the least number of marks is the winner of the trial. If there is a draw, then the rider who has completed most sections 'clean' (without penalty) is the winner.

The big-money international trials scene of today is a comparatively recent development. Until the 1960s, it was very much an amateur sport with no prize or bonus money, just a pewter mug or some other trophy awarded to the winners.

Machines ridden in the early days were basically roadster motorcycles equipped with knobbly tyres for extra grip in the muddy off-road conditions. After World War II and for many years, the most prestigious event was the Scottish Six Days Trial, in which competitors would set off each day to tackle different routes and sections in the highlands of Scotland. The motorcycle manufacturers supported the event because of the prestige of being involved and possibly winning. Outstanding riders of the day usually received works support, not only in the provision of factory-prepared machines but also, in many cases, in the offer of a job in the

PREVIOUS PAGE A Yamaha IT465 two-stroke making light work of a steep incline on one of the many American enduros held throughout the year.

RIGHT The Scottish Six Days Trial attracts an international entry. Here Yrjo Vesterinen, three times World Trials Champion, negotiates a rocky stream on his Bultaco, under the critical eye of another competitor.

BELOW Rocks, mud, even fast-flowing streams have to be negotiated in the cause of 'mudplugging'. Martin Lampkin (Bultaco) takes to the water in the St David's Trial.

Purpose-Built Machines

The first dent in the armour of the British four-stroke, single-cylinder trials bikes came in the late 1950s when Greeves (a tiny company in Essex which until then had manufactured invalid carriages) and the DOT motorcycle company (which, by contrast, had had considerable experience of TT racing before the war) produced lightweight two-stroke, purpose-built trials motorcycles. Although they had to use proprietary Villiers motors which were not entirely suited to trials riding, Greeves had a number of successes, with Don Smith aboard one of their two-stroke motorcycles, which should have made the other British manufacturers sit up and take notice.

Then, in 1961, Sammy Miller, who had reigned supreme in trials riding his legendary Ariel 500 cc single-cylinder four-stroke, GOV 132, left the BSA-owned company to design a trials bike for a small Spanish motorcycle company, Bultaco. Using the established Bultaco 250 cc single-cylinder, two-stroke motor, he designed and built the Bultaco Sherpa, a revolutionary machine which was to set the trend for all future trials-bike designs. Almost immediately established design thinking was swept aside and the lighter, easy-to-control two-stroke superseded the heavy and often cumbersome British four-stroke. Demonstration tours of the United States by Sammy Miller and Don Smith increased interest in the sport, and within a few years it had swept Europe and was making inroads into traditional American motorcycle sports.

Surprisingly, it was not until 1966 that the controlling body of international motorcycle sport, the FIM, almost condescendingly agreed to grant championship status to a series of European events. The winner of the first European Trials Championship was Don Smith on his works' Greeves, with Sammy Miller winning for Bultaco in 1968. Smith left Greeves to join another Spanish company, Montesa, to design and build a two-stroke for them, and it was aboard this that he recaptured the title from Miller in 1969. Miller regained it in 1970, and in 1971 and 1972 a first double was achieved by yet another Spanish motorcycle company, OSSA, with Mick Andrews riding the bike he had designed himself.

In 1975 the FIM finally submitted to mounting pressure and announced that the event would be given world championship status. At long last trials riding had earned the credit it deserved and the top riders were in the big-money league. Continental (notably Scandinavian) and Japanese riders have joined the fray and it is now the Spanish and Japanese two-strokes which dominate the sport.

Six Days of Speed

If you think mudplugging or trials riding is too tame and moto-cross lacks finesse, then what about time trials or *enduros*, as they are called in the United States?

Competitors in time trials set off at one-minute intervals and pace themselves against the clock to average a set speed over a section of road and rough track to reach a checkpoint on time. Every minute late means points lost and the winner is the competitor who arrives at the finish with the least penalty points. The riders are expected to cover sections of anything up to 320 km (200 miles) a day on the road and across some of the toughest and most rugged countryside that can be found.

No outside assistance may be given and running repairs have to be made at the roadside from equipment carried on the bike or on the rider. This means that not only does the rider have to have the stamina of a moto-cross competitor but he must also be a first-class mechanic.

One of the oldest of time trials and an event which still carries tremendous international prestige is the International Six Days Trial. It was first held in Britain in 1913, with the idea of proving to the world that motorcycles were a reliable means of transport and also to encourage manufacturers to build into their machines the necessary stamina and durability to last six days of endurance riding. The routes chosen were not nearly as arduous as those used today, but one has to remember that the motorcycles used then were still basically the roadster models of the day.

Member countries of the FIM entered teams of riders for the ISDT to compete for the International Trophy, and the most important stipulation was that the teams must ride motorcycles manufactured in their own country. This created problems for some countries with only a small motorcycle industry and, in 1924, the Silver Vase Trophy was established as a second award for national teams of three riders entered on foreign-made machines.

Each year a different country hosts the ISDT and to win either the Trophy or Silver Vase is a serious matter of national prestige. In the 1930s there were some tremendous struggles between the British and German teams. Then, after World War II, the British manufacturers had to contend with a strong challenge from Czechoslovakia; and, as ISDT motorcycles became more and more specialized, domination of the sport moved to the West Germans, East Germans, and Czechs. Most riders from the Iron Curtain countries are members of service or factory teams; they ride their motorcycles every day and know every nut and bolt on them. This, and the fact that their countries organize far more enduro events, has made the

Czech and East German teams almost invincible. The only major enduro-type event now held in Britain is the Welsh Two Days Trial and it is from the results of this that the British team is usually selected.

The ISDT is now similar to a six-day moto-cross event. That the men and the machines can stand the pace is incredible. Competitors are allowed only 10 minutes per day to maintain the machines, plus whatever time can be stolen by riders gaining a few minutes on the very tight time schedules. Makeshift repairs to bikes to keep them going are often ingenious: broken frames lashed together with chains strapped round tyre levers, exhaust systems tied on with wire, broken throttles set wide open with speed being controlled by the ignition switch or 'kill' button; anything goes to get the bike to the final checkpoint of the day. At night the machines are locked away in an enclosure called a *parque fermé* and closely guarded to ensure that no one tampers with them, and then the following morning they are wheeled out by the competitors, and they must start within a specified time or points are lost by the riders concerned.

As it is a team event, any one competitor can be responsible for his team's downfall. Consequently, there have been cases of unbelievable courage and bravery by individuals riding with broken fingers, smashed toes, or torn muscles, purely to keep their team in the running for an award. In many cases only pain-killing injections have enabled them to continue.

Enduro riding is probably the toughest motorcycle sport ever devised by man. And it is a sport where only the fittest men and machines survive.

LEFT Not all sections of the SDTs are located in the wilderness, as Rob Edwards demonstrates while easing his Montesa over a mound of concrete in the Scottish event. Edwards, a works rider for the Spanish factory, is one of the elite group who ride successfully as full-time professional trialsters.

165

LEFT Mick Andrews helped develop the Spanish OSSA trials motorcycle—becoming European Trials Champion in the process. He later transferred his allegiance to the Japanese Yamaha factory and gave them their first victory in the Scottish Six Days Trial. Here he rides a works 400 cc Yamaha in the 1977 World Trial.

BELOW Ulf Karlson, of Sweden, demonstrates the delicate art of 'rock-climbing' while maintaining perfect control over his Montesa.

RIGHT Suzuki was late to enter the
international trials scene, but Graham
Beamish, a British importer of Suzuki trials
machines, soon fielded a strong team of young
riders. Here Alan Wright competes in the 1977
World Trial aboard his 325 cc two-stroke
Suzuki.

MOTO-CROSS

Moto-cross or *scrambling*, as it used to be called, is one of the most spectacular sports to watch and calls for tremendous physical fitness and stamina from the riders and outstanding strength and reliability from the motorcycles. The sport as it is today is a far cry from its origins, when almost standard roadsters were raced over scrubland circuits.

The first recorded scramble took place in the early 1920s, when a Harley-Davidson ridden by A. B. Sparks won a two-leg race over a 48 km (30 miles) course at Camberley in Surrey. The usual procedure in those early days was for enthusiasts to ride to the race venue and then to lighten the weight of their machines by stripping them of components such as lights, mudguards, and anything else superfluous to the needs of the race. The motorcycles had little in the way of suspension to protect the rider from the ruts and bumps on the course. After one lap of the testing off-road circuit, competitors would relax for lunch, carry out any repairs needed, and then tackle the circuit a second time to decide the overall winner. The results of the scramble were decided on the positions achieved in both legs of the event, with time being the deciding factor in the case of a tie. Much the same system of scoring is used in present-day moto-cross.

Although scrambling continued to develop in Britain, with circuits becoming shorter and manufacturers taking an increasing interest in the sport and slightly

LEFT Only the hardy need apply. Typical motocross action from a special event held at Daytona International Speedway. At the first corner, Yamaha No 4 has fallen and the rest of the bunch have to find their way around.

modifying their roadster designs, it was in France and Belgium in the 1950s that the boom took place. (It was there that the term *moto-cros* was coined. The name soon caught on in Britain and replaced our own, more picturesque term.)

The Continentals saw a future in this exciting off-road sport and established permanent rough-riding circuits about 2 km long with excellent spectator facilities. By the mid-1950s important meetings were attracting anything up to 50,000 spectators. As the crowds paying to see the sport continued to grow, so more prize money could be paid to winning riders, which in turn made the sport more fiercely competitive.

The works-sponsored riders of the 1950s rode giant 500 cc, four-stroke, single-cylinder motorcycles weighing up to 136 kg (300 lb). In spite of being fitted with telescopic front forks and swinging-arm rear suspension, they offered very limited movement of suspension to damp out the ruts and bumps of the circuits. Until the early 1960s the Matchless, AJS, BSA, and Norton bikes, plus Husqvarna

from Sweden and FN from Belgium, reigned supreme in the 500 cc class. Even experienced riders had often to fight for control over these powerful but unwieldy machines.

The breakthrough in moto-cross, as in trials, came with the development of a new generation of two-stroke machines, which set the circuits alight with their remarkable handling and speed. Until this time, small-capacity bikes had been under-powered, over-weight, and considered more suitable for beginners; but this new breed of 250 cc two-strokes from Greeves of Britain, CZ of Czechoslovakia, and Husqvarna was so fast and yet controllable that many competitors began entering the senior racing classes on their lightweight machines—and quite a few of them beat the 500 cc racers.

The FIM then ruled that the lightweight machines must remain in their capacity class; but with the trend toward smaller motors already established, the manufacturers of the two-stroke machines simply brought out designs of over 350 cc, which allowed them to compete in the senior

events. The impact on the sport was dramatic. In a matter of two seasons, the entire scene changed: of the older British manufacturers' machines, the Matchless, AJS, and Norton four-strokes became obsolete and only the BSA bikes remained to dispute two-stroke dominance.

BSA were fortunate in having the services of two superb development riders: Britain's one and only world moto-cross champion, Jeff Smith, and Vic Eastwood, who had left the AJS team to join BSA. Eastwood had realized that the BSA unit-construction 500 cc, which was reasonably light with a good power-to-weight ratio, was the only remaining competitive four-stroke among British bikes. In fact, when BSA discontinued their moto-cross team at the end of the 1960s, the unit-construction 500 cc four-stroke design was taken up by Alan Clews, who continued development of the machine under the CCM banner and has since enjoyed a fairly reasonable run of success.

There are still many who believe that, with continued development, there could have been four-stroke moto-cross machines

LEFT The tension mounts as riders wait for the starting barrier to drop. The first rider into the first corner has the advantage, as his rear tyre sprays dirt, mud, or stones into the faces of the pack behind. Note the striking similarities of frame and suspension in these machines: more than half a dozen different makes are visible in the picture.

BELOW Vic Allan aboard a CCM four-stroke, the only remaining all-British moto-cross machine capable of offering a challenge to Japanese and Continental makes. Although in 1976 he and Vic Eastwood seemed likely to form the basis of an excellent CCM team, Allan was later lured back to the Bultaco works team.

equal in performance to any of the current two-stroke models, and some experts consider that the torque and flexibility of the large-capacity four-stroke are potentially much more suited to scrambling than are the high-revving two-stroke designs. This has yet to be proved. Meanwhile, what cannot be disputed is that the development of the two-stroke moto-crosser not only increased the popularity of the sport but brought similar machines within the price range of thousands of enthusiasts. The manufacturers built not only the works competition machines, but also replicas for sale to the general public. The result was that, by the mid-1960s, moto-cross was growing more rapidly than any other sport in Europe. Practically every manufacturer of two-strokes on the Continent saw moto-cross as an outlet for their machines. Montesa, Bultaco, and OSSA of Spain, Maico of Germany, and Puch and KTM of Austria joined the established Husqvarna and CZ companies in the fierce struggle for supremacy in the Continental moto-cross scene.

LEFT Even on relatively smooth surfaces, moto-cross machines spend almost as much time in the air as on the ground. Here, at a German moto-cross, a rider crests the brow of a hill and plunges from bright sunshine into the dark of a wood.

NEAR RIGHT Front wheel up, Roger DeCoster negotiates a relatively easy section in the 1977 British 500 cc Moto-Cross Grand Prix aboard his 376 cc, single-cylinder, two-stroke Suzuki. The Japanese factory hired DeCoster and his fellow-Belgian Joel Robert to help develop their world-championship-winning machines. The pair provided the most formidably gifted spearhead of any of the works teams.

FAR RIGHT From modest and informal beginnings in Britain, moto-cross has developed into an international sport that attracts crowds of over 50,000 to major Continental events. Its cosmopolitan flavour is symbolized in this picture of the Russian ace Gennady Moisseev, winner of the World 250 cc Moto-Cross Championship for the Austrian KTM factory in 1978 and 1979.

BELOW Like a herd of stampeding cattle, the riders hurtle away at the start of the 1977 Spanish Moto-Cross Grand Prix. With the field as closely bunched as this, the inevitable scrimmage at the first corner becomes a major test of nerve and skill.

The Japanese Intervene

This tremendous enthusiasm spread from Europe to the United States, and, with over-the-counter works replicas available, the American market soon boomed. At this point the Japanese manufacturers, who by now were completely dominating the road-racing scene but who had hitherto ignored the potential of off-road runners, realised that here too was a vast market to be exploited. Once more, their intervention was to prove decisive.

Suzuki was the first to plunge headlong into a moto-cross development programme by buying the services of the best available riders, namely world champions Roger De-Coster and Joel Robert. In an enormously expensive crash-development programme, Suzuki designed and built, with the advice and assistance of Joel Robert, a grand-prix moto-cross motorcycle weighing a mere 72.5 kg (160 lb). In one of the most astonishing examples of rapid success flowing from high capital investment allied to engineering knowhow, Suzuki won the World 250 cc Moto-cross Championship at its first attempt. It also captured the title the following two seasons, and then moved into the 500 cc moto-cross scene with DeCoster as its number one rider in the class; the Belgian ace did equally well in the big-bike grands prix.

The Japanese had proved yet again that enormous but carefully planned expenditure on research and development, the signing of top riders, and the use of one-off, hand-built 'titanium specials' secured results. Then, in order to bring a more competitive element back to the sport, the FIM imposed a minimum weight limit of 95 kg (210 lb), which meant that there was no advantage in building highly expensive, ultra-lightweight, titanium-framed motorcycles. Designers turned next to the problems of handling.

The 1970s saw the beginning of renewed efforts to improve frames so that the rear wheel of the bike remained in contact with the track surface no matter how severe the undulations. The result was a tremendous increase in suspension movement, or travel, which in turn brought about problems in damping out the 'bounce' factor of the suspension springs. Damping fluids reached boiling point under racing conditions and lost their effectiveness. Cooling-oil reservoirs were fitted to deal with the problem, and inert-gas suspension was tried.

Yamaha came up with a triangulated rear fork which pivoted at the rear of the main frame and was suspended on a single, very large damping unit. Suspension movement on their machines was approximately 25 cm (10 in) at both front and rear, which meant that the wheels could follow all the undulations of even the bumpiest surfaces with ease. With contact with the ground maintained at all times, the power and flexibility of the engines could be fully exploited and the machine controlled more easily by the rider. It also meant that the moto-cross rider was considerably more comfortable than ever before. Yamaha's 'monoshock' 250 cc moto-crosser was an immediate success and captured the world championship for the Swede, Hakan Andersson.

During the last five years more research has gone into suspension and frame design than into the development of the engines. The enormous significance of this research can be gathered from the fact that the present-day 125 cc moto-cross machines travel as fast as the 500 cc machines, simply because all the power they develop can be put firmly on the track at all times, whereas only part of the power from a 500 cc machine can be used effectively.

TOP LEFT Britain's Graham Noyce seen here off the deck with his West German Maico mount. It was his performances with this bike that gave him a works Honda contract in 1978 and then the 500 cc World Championship in 1979.

LEFT When Honda entered the moto-cross scene with single-cylinder two-strokes, it looked to the United States, in the shape of Brad Lackey, for its leading works rider. Lackey competes regularly in Europe, where his fearless style has made him a favourite with spectators. Here he seems to be both flying and cornering in a 1977 500 cc event at Farleigh Castle.

ABOVE While the majority of riders in moto-cross leap about on lightweight, if powerful, two-strokes, a number of riders still prefer the gutsy pulling power of the four-strokes. One such rider is Bengt Aberg of Sweden, seen here demonstrating the pace of the 500 cc, four-stroke machine he has helped Yamaha develop from the XT500 overhead-camshaft, single-cylinder trail motorcycle.

LEFT Vic Eastwood and his CCM 498 cc, both carrying their share of Berkshire mud at a 1977 moto-cross meeting at Newbury. One of the ablest British moto-crossers, Eastwood has also ridden bikes for AJS and BSA, and has vast experience as a development rider.

Sidecar Racing

The only section of the sport where the two-stroke power unit has not taken over is in sidecar-cross. Here the big twin-cylinder four-strokes continue to reign supreme. The machines are all hand-built specials that do not have a mass-market sales potential. Consequently, none of the major manufacturers has given support or contracted riders to compete on works specials. Successful riders rely on sponsorship from motorcycle dealers, who are prepared to cover costs purely for publicity value and for the enjoyment they obtain from being involved in the sport.

The big Norton Commando 850 and Yamaha 750 four-stroke engines fitted into Wasp moto-cross frames have been the most consistently successful machine in the world championship over the past few seasons. It is the latest expression of a design principle that has thrown up a variety of heavyweight raceware, including TriBSAs, TriNors, Nor-BSAs, and other combinations of powerful four-stroke twins that could be built into a moto-cross chair outfit.

Although sidecar-cross racing has failed to attract anything like the enormous investment that the major manufacturers have channelled into solo moto-cross, it is quite as exciting and skilful a sport in its own way. It is a great pity that the enthusiasm of the combination riders and their passengers, who devote so much time and skill to the sport, receives only a fraction of the rewards enjoyed by the professional solo riders.

TOURING

Probably the most exciting aspect of owning a motorcycle, apart from sharing the exhilaration and fun of riding with friends, is planning a tour. For the touring motorcyclist, the world is his oyster. He sets the pace and chooses the kind of scenery through which he travels, and he can either stick rigidly to his original plan or change his route as he goes along, for he only has himself to please. Even riders who have been touring for years say that each new tour is a fresh adventure; and the pleasure starts at the moment a touring idea is conceived, continues with the excitement of anticipation, and culminates with the feeling of unity between the rider, his machine, and the open air, as the miles roll by. Every rider who has ridden a tour comes home with tales to tell; a tour offers adventure and presents a challenge to all motorcyclists.

Unlike so many activities associated with motorcycles, touring is not a race; its aim is to enable the rider to visit previously unseen regions at a pace which can be comfortably accommodated day after day. There is no harm in setting a target distance for each day, unless it leads to disappointment if that goal is not reached; the first-time tourer should not be too ambitious. British journalist Dave Minton rode a BMW to the Norwegian Arctic Circle and back in freezing blizzards. It was an heroic ride, but one which was carefully planned after the rider had ridden a great many long-distance tours. He wanted a new challenge, to see if his riding talents could be extended along with the boundaries of his touring experience. Some riders would not regard this kind of ambitious venture as true touring, but more a test of endurance and resolve. However, the essential factor in touring is that the rider finds satisfaction in a long-distance motorcycle ride, and any beginner may aspire to the sort of journey made by Minton once he or she has discovered the measure of his or her own capabilities.

Many American riders think nothing of clocking up 1000 or 1500km (500 or 1000 miles) in a day on their vast interstate highways, listening to the stereo radios on their 'full dress' tourers. A European rider would find it exhausting even to approach a similar distance, unless it were all on motorways. Nevertheless, for some riders simply 'hitting the road' for as many hours in the day as possible is rewarding for its own sake. Stopping to observe the countryside, and for leisurely meals and conversation, are activities which play no part because, for this tourer, covering enormous distances is the sole object of the exercise, and such riders derive their pleasure simply from watching vast stretches of road roll beneath them. Most riders are not cast in this mould, but even so the problem of over-scheduling, mentioned earlier, may arise. If something catches the eye on route to a planned destination and an extra stop is made, time will be lost, and this may lead to a sense of failure if the distance planned for that day has not been travelled. Disappointment should be guarded against or it may result in dissatisfaction about the whole trip.

A whole day in the saddle, irrespective of the number of miles covered, can teach a rider a lot about himself and his bike. That 'comfortable' seat becomes distinctly uncomfortable after four solid hours, and

Average Temperatures Around the World—in degrees Centigrade [degrees Fahrenheit in brackets].											
	Jan	**Feb**	**Mar**	**Apr**	**May**	**June**	**July**	**Aug**	**Sept**	**Oct**	**Nov**	**Dec**
Amsterdam	3(37)	3(37)	5(41)	8(47)	12(55)	16(60)	18(64)	17(63)	16(60)	11(52)	6(44)	4(38)
Athens	8(48)	9(49)	11(53)	15(59)	20(69)	24(76)	27(81)	27(81)	24(75)	19(67)	14(58)	10(51)
Bangkok	25(78)	27(81)	29(84)	30(86)	29(85)	28(83)	28(83)	28(83)	28(83)	27(81)	26(79)	25(77)
Bombay	24(75)	24(75)	26(79)	28(82)	29(85)	29(84)	27(81)	27(80)	27(80)	28(82)	27(81)	25(78)
Brussels	3(37)	3(37)	5(42)	8(47)	12(55)	16(60)	17(63)	17(63)	15(59)	10(51)	5(41)	3(37)
Buenos Aires	23(73)	24(75)	21(70)	20(68)	16(61)	14(57)	10(50)	11(52)	13(55)	13(55)	17(63)	20(68)
Caracas	18(64)	18(64)	19(66)	21(70)	22(72)	21(70)	20(68)	20(68)	20(68)	21(70)	20(68)	19(66)
Copenhagen	1(33)	0(32)	2(36)	6(43)	11(53)	15(59)	17(63)	16(61)	13(56)	8(47)	3(39)	2(35)
Florence	5(42)	7(45)	10(50)	13(57)	18(64)	21(71)	25(76)	24(75)	20(69)	16(60)	10(50)	6(43)
Frankfurt	−1(30)	0(32)	4(39)	7(46)	13(55)	15(60)	18(64)	17(63)	14(57)	9(48)	4(38)	1(33)
Hong Kong	24(75)	24(75)	27(80)	27(80)	32(90)	32(90)	32(90)	32(90)	32(90)	29(85)	29(85)	27(80)
Lisbon	10(51)	11(52)	12(55)	14(58)	17(63)	19(67)	21(71)	22(72)	20(60)	17(63)	13(57)	11(52)
London	3(39)	4(40)	6(43)	8(47)	11(53)	15(59)	17(63)	16(61)	13(57)	9(49)	6(44)	5(41)
Madrid	4(40)	6(43)	9(49)	12(54)	16(61)	20(69)	24(75)	23(74)	19(67)	13(57)	8(47)	5(41)
Milan	2(35)	4(40)	8(47)	13(56)	17(63)	21(71)	23(74)	22(73)	19(67)	13(57)	7(45)	3(37)
Montreal	−11(12)	−11(12)	−4(25)	5(41)	12(54)	18(64)	20(68)	18(64)	14(58)	8(46)	0(32)	−8(18)
Moscow	−18(0)	−15(5)	−5(23)	2(36)	10(50)	16(61)	20(68)	18(64)	11(52)	5(41)	−2(28)	−10(14)
Nairobi	27(81)	27(81)	26(79)	22(72)	20(68)	18(64)	17(63)	15(59)	16(61)	18(64)	20(68)	22(72)
New York	0(32)	0(31)	4(39)	9(49)	15(60)	20(69)	23(74)	23(73)	19(67)	13(56)	7(45)	1(34)
Paris	3(37)	4(39)	6(44)	10(51)	13(57)	17(63)	18(65)	18(65)	15(59)	10(51)	6(43)	3(38)
Rio de Janeiro	30(86)	30(86)	30(86)	27(81)	26(79)	22(72)	22(72)	22(72)	24(75)	24(75)	26(79)	28(82)
Rome	8(47)	8(47)	11(52)	13(57)	18(65)	21(71)	24(76)	24(76)	22(72)	17(63)	12(55)	9(49)
Singapore	27(80)	27(80)	27(81)	28(82)	27(81)	28(82)	28(82)	27(81)	27(81)	27(81)	27(80)	27(80)
Stockholm	−3(27)	−3(27)	−1(31)	3(39)	9(49)	13(57)	17(63)	15(59)	11(52)	6(43)	2(35)	−2(29)
Sydney	21(71)	21(71)	20(69)	18(64)	15(59)	12(54)	12(53)	13(55)	15(59)	17(63)	19(67)	21(70)
Tokyo	3(38)	4(39)	6(44)	13(55)	16(62)	21(70)	25(77)	26(79)	22(72)	16(61)	11(52)	6(43)
Vienna	−1(30)	1(33)	5(41)	9(49)	14(58)	17(63)	19(67)	18(65)	15(59)	9(49)	4(40)	1(33)
Zurich	0(32)	1(33)	5(41)	8(47)	14(58)	18(64)	20(68)	18(65)	14(58)	9(49)	4(40)	0(32)

prolonged periods on a bike with minor vibration only make that problem worse as the rider begins to ache from muscles he never knew he had. After a day or two on the road some riders experience an incapacity to eat more than a few mouthfuls of food even though they feel hungry enough for a three-course meal. Mental fatigue may set in before there are 300km (200 miles) on the speedometer. A first-time tourer charts new ground in discovering such things.

If possible, talk to people who have made longer trips than yourself, to hear their opinions on points which may be troubling you. Most riders are only too pleased to pass on their experiences and hints. There is no substitute for correct preparation, and other people's advice could well contribute much to yours.

This chapter represents the cautious man's approach to touring. Riders who are ready to set off almost at the drop of a hat will wish to skip much of the prudence which follows and, happily for their riders, many of today's machines are so reliable that journeys of great distances can be accomplished without so much as a glance at the toolkit. But should the imprudent tourer require assistance it is likely that the well-prepared rider will be his saviour.

The rider who wishes to tour his home country may of course omit the paragraphs which deal with taking a bike abroad. A rider contemplating a tour may look at the matter in three main parts: planning the trip; preparing the bike; loading the bike. Each of these three parts contains many sub-headings to be considered. Much of it, however, is common sense, and the newcomer to touring will find that the sooner he makes a tour the sooner he will learn.

Planning the trip

Planning the trip involves selecting clothes and camping equipment, discovering in advance the sort of paperwork you may have to tackle, organising finances, and mapping out the route.

The Route When planning your route, obtain the most up-to-date maps. New roads, particularly by-passes for towns, are springing up all the time. Good maps will show you exactly where you are heading and allow you to make a choice at an unexpected diversion. If you wish to examine one particular area in great detail, buy Ordnance Survey maps which have scales of up to 40mm per km (2½in to the mile) and elevation points. Always buy maps which can be folded and placed in the transparent pocket of a tank bag for quick reference. They can be made more durable and water-proofed by spraying with clear varnish.

Some riders cut their large maps into strips to save unfolding them, and write the names of towns and villages which they will pass through on a separate sheet of paper. Others mark their route straight on to the map with crayon or felt-tip pen, or put the map in the tank bag flap and mark the route with a felt-tip pen on the clear plastic sleeve top. Insert the map into the tank bag flap so that the map points in the direction you are going. (Since all maps have north at the top and south at the bottom, it will be necessary to turn the map upside-down when you are travelling south, but most riders find it easier to read the names of towns upside-down and follow the road plan exactly as it is laid out before them when heading south, than suffer the constant strain of re-orientating by 180 degrees.)

For travelling long distances, fast multi-lane roads are the most expedient means. They also have the advantages of food and petrol being available 24 hours a day. Their drawbacks may include having to pay for their use, as in France, and most riders find them boring. Taking single-lane roads may slow the overall pace, but they offer a better and more enjoyable means of seeing the countryside and meeting local people. Riding in company with other motorcyclists is also likely to slow the pace because of probable extra stops.

Paperwork If you are planning to ride abroad the following matters will have to be attended to: passport, visas, inoculations, international driving licence or driving permit, and additional insurance to cover both the vehicle and personal injury. Depending on the country or countries you are to visit, bail bonds may be advisable to avoid possible detention following an accident or traffic offence. Consult your travel agent on these points.

Other considerations include joining a body which offers a breakdown or recovery service, and, if you intend to camp, obtaining a camping 'carnet', which the French particularly like to see. The British take their national health system for granted, but elsewhere medical services have to be paid for, which means more homework on insurance.

Cargo space must be booked on a ferry or ship if water has to be crossed. Solo riders can often make crossings without prior bookings because their machines take up so little room, but it is best to check on the situation first. Owners of motorcycles with sidecars must make a firm booking. All riders who wish to go by hovercraft, and those who intend to have their machines air-freighted must also make firm bookings.

The most important point of all is to get all bookings, visas, insurance, etc. settled well in advance of the departure date. As most tours take place during the precious two or three weeks' summer holiday which the rider looks forward to each year, it is important that none of those days is lost through lack of adequate preparation.

You should also take your machine's log book and certificates of roadworthiness, if applicable, as proof of your ownership and the good condition of the machine. Obtain details of traffic signs and regulations for the countries to be visited from either a travel agent or the body you have joined for breakdown cover, and obtain stickers or plates bearing the international abbreviation for your country of origin.

Always take your national driving licence in addition to an international licence to make all border crossings as smooth as possible. Some border police can be hard to satisfy. Complete documentation can win them over and in some cases could even save you being turned back. Sometimes none of the documentation will be necessary. For example, when passing from Belgium to Holland, the green light at the customs point is often left on, allowing you to pass through without dropping speed. But the rule should be: 'when it comes to red tape, play safe'.

In case your machine breaks down it is a sensible idea to arm yourself with a list of dealers catering for the marque of machine you ride. If you are travelling abroad your local dealer may be able to give you some addresses in the country or countries you intend to visit. Otherwise write to the marque's importers in your country, or obtain motorcycle magazines from the countries you intend to visit, either before you go or while you are there. The advertisements in these magazines will yield dealers' addresses and possibly a guide to the scale of charges for parts. If your tour is to be a national one, watch out for advertisements in the specialist press which give all the dealers in your country for your brand of motorcycle. Put the addresses and telephone numbers of all dealers on one sheet of paper, so that, should you break down, it will be easy to check with your map and address list which is nearest. Ideally a telephone call should be the first step, to check whether the part or work you require can be provided. This can save a lot of wasted mileage. Even if you are abroad and cannot speak the language, it is worth a try; someone there may speak your tongue.

To complement your list of dealers, it is worth compiling another containing the addresses and telephone numbers of the branches of the owners' club for your brand of machine although obviously you would have to join the club if you were going to take advantage of any facilities it may be able to provide. The club should also have details of affiliated clubs in foreign countries.

Another safeguard would be to obtain, if one is available in the country in which you are to travel, a collated list of fellow motorcyclists who have publicly stated that they are willing to help riders in trouble. Such a scheme has been started in the UK by the weekly newspaper *Motor Cycle News*.

For details of foreign road signs and traffic regulations, inquire at major bookstores for travel books covering these details, or call on your nearest automobile association. The latter are also the people to see for an international driving licence. You should also explore both avenues for details of accommodation, be it hotels or camp sites. Tourist offices and libraries can be of help too. Some of the guides available are quite comprehensive, and many are written for those travelling on a low budget.

Finance Touring one's own country is, of course, a relatively straightforward proposition, financially: you know approximately how much you will be charged for goods and whether you are getting value for money. If the cash is running out, a trip to your nearest bank is the easy remedy, and there is no need to worry about currency exchange loss. For major expenditures you can use your cheque book.

Some of these conveniences also apply to a trip abroad, however, because in most European countries banks will cash a cheque supported by a banker's card and some other means of identification. If you have any queries about the system, ask your local bank for advice when you go in to arrange for traveller's cheques or to buy the foreign currency you require. Most countries limit the amount of national currency you are allowed to take with you, so you may need additional resources, such as foreign currency which can be obtained from your own bank. Again, most countries limit the amount you can have, but this is likely to be far greater than the national currency limit. The advantage of having ready cash is that the commission charge made by your bank for changing the money will work out cheaper than for changing traveller's cheques in hotels, currency exchange offices and banks abroad. On the other hand traveller's cheques are a more secure system in the event of a theft. Just remember to take your cheque book or credit card with you in case you overreach your budget. Once you have sorted out your finances you will need to make sure that you have a currency exchange guide included in your document folder so that you can translate the value of the new money you are spending. You may even consider it worthwhile taking a pocket calculator with you to aid you in this respect. Some are small enough to fit into a pocket and are also a valid part of the tourer's equipment if he is inter-

ested in keeping track of how far his bike is going to the gallon or litre.

If travelling abroad the question of conversions is almost certain to arise with regard to fuel, distances and tyre pressures. Accompanying this chapter are tables which include these conversions and give conversion factors. Again a pocket calculator will help. Bear in mind that when it comes to tyre pressures you may even have to learn the equivalents: one for the bike unloaded and one for the bike loaded.

Health In addition to a first aid kit, tablets for headaches are a prudent precaution. If travelling abroad for the first time, the local food may upset the digestive system, so medicines for indigestion, diarrhoea and constipation should be taken along. Sea-sickness pills may be needed too, if a sea crossing is to be part of the tour. Ointments for abrasions, insect bites, burns etc., complete a sensible health kit.

Weather and Terrain Once you have decided on where to tour, find out about the weather prospects and the types of road you are likely to be travelling on. The south of France can be very hot in September, but it is also a month noted for torrential downpours, so a lightweight waterproof suit would be necessary if you go there at that time of year. If your planned route involves even the remotest chance of snow, your progress could be brought to a complete halt if conditions become too severe. To help you anticipate weather conditions, a chart giving average temperatures for the world's major cities is included with this chapter. When calculating daily distances, remember that tackling mountain roads will bring your average speeds down, and being stuck behind a coach or lorry on a narrow road could mean speeds well below 50kph (30mph) for long periods. Maps with contour lines or elevation points, or both, will help in determining your daily routes and distances.

Geographical/Historical Appreciation Read about the place you are going to visit if you wish to gain maximum benefit and satisfaction from your tour. One place can look much like another unless you learn something of its background; then it becomes far more interesting and significant. It can also help in getting into discussions with the local inhabitants, providing you share a common tongue, and this can add a dimension to your touring, making you feel as if you have become a part of the places you have seen.

Being on the road has a kind of magic about it, and actually going places is more exciting than the point of arrival to many people. Often the tourer is viewed with reverence by the inhabitants of the towns and villages he passes through, particularly when he is touring foreign lands. Once the ice has been broken, friendships can be

made, and the traveller often experiences more than his fair share of hospitality simply because he is a traveller. The tradition of extending a friendly and helping hand to the man on the road lives on. If you get stuck with a problem with your bike, stopping a local rider and asking his advice may lead to your being invited to his home and given the use of his tools and any workshop facilities he may have. The common bond of motorcycling transcends barriers of nationality. However, motorcyclists can also meet with indifference and downright hostility. Should such unfortunate circumstances arise, the only answer is to press on.

Language Another problem for the rider going abroad may only be academic: that is, the language problem. If you have had no grounding in the language of the country which you are to visit, taking a phrasebook will be no good at all unless you learn to pronounce the words, and even if you get that far the reply will leave you utterly in the dark. You could count the whole matter as no problem and simply smile your way through, or take a course in the language before you leave. If the latter sounds like too much hard work, at least learn a few essential phrases such as 'please' and 'thank you'.

Camping The question of a good night's rest is very important to the touring motorcyclist. Lack of it over several nights can build up and spoil your enjoyment of the trip. Those who can afford to stay in hotels or boarding houses may encounter the problem of finding one with a vacant room. Booking beforehand can solve the problem but if the rider does not wish to plan his tour in such detail he will have to take a chance and may well find that discrimination against motorcyclists is the biggest drawback in finding accommodation.

Motorcycling is an open-air pastime, and many motorcyclists prefer to remain out of doors at night by camping. When selecting camping gear, buy the best you can afford. Careful thought has to be given to the size and weight of individual camping items with regard to carrying them on the motorcycle. Camping shops realize that the motorcycling fraternity makes up a fair percentage of their custom and some special articles of camping equipment are now for sale to the touring motorcyclist. For example, a British camping firm now sells a two man and motorcycle tent, featuring an extra portion to cover the machine. This may sound like taking pride of ownership a little too far, but the 'garage' space afforded by this design can be of further use if emergency repairs have to be made in poor weather. A visit to a large camping store to discover articles such as this should be undertaken before the rider commits himself.

For riders touring warm countries sleeping in the open air may sound romantic, but is often far from practical. Insects, rain, and condensation are all possible occurrences which will make a tent seem like a palace. The main problem in most areas is keeping warm at night, and a tent helps to retain warmth as well as protecting the camper from the elements. A tent with a waterproof groundsheet will prevent puddles inside the tent and keep insects out. If the camper is likely to encounter conditions which are too warm he should ensure that his tent has vents at the top and bottom so that the bottom vents draw cool air in and, as the air warms, and rises, it can be expelled through the top, thereby creating a flow of cooling air. If there is no movement of air then cooling will be impossible.

For bedding, air mattresses are best as they can be deflated after use, rolled up and only take up a small space as part of the luggage. Some air mattresses now on the market are self-inflating; others have channels which can be individually inflated. Air mattresses which can be inflated by lung power rather than by a foot pump will of course save on luggage volume and weight.

A good-quality sleeping bag filled with down or some other material with good heat conserving properties is essential for a good night's rest. However, there is no need to buy an expensive goose-down-filled sleeping bag for extra warmth if most of your camping is to be done during the warm days of summer. A less expensive synthetic-filled sleeping bag would be more appropriate. If you intend to use your camping gear a great deal then choose a sleeping bag which can be machine-washed rather than dry cleaned. A sleeping bag which can be compressed to take up the least possible amount of room when packed for travelling also makes sense. Often it is possible to buy a 'compressor bag' with a sleeping bag. The compressor bag has draw strings to compress and protect the sleeping bag for easy storage. It also helps to keep the sleeping bag clean. Another important consideration is to choose a sleeping bag which dries quickly, should it become damp or wet.

For extra warmth in a sleeping bag, cotton underwear or pyjamas are a far better solution than blankets on top of a sleeping bag; anything placed over the bag will compress the stuffing, thereby reducing the all-important air spaces within it which help to trap body heat. Wearing garments heavier than pyjamas will not aid heat retention: the two warmest areas on the human body are between the arms and the sides and between the legs, so heavy trousers and jackets would hinder the generation of heat in these areas. Wrapping a jacket around the body rather than wearing it is a better solution. Better still, a light blanket wrapped around the body inside the sleeping bag is a good way of retaining body heat, because more 'dead air' space is gained. ('Dead air' spaces prevent the natural movement of air, or convection, and so stop warm air escaping and act as a barrier against cold air. However, the largest space which will work by this principle is less than one centimetre (0.5in) in diameter.)

The extremities of the body are the areas most likely to feel the cold, so a pair of warm socks and a sleeping bag which forms a collar around the neck, reducing heat loss from the shoulders, will be a great benefit. Loss of heat from the head may also be considerable, and some campers use a sleeping bag which covers the head, leaving only the face exposed; and some wear hats. If the comfort of a pillow is required, an air pillow or folded towels will work admirably and keep the luggage list from becoming too long. For a husband and wife touring together, sleeping bags which zip together will allow more heat to be generated and conserved than individual sleeping bags.

For the touring rider who wishes to cook his own food, a tent with a canopy to provide shade or shelter while cooking is done makes sense. Cooking utensils should be chosen for lightness as well as durability, and there are many ingenious space-saving pan and crockery sets on the market. A list of essential cooking utensils need only include a gas stove, matches and one pot for boiling water (if you buy canned foods, they can be cooked in the can in boiling water), and a cup, plate, spoon, knife and fork per person. A means for storing water will be needed: a plastic water envelope which can be folded flat when not required is the most convenient way. A can and bottle opener, washing-up liquid and a drying cloth are also essential.

Camping can be so sophisticated that even perishable goods can be carried in

refrigeration, but the problem for the motorcyclist is bulk and weight. A tin of dried milk may not taste as good as the real thing but it lasts much longer, does not leak and takes up very little room. The tourer has to make up his own mind about this, and about the amount of clothing taken. A few plastic bags will help in this respect by keeping all items dry, and by separating clean clothes from used ones. Do not forget to take toilet rolls and towels as part of your list of personal effects.

Setting up camp must be done with thought if all the camping gear and utensils you have assembled are to be of the greatest benefit. A piece of level ground is the first important factor. Small rocks and irregularities in the surface should be removed or smoothed over. If the tent has a separate groundsheet it is a good idea to lay it down so that the camper can lie on it to make sure that the surface is smooth enough for a good night's sleep. Facing the tent so that the sun falls on it in the early hours is a good way of ensuring an early start to the day and a dry pack. If the camper is staying more than one night in the same spot however, a shaded area is preferable for the daytime use of the tent.

Finally, the all-important time factor has to be considered. Packing camping gear to be carried on a motorcycle has to be done neatly and therefore requires time. The same is true of setting up camp and the rider who leaves himself insufficient time for both will find his temper becoming shorter as he tries to rush the job, which, more likely than not, will result in a less efficient and less enjoyable operation.

An important rule to follow before setting off is: if it's new, test it through. In other words, if you buy a new tent do not wait until you are on tour before you erect it. Try it at home first to make sure that all the pegs, holes, etc. are present. This would also give you an opportunity to time yourself to find how long it takes to put up, and you will also be able to discover if you can fold the tent up as neatly as the manufacturer's packaging, ready for reloading on the motorcycle. The same approach should be applied to all new articles of equipment.

Clothing Comfort and protection are the main requirements, and a two piece leather suit meets them admirably; it is still the best form of clothing for a touring motorcyclist. It stops the rider becoming too hot on a warm day, and in cold weather and at night the insulating properties of leather keep in body heat. The suppleness of leather means that it moulds itself comfortably to the contours of the body, it is highly wind- and water-proof and, in the event of an accident, its toughness protects the rider against abrasions. A two-piece suit is more convenient than a one-piece suit: it is far simpler to be able to remove a jacket than to undo the top half of a one-piece suit and tie the arms around the waist. However, with an ordinary two-piece suit the jacket can 'ride up' the wearer's back, leaving it exposed, so it is worth considering the extra expense of a suit which zips the top and bottom halves together. The idea is to prevent the possibility of back abrasions in a fall. Leather boots and gloves should be worn for the same reason as a leather suit: they also allow the skin to breathe, absorb sweat, and protect the rider. They should be worn even in warm climates, although obviously in lightweight leather. Never, even on the hottest day, ride bare-armed or bare-legged, but always keep all parts of the body covered to guard against skin abrasions from a possible fall.

The rider heading for colder climes usually prepares adequately for the weather conditions he is likely to encounter, but the rider setting off for the first time to a warmer climate is often tempted to leave behind items which he finds he needs. A lightweight waterproof suit should always be included, if only for night riding when the temperature drops and an extra layer of clothing is needed. Also bear in mind that for approximately every 100m (300ft) above sea level the temperature drops by about 0.6°C (1°F). (One should also mention here that engine horsepower falls at altitude because of lower relative air density. A chart giving approximate power loss is included with this chapter.) Easily stowed waterproof overboots and overmitts should also be considered by the summer tourer. Again, when kitting out for a tour, buying the best quality goods one can afford is the best approach.

The all-important choice of headwear should also be considered. Comfort is of prime importance: a helmet which remains comfortable all day without developing any nagging tight spots is essential. If you have worn your helmet for only short

America's ultimate production touring bike, the Harley-Davidson 4-stroke V-twin Electraglide 'full-dress tourer' (this is the earlier 1,200 cc version), symbolizes freedom to touring motorcyclists throughout the world.

periods at a time and are planning a tour which involves long riding spells, go for a long ride before the tour date to see how the helmet feels. (This would also provide an ideal opportunity to break in any new clothing items you may have purchased, particularly boots.) If you wear a visor attached to your helmet, take a spare. One should be clear and the other tinted for riding into the sun. Scratch-resistant visors have recently been introduced on the motorcycle market and are far better for prolonged use than the standard types which scratch easily. If you have a standard one buy a visor cleaner which will rub off superficial scratches in addition to cleaning the visor. Also take anti-misting spray or cloths along. Good vision as well as comfort is essential for primary safety. Whether you wear an open or full-face helmet choose one made of fibreglass if you can afford it. Fibreglass is said to be superior to polycarbonate for its shock-absorbing qualities, largely because it spreads the shock load.

Preparing the bike

Preparing and loading the bike involve many of the same routines, so this section in some respects overlaps with the final section on loading the bike. Both sections should be read to complement each other. (For example, fitting a fairing could come under the above heading but has been dealt with in the final section as part of the discussion on the effects of various loadings on a motorcycle.)

Whether your touring plan is simple or complicated, it will have a good chance of being undermined if preparation of the motorcycle is neglected in any way. A well-prepared machine gives the tourer confidence, whereas the rider who leaves its reliability to chance can only blame himself if he loses time through having to do roadside repairs.

There are two stages in preparing the bike: servicing to bring the bike to top condition; and equipping it with necessary spares and accessories.

Servicing It is important to remember that the more miles you intend to cover, the more careful servicing counts. If your bike is maintained by a dealer, emphasize the importance of the pre-tour service to him.

When doing the service with the aid of a workshop manual, the home mechanic should bear in mind the points which follow.

Points and ignition timing. Clean the contact breaker points faces 'square' and set them to the recommended gap. When examining the ignition timing check the advance with the engine running. If you do not have a strobe light you will have to carry out any timing adjustment statically. Then you should make sure that the ignition advance is working, since most of the time your engine will be running at full advance. If your engine runs on high octane fuel and you are going to visit a country where only low octane fuel is available, you can compensate for it by retarding your ignition. Consult your dealer or an expert if you need advice. Riders whose machines feature electronic ignition should read their workshop manuals carefully or seek advice from a dealer before attempting any adjustments, assuming that they can be made.

Carburation. Before attempting any changes to the carburation, always set the ignition system to the maker's specifications first. Next check and clean the air filter. Only then should any attempts at adjusting carburation be made. As a precaution against dirty fuel, a transparent filter could be fitted to the fuel line.

Suspension. Check for wear in the swinging arm bearing surfaces if your machine features this type of rear suspension. The only other problem likely to appear with modern suspension is oil seal wear in the front forks. If one or both legs are losing oil, renew the seals. Loss of oil means loss of suspension damping and hence loss of roadholding and comfort. If you are likely to encounter particularly dirty conditions, fit gaiters to your fork legs to prevent oil seal wear. The front forks may also need a steering damper fitted to them if they develop a tendency to flutter because of the extra weight being carried on the bike.

Steering. Check the condition of the steering head bearings and steering damper if one is fitted. Wheel alignment should also be checked: on most modern bikes this is simply a matter of verifying that the front wheel has been installed correctly, and that the index marks on either side of the rear suspension fork for chain adjustment align.

Electrical. The condition of the battery is most important. Check that all the cells are in a good condition with the aid of a hydrometer. The general condition of the wiring loom should be checked and all bulbs should be in working order. A headlight with an asymmetric dip beam may have to be replaced if you are visiting a country which has traffic flow on the other side of the road. A headlight with a dip beam which points straight ahead is therefore the easiest answer for all countries.

Tyres. Some big bikes now on the market can wear out tyres at a phenomenal rate, so work out whether your tyres have enough tread to last the distance of the tour. If not, fit a new pair before you set off, as you may not be able to obtain the brand you want if you decide to wait until your present tyres wear out while on tour.

Fitting tyres you are not happy with reduces confidence which will take away much of the fun of your riding. Balance your wheels and check with your tyre dealer or manufacturer how much extra pressure the tyres should be run at, considering the extra load and speed they will be required to cope with, not to mention the extra mileage they must cover.

Brakes. Examining the brakes is of the utmost importance. Check both wheels thoroughly to ascertain the level of wear, and fit new pads or shoes, as the case may be, if necessary. Most modern machines have wear indicators in the form of a pointer on the brake drum, and a red line on a disc pad. Often the disc pad is covered in so much dust that the red line cannot be seen, and although a drum brake pointer should be fairly accurate there would be no harm in checking. This check could be extended to the removal of both wheels, as a practice run, in case you have a puncture en route, and to find out exactly what tools would be needed for the job. Some standard bike toolkits would not be able to cope with it.

General maintenance. Items such as valve clearances, cam chain adjustment (where applicable), and rear chain adjustment and lubrication come under this heading. An oil change and oil filter renewal may also be necessary.

Carry out any work which has to be done on your bike well in advance of your departure date, to make sure the work has been effective. Attend to everything which shows signs of giving trouble. A slight problem such as an oil weep will undoubtedly get worse and become a constant annoyance when the motor is running all day.

Equipment A rider can load himself down with spares he will never need. Being sensibly selective is an art born of touring experience and an increasing knowledge of one's machine.

The following spares and tools should be considered as essential items: a chain joining link; a chain breaker; a puncture repair outfit; a headlight bulb; cables; fuses; spark plug(s); a valve core; open-ended and ring spanners; an adjustable spanner; tyre levers; a Mole grip; wire; a plug spanner; a feeler gauge; a tyre pressure gauge; pliers; insulating tape; screwdriver(s); a multi-purpose pen knife (with can opener, bottle-top remover and corkscrew attachment); assorted nuts and bolts; a spoke key; a rear suspension adjuster; duct tape; electrical wire; a torch; and a tent peg hammer.

In addition to a spare valve core, Schraeder dust caps should be fitted to the threaded valve stems of each wheel. These enable swift removal of the valve core and provide an effective seal against sudden inner tube deflation, should a valve core become faulty. A bicycle pump with a connector to fit the inner tube may be considered useful, particularly if it can be attached easily to the machine's frame or stowed with the other luggage. (It would be of further use if air beds are included in the camping equipment.) The puncture repair outfit and tyre levers could be discarded in favour of a puncture sealant, but the problem would be that a large hole in the inner tube might be too much for the sealant. Equally, it may be too much for a patch, in which case a replacement tube is the only answer. If you feel happier armed with a tube you are in luck if both wheels are the same size. If not, and you do not want the encumbrance of two tubes, take the biggest because, as an emergency measure only, it can be folded to fit a smaller wheel.

Not mentioned in the list but recommended is a first aid kit, a legal requirement in some countries. Recent BMW models have them as standard. They also have shaft drive, obviating the necessity for chain lubrication and tensioning. Owners of chain-driven motorcycles should carry chain lube while on tour and make it a ritual to lubricate the chain after each day's travelling. This will allow the lubricant to penetrate overnight and pay dividends in extended chain life.

Pack all spare fuses and bulbs in foam to protect them. Gap new spark plugs and protect the electrodes before putting them with the toolkit. Two types of wire are mentioned in the list, one for emergency electrical repairs, the other for holding on parts which may have loosened. Duct tape is also useful, as it is extremely strong and can be used for repairing items of clothing as well as patching seats and holding on parts of the bike which may have worked loose. Some riders have used it successfully to cover holes in fuel tanks and engine cases. Alternatively, an epoxy resin kit could be carried for repairing holes in metal and plastic parts. Be sure to carry the kit in a plastic container in case of leakage.

Wheel balancing has already been mentioned in the section on servicing, but it might be worth taking some solder wire, in case a wheel has to be rebalanced following a puncture or the fitting of a new tyre. The solder is simply wrapped round the spoke opposite the heaviest part of the wheel, which is determined by spinning the wheel several times and marking the lowermost point of the tyre. Several marks in the same area of the tyre indicate the heaviest spot. While this method is not foolproof, it usually works and is the only course open to the roadside repairer.

A rag and hand-cleaning substance of some kind ought to be included in the toolkit. Another item, used by some top motorcycle mechanics, could be a pair of close-fitting cotton gloves for keeping the hands clean while working on the bike. Another useful idea, practised by long-distance road riders and competition enduro riders alike, is to paint tools in a bright colour. If a breakdown occurs at night and the toolkit has to be used, the chances are that the tools will tend to be somewhat scattered as work proceeds. When it comes to reassembling the kit, tools which are easily seen by torchlight will make the job much quicker and reduce the possibility of leaving some behind. Always carry all tools on the motorcycle itself and never in the pockets of a riding jacket; a pocket containing screwdrivers and spanners could be extremely dangerous in the event of a fall.

Tourers visiting foreign countries where they have to ride on the other side of the road might find it worth fixing an easily seen notice to the machine as a reminder of this. No tourer should be put off by the thought of riding on the 'wrong' side of the road for the first time, but it is all too easy, after a prolonged stop, to remount and instinctively head up the road as if on home ground, to suddenly find a truck or car on a direct collision course round the next corner.

If a pillion passenger is included in the tour his or her comfort should be considered. A backrest, and footboards instead of footrests, which allow variation in the riding posture, plus a comfortable seat would go a long way to smoothing out the miles. A rider-to-passenger communication system with radio and tape player are further luxury possibilities. The pillion rider can earn some of his or her comfort by carrying the camera, if one is to be taken along. This would protect it from vibration and keep the camera readily available for pictures en route. Some photographic shops stock strong cases specifically designed for outdoor use.

Further information on tools and their uses may be found in the chapter beginning on page 104, dealing with the enthusiast's toolkit.

Loading the bike

To the uninitiated tourer, loading a bike may seem to be simply a matter of sticking weight where it is most convenient. The hardened tourer will know that weight distribution and paring of luggage to the minimum weight possible is a fine art, if the machine is to handle in an acceptable manner. Anyone can abuse the handling and braking qualities of a motorcycle by putting too much weight in the wrong places.

In America it is possible to fall foul of the law because 'gross weight restrictions' apply there. In other parts of the world, too, it is possible to attract attention of the wrong sort by having too much weight on the bike. The British *Daily Telegraph* in 1978 carried an amusing story of a 150cc scooter rider who was stopped in London's Regent Street by police. He was carrying 51kg (112lb) of potatoes, 16kg (35lb) of cabbages, 16.4kg (36lb) of other vegetables, a bird cage . . . and a parrot perched on his right shoulder! If it had not been for the parrot, perhaps he would have got away with it.

Even serious motorcyclists find it all too easy to upset the balance of the original design, even to the extent of rendering the machine unsafe. Owners of new 750cc Triumph Bonnevilles whose machines come complete with a rear carrier will have noticed a warning statement saying that a 6.8kg (15lb) weight limit is recommended for the carrier. Above this weight the effect on the machine's handling, particularly at speed, can be serious; the warning has nothing to do with the strength of the carrier. BMW owners have an even lower weight threshold before handling quality is affected: the factory recommends only 4.5kg (10lb) as the maximum weight for a rear carrier. All owners should therefore consult their handbooks as the first step in loading their bikes, to find out exactly what the weight carrying limits are. This is particularly important for American riders who have to conform with regulations concerning gross vehicle weight rating. A plate stating this figure should be affixed to all motorcycles sold in America after 1972. The plate also gives 'gross axle weight ratings' and these limits are designed to prevent a weight imbalance on any laden machine. In America tyres are also subject to a loading capacity law. The figures should be given in small print on one side of the tyre.

When loading his motorcycle the rider ought to reflect on the physical forces which apply to his machine when it is in motion, so that he can appreciate the effects that extra weight and where it is placed can have on the machine. While the motorcycle is in motion it can turn about three different axes: horizontal, longitudinal and vertical. Pitch occurs about the horizontal axis, roll occurs about the longitudinal axis and yaw occurs about the vertical axis. The pitch alters when the front forks are compressed or when the motorcycle is acted upon by some other force about the horizontal axis. When a motorcycle leans into a corner, its attitude is changed within the roll plane. Yaw occurs when the motorcycle changes position in relation to its straight-ahead motion. It pivots about the vertical axis, and this can result in some spectacular manoeuvres such as full-lock slides. In a situation such as this the machine moves straight ahead while the bulk of it is pointing in a different direction. All three physical forces can occur together while the machine is in motion. Since momentum equals force times weight and a laden touring motorcycle weighs more than an unladen motorcycle, the momentum in all the planes so far mentioned will be increased because the weight factor is increased. Any rider who has taken extra weight in the form of a pillion passenger, extra luggage, or both, will know that it takes more time to stop the machine than if the machine were not loaded. To stop the machine in the same distance, more braking effort is required when the machine is laden.

When carrying extra weight on a motorcycle, always place it within the machine's wheelbase and as low as possible. Therefore, if side panniers have been fitted they should be moved as far forward as is convenient, and the heaviest items they are to carry should be placed in the bottom. For a rear rack and rear top box only light loads should be considered. Many tourers like to have a top box which can form a backrest for the pillion rider and house crash helmets when they are not in use.

Accessories In many respects, soft luggage goes a long way to reducing the possibility of erratic handling. Soft saddle bags for the tank and seat keep the weight within the wheelbase and close to the machine's centre of gravity. Soft luggage is also very accommodating in that it stretches to take awkward shapes and moulds itself into available spaces on the motorcycle. Though a tank bag is fairly high on a machine, it too falls within the wheelbase and is ideal for carrying light loads as well as information which can be seen by the rider while he is astride the bike.

If rigid rear panniers are to be fitted, care should be taken when you are choosing them. Parallelogram shaped panniers may look smart but often they will not accept a solid square object such as an attaché case, whereas plainer looking rectangular panniers might. Panniers which unclip from their framework and can be carried like suitcases are useful because they allow packing and unpacking to be done in a hotel room or tent. The type of panniers with lids which hinge to open away from the machine can act as trays for holding items required when you stop for a snack or at the campsite.

All panniers should feature sturdy locks. Glove compartments in a fairing should also lock and, in addition to the machine's steering lock, supposing one is fitted, an additional method of immobilizing the machine is essential.

Other accessories which could be attached to the bike are front and rear crash bars to protect the machine and its fibreglass ancillaries in the event of an accident. There is not enough space to detail all the options such as engine oil coolers for hot countries and heated handlebars and gloves

for cold climates, and the rider must decide for himself which extra items merit inclusion on his list of accessories.

One piece of equipment needed by all riders is the aerolastic or, in American terms, bungee cord. This can have an infinite number of uses, particularly in emergencies (some riders even do their jackets up with one). Its main use is obviously for strapping down luggage. A small one conveniently placed to hold the rider's gloves when they are not in use is just one other application.

Sidecar users who do not wish to overload their machine and sidecar have the advantage of being legally allowed to tow a trailer. American riders, unlike European riders, have this privilege extended to solo machines and their accessory market for touring is an enormous one. Trailer tents, beautifully tailored custom seats, audio equipment and even citizen-band communication systems to allow conversations with riders up to two miles away, are available.

Fairings As a general rule loads should not be attached to the forks or handlebars. This rule has been and always will be widely ignored, especially by riders with handlebar-mounted fairings and windscreens. Thanks to the good design of today's motorcycles, however, handling characteristics for the most part are not unduly upset, though some riders have woeful tales of expense and physical discomfort to relate, following an unexpected fall due to steering instability with a handlebar fairing. Fairings sturdily attached to the frame are safer. Gusts of wind have to be strong enough to move the entire machine off course before they pose any real threat to a frame-mounted fairing, whereas strong wind against a handlebar-mounted fairing can deflect the front wheel from its path and set up a wobble as castor action overrides the self-centring effect of trail, first in one direction and then the other. Thousands of handlebar fairings have been sold and have been of great benefit to their owners in terms of weather protection. Nevertheless, the fact that problems can arise should be realized by the prospective purchaser.

Air valves, stronger fork springs or, simplest of all, thicker oil could be used in the front forks of a machine which has been fitted with a heavy fairing and accessories and as a result has had its springing and damping qualities overloaded.

Before fitting a fairing, an owner should give very careful thought to exactly what he wants from it. For example, a full fairing which gives excellent wind and weather protection may become unbearably hot in summer if the bottom section cannot be removed. All fairings, and even windscreens to a certain extent, throw engine noise back to the rider. Fairings also

catch sidewinds. The further a fairing is mounted away from the rider, the less protection it is likely to give him. On the other hand, the rider in this instance would have the convenience of being able to mount accessories such as clock, radio, temperature gauge and so on, and still have the benefit of a cooling breeze in the summer as well as additional load-carrying space in the form of side pockets on some models.

Also to be considered is the height of the screen. The rider should be able to see over the top so that in poor weather, when the screen is covered in grime, he still has forward vision. Another less obvious factor in fitting a fairing is the riding position. Most machines have a riding position which requires the rider to lean forward slightly, but the weight on the arms is partially alleviated by wind resistance while in motion. With a fairing this wind resistance is eliminated, so the full weight of the torso is supported by the arms and wrist, and this can lead to complete numbing of the wrists and hands. Different handlebars allowing a more upright riding position would be the answer. However, fairings *do* protect the rider against road grime, insects and the weather, and these advantages are very often considered important enough to outweigh the disadvantages, and are the reason why a high percentage of long-distance riders use them.

Adjustments When the bike has been fully loaded, a short run should be undertaken to confirm that no further alterations to the machine or luggage need to be made. If a rider has changed from a standard solo to a full-dress tourer with pillion passenger, he cannot expect it to feel the same. Braking distances will be much longer, the bike will not be as nimble round corners, and there is likely to be a marked reduction in ground clearance. The latter can be overcome to some extent by setting the rear shock-absorber springs at their hardest preload position. This adjustment is also possible on the front forks of some big-bore Japanese mounts. Air shock-absorber systems to replace standard rear units are available to the motorcyclist and give infinitely variable suspension settings. It is also possible to have air valves inserted in the front forks to give air-assisted front suspension. This refinement is a standard fitting to the Suzuki GS1000 and may be the start of a trend which would be welcomed by touring enthusiasts.

The best touring equipment does not of course necessarily mean the best fun and satisfaction. Riders of humble mopeds have gained as much enjoyment from long-distance riding as the rider with all the latest equipment, and whatever type of powered two-wheeler you have, touring has much to offer.

Kilometres into Miles

Km	Miles	Km	Miles	Km	Miles	Km	Miles	Km	Miles	Km	Miles
1	0.62	20	12.42	39	24.23	58	36.04	77	47.84	96	59.65
2	1.24	21	13.04	40	24.85	59	36.66	78	48.46	97	60.27
3	1.86	22	13.67	41	25.47	60	37.28	79	49.09	98	60.89
4	2.48	23	14.29	42	26.09	61	37.90	80	49.71	99	61.51
5	3.10	24	14.91	43	26.72	62	38.52	81	50.33	100	62.14
6	3.72	25	15.53	44	27.34	63	39.14	82	50.95	200	124.28
7	4.34	26	16.15	45	27.96	64	39.76	83	51.57	300	186.42
8	4.97	27	16.77	46	28.58	65	40.39	84	52.19	400	248.56
9	5.59	28	17.39	47	29.20	66	41.01	85	52.81	500	310.70
10	6.21	29	18.02	48	29.82	67	41.63	86	53.44	600	372.84
11	6.83	30	18.64	49	30.44	68	42.25	87	54.06	700	434.98
12	7.45	31	19.26	50	31.07	69	42.87	88	54.68	800	497.12
13	8.07	32	19.88	51	31.69	70	43.49	89	55.30	900	559.26
14	8.69	33	20.50	52	32.31	71	44.11	90	55.92	1000	621.40
15	9.32	34	21.12	53	32.93	72	44.74	91	56.54		
16	9.94	35	21.74	54	33.55	73	45.36	92	57.16		
17	10.56	36	22.37	55	34.17	74	45.98	93	57.79		
18	11.18	37	22.99	56	34.79	75	46.60	94	58.41		
19	11.80	38	23.61	57	35.41	76	47.22	95	59.03		

1 km = 0.6214 mile

Miles into Kilometres

Miles	Km	Miles	Km	Miles	Km	Miles	Km	Miles	Km	Miles	Km
1	1.60	12	19.31	23	37.01	34	54.71	45	72.41	80	128.74
2	3.21	13	20.92	24	38.62	35	56.32	46	74.02	85	136.79
3	4.82	14	22.53	25	40.23	36	57.93	47	75.63	90	144.83
4	6.43	15	24.13	26	41.84	37	59.54	48	77.24	95	152.88
5	8.04	16	25.74	27	43.45	38	61.15	49	78.85	100	160.93
6	9.65	17	27.35	28	45.06	39	62.76	50	80.46	200	321.86
7	11.26	18	28.96	29	46.66	40	64.37	55	88.51	300	482.79
8	12.87	19	30.57	30	48.27	41	65.98	60	96.55	400	643.72
9	14.48	20	32.18	31	49.88	42	67.59	65	104.60	500	804.65
10	16.09	21	33.79	32	51.48	43	69.19	70	112.65		
11	17.70	22	35.40	33	53.10	44	70.80	75	120.69		

1 mile = 1.6093 km

Tyre pressure equivalents

Pounds per sq. inch	Kilogrammes per sq. centimetre
14	0.98
16	1.12
18	1.26
20	1.40
22	1.54
24	1.68
26	1.83
28	1.96
30	2.10
32	2.24
36	2.52
40	2.80

1 kg-cm² = 14.22 psi
1 psi = 0.0703 kg-cm²

OIL

Pints	Litres
1	0.57
2	1.14
3	1.70
4	2.27
5	2.84
6	3.41
7	3.98
8	4.54

1 pint = 0.5683 litre
1 litre = 1.761 pint

PETROL
Litres to British Gallons

Litres	British Imperial Gallons	Litres	British Imperial Gallons
1	0.22	10	2.20
2	0.44	20	4.40
3	0.66	30	6.60
4	0.88	40	8.80
5	1.10	50	11.00
6	1.32	100	22.00
7	1.54	300	66.15
8	1.76	400	88.20
9	1.98	500	110.25

British Gallons to Litres

British Imperial Gallons	Litres	
1	4.54	
2	9.09	
3	13.63	
4	18.18	
5	22.73	
6	27.27	
7	31.82	*1 litre = 0.2200 gal*
8	36.36	*1 gal = 4.546 litre*
9	40.91	*1 US gal = 3.7853 litre*
10	45.46	*1 litre = 0.264 US gal*

THERMOMETER SCALE EQUIVALENTS

F°	C°	F°	C°	F°	C°	F°	C°	F°	C°
212	100.0	96	35.5	70	21.1	44	6.6	18	− 7.7
200	93.3	94	34.4	68	20.0	42	5.5	16	− 8.8
190	87.7	92	33.3	66	18.8	40	4.4	14	−10.0
180	82.2	90	32.2	64	17.7	38	3.3	12	−11.1
170	76.6	88	31.1	62	16.6	36	2.2	10	−12.2
160	71.1	86	30.0	60	15.5	34	1.1	8	−13.3
150	65.5	84	28.8	58	14.4	32	0.0	6	−14.4
140	60.0	82	27.7	56	13.3	30	− 1.1	4	−15.5
130	54.4	80	26.6	54	12.2	28	− 2.2	2	−16.6
120	48.8	78	25.5	52	11.1	26	− 3.3	0	−17.7
110	43.3	76	24.4	50	10.0	24	− 4.4		
100	37.7	74	23.3	48	8.8	22	− 5.5		
98	36.6	72	22.2	46	7.7	20	− 6.6		

Conversion examples:
50 deg F into C

$$\frac{5[50 + 40]}{9} - 40 = 10 \text{ deg C}$$

30 deg C into F

$$\frac{9[30 + 40]}{5} - 40 = 86 \text{ deg F}$$

Time it will take

Distance in kilometres (miles in brackets)

Time it will take to complete distance
Average miles driven in an hour (mph)

Distance in kilometres (miles in brackets)	30 mph	40 mph	50 mph
20 (12.4)	25 min	19 min	15 min
30 (18.6)	37 min	28 min	22 min
40 (24.9)	50 min	37 min	30 min
50 (31.1)	1 hr 2 min	47 min	37 min
60 (37.3)	1 hr 15 min	56 min	45 min
70 (43.5)	1 hr 25 min	1 hr 5 min	52 min
80 (49.7)	1 hr 39 min	1 hr 15 min	60 min
90 (56.0)	1 hr 52 min	1 hr 24 min	1 hr 7 min
100 (62.1)	2 hr 4 min	1 hr 33 min	1 hr 15 min

The effect of Altitude upon Horsepower

In high regions, slight falling off of engine performance is sometimes noticed. The loss of horsepower at various altitudes may be reckoned as shown:

Altitude

Altitude		
Sea Level	100	
1000 feet	96.5	
2000 feet	93	
3000 feet	89.5	Percentage of normal horsepower.
4000 feet	86	
5000 feet	83	
6000 feet	80	
7000 feet	77.5	

GRADIENTS

The ascent in feet for every mile climbed on a given gradient is shown below, together with the relevant gradient percentage.

Grade (feet)		Feet per mile	Percentage
1 in 5	=	1,056	20
1 in 6	=	880	16.4
1 in 7	=	754	14.2
1 in 8	=	635	12.4
1 in 9	=	586	11.1
1 in 10	=	528	10
1 in 11	=	480	9.1
1 in 12	=	440	8.4
1 in 13	=	406	7.9
1 in 14	=	337	7.2
1 in 15	=	352	6.6
1 in 16	=	330	6.4
1 in 17	=	310	5.8
1 in 18	=	293	5.5
1 in 19	=	227	5.2
1 in 20	=	264	5
1 in 25	=	218	4
1 in 30	=	155	3.3
1 in 35	=	151	2.8
1 in 40	=	132	2.5

Hundredweights to Kilogrammes

Cwt	Kg	Cwt	Kg
1	50.8	31	1574.8
2	101.6	32	1625.7
3	152.4	33	1676.5
4	203.2	34	1727.3
5	254.0	35	1778.1
6	304.8	36	1828.9
7	355.6	37	1879.7
8	406.4	38	1930.5
9	457.2	39	1981.3
10	508.0	40	2032.1
11	558.8	41	2082.9
12	609.8	42	2133.7
13	660.4	43	2184.5
14	711.2	44	2235.3
15	762.0	45	2286.1
16	812.8	46	2336.9
17	863.6	47	2387.7
18	914.4	48	2438.5
19	965.2	49	2489.3
20	1016.0	50	2540.1
21	1066.8	51	2590.9
22	1117.6	52	2641.7
23	1168.4	53	2692.5
24	1219.2	54	2743.4
25	1270.0	55	2794.1
26	1320.8	56	2844.9
27	1371.6	57	2895.7
28	1422.4	58	2946.5
29	1473.2	59	2997.3
30	1524.0	60	3048.1

1 cwt = 50.802 kg   1 kg = 0.0197 cwt

Pounds into Kilogrammes

lb	Kg	lb	Kg
1	0.45	20	9.07
2	0.91	30	13.61
3	1.36	40	18.14
4	1.81	50	22.68
5	2.27	60	27.22
6	2.72	70	31.75
7	3.18	80	36.29
8	3.63	90	40.82
9	4.08	100	45.36
10	4.54	112	50.80

Kilogrammes into Pounds

Kg	lb	Kg	lb
1	2.20	20	44.09
2	4.41	30	66.14
3	6.61	40	88.19
4	8.82	50	110.23
5	11.02	60	132.28
6	13.23	70	154.32
7	15.43	80	176.37
8	17.64	90	198.42
9	19.84	100	220.46
10	22.05	250	551.15

1 lb = 0.4536 kg
1 kg = 2.2046 lb

Metres to Feet					Feet to Metres			
Metres	Feet	Metres	Feet		Feet	Metres	Feet	Metres
1	3.2	17	55.7		1	0.3	17	5.1
2	6.5	18	58.0		2	0.6	18	5.4
3	9.8	19	62.3		3	0.9	19	5.7
4	13.1	20	65.6		4	1.2	20	6.0
5	16.4	21	68.9		5	1.5	21	6.4
6	19.6	22	72.1		6	1.8	22	6.7
7	22.9	23	75.4		7	2.1	23	7.0
8	26.2	24	78.7		8	2.4	24	7.3
9	29.5	25	82.0		9	2.7	25	7.6
10	32.8	50	164.0		10	3.0	50	15.2
11	36.0	75	246.0		11	3.3	75	22.3
12	39.3	100	328.1		12	3.6	100	30.4
13	42.6	200	656.2		13	3.9	200	60.9
14	45.9	300	984.3		14	4.2	300	91.4
15	49.2	400	1312.4		15	4.5	400	121.9
16	52.4	500	1640.5		16	4.8	500	152.4

1 m = 3.281 ft
1 ft = 0.3048 m

Collector's choice

The recent world-wide increase of interest in motorcycles both old and new has meant that there are now many people who wish to make collections of motorcycles. In fact, the numbers of people who wish to do so is so great that collectability rather than quality is now what counts. Humble machines which no self-respecting collector would have considered ten years ago are now being restored. The new interest has also made people more aware that machines rolling off production lines today will doubtless be the collectors' items of tomorrow.

Because more and more collectors are trying to acquire fewer and fewer machines of genuine historical interest, the Vintage Motor Cycle Club, formed in the UK immediately after the Second World War to safeguard the survival of old motorcycles, has altered its rules to accommodate the new interest. Previously conceived ideas of which machines are of 'good and rare quality' (the original VMCC yardstick) have been abandoned, and all motorcycles which have survived for more than 25 years are now regarded by the club as 'vintage'. The club now allows such machines to race in vintage events. To-day's machines are therefore collectable by virtue of the fact that once they reach their 25th birthday they will be eligible to compete in vintage events run by the VMCC, the leading authority in this field.

The new collector therefore has *carte blanche*: he may either collect whatever comes his way or take a more purist approach and search out examples of true significance.

In the following table a dozen machines from each period of motorcycling history have been chosen as suitable for forming the basis of a worthy collection. All the machines have, at one time or another, been on sale to the public, and so the collector has a good chance of being able to obtain examples.

Not included are racing machines and motorcycles which never reached the production stage. These are all highly desirable. Machines with famous and nostalgic backgrounds are the aces in the collector's hand. Who would not be envious of, for example, the custodian of a Brough which had once been owned by the manufacturer himself, or by Lawrence of Arabia, one of his best customers?

Machines which today have competitive events held for them are attractive to the collector's eye. Pride of ownership can be extended to pride in displaying and racing a 'living' example of a vintage machine. One-make clubs catering for machines of discontinued production, such as Vincent, Rudge and Scott, who admit all models produced, make these brands top priority for a collector.

Veteran: machines manufactured up to the end of 1914.

Werner (front wheel drive), Singer (engine in front or rear wheel), Excelsior (British), Rex, Triumph (hub clutch or hub gear), P and M, FN (Belgian four-cylinder), Rudge Multi, Douglas, Zenith Gradua, Scott, BAT.

Vintage: machines built between 1915 and the end of 1930. (These dates are arbitrary. Events held by the Vintage Motor Cycle Club are now open to machines 25 years old.)

ABC, Ascot Pullin, Scott, 'Flat tank' Norton, 'Long-stroke' Sunbeam side valve, ohv Sunbeam, ohc Velocette, Rudge four valve, James V-twin, Harley-Davidson, Indian (USA), Cotton.

Post Vintage: 1930–1945.

Norton International, AJS (overhead camshaft model), Excelsior Manxman, Douglas Endeavour (transverse twin), Ariel ohc Four, OEC duplex steering, Scott, Triumph twin, Vincent HRD, Velocette two-stroke, BSA V-twin ohv.

Post War: machines manufactured after 1946. (Some collectors regard 1960 as the end of this period.)

Vincent HRD, BSA Gold Star, Triumph 650, Norton Dominator, AJS (or Matchless) single cylinder, NSU Max (Germany), BMW, Moto Guzzi, Gilera, Velocette Venom, Ariel Four, Sunbeam twin.

Modern: machines manufactured after 1960 (not yet an officially recognized category).

Kawasaki Z1900-4, Norton Commando, Hercules 2000 Wankel, Honda P50 moped (engine in rear wheel), 250cc Suzuki Super Six, 750cc MV Agusta, 250cc Yamaha YDS2, 250cc Honda CB72, 450cc Honda twin, Triumph (or BSA) 750cc three-cylinder, Honda 125cc Benly, Kawasaki 750cc three-cylinder two-stroke.

Museums

For those interested in motorcycling history, museums are the obvious places to visit. However, the enthusiast should bear in mind that there are many more private collections of historical machines than public ones, and obtaining an introduction to such a collection will involve a little more trouble than simply visiting a state-run institution. However, it usually has the advantage that the visitor is able to talk to the owner about the exhibits.

Most people will nevertheless settle for a visit to a public museum for their further appreciation of motorcycles and their past. Museums devoted solely to motorcycles are rare, and most of the museums listed below mainly have cars and only a few motorcycles. Not listed are exhibitions of cars and motorcycles which are put on occasionally at seaside resorts during the summer season only.

Austria
Steyr Daimler Puch AG, Steyr.
Technisches Museum, Wien.

Belgium
Olivier Herbosch Sammlung, Antwerp.
Automobilmuzeum Mahy, Gent.

Czechoslovakia
Technicke Muzeum, Koprivnice.
Narodni Technicke Muzeum, Prague.

Canada
Canadian War Museum, 330 Sussex Drive, Ottawa, Ontario KIA OM8.
Harley-Davidson of Edmonton, Edmonton, Alberta.
Ontario Science, Toronto, Ontario.

Denmark
Egeskov Veteranmuseum.
Jysk Automobilmuseum, Gjern.
Danmarks Tekniske Museum, Helsingor.
Aalholm Automobil Museum, Nysted.

France
Collection Bonnal Renaulac, Bègles.
Musée Automobile du Val de Loire, Briare.
Musée de l'Automobiles de Normandie, Clères.
Musée National de la Voiture et du Tourisme, Compiègne.
Le Musée de l'Automobile du Mans.
Musée de l'Automobile de Lourdes.
Musée de l'Automobile du Centre, Vatan.
Musée Automobile de Provence, Orgon.
Autobiographie Renault, Paris.
Musée des Techniques, Conservatoire National, Paris.
Auberge Musée Automobile et Technique, Petit-Arran.
Musée Automobile de Bretagne, Rennes.
Musée de l'Automobile, Rochetaillée.
Musée d'Automobiles du Forez, Sury-le-Comtal, Loire.
Museon di Rodo, Uzès, Gard.
Musée d'Automobiles M. Berliet, Vénissieux, Rhône.
Autorama, Musée d'Automobiles, Yerres.

Holland
Het Nationale Automobiel Museum, Veurschestraatweg 280, Leidschendam.
Lips Autotron, Drunen.
De Klinze, Oudkerk.

Hungary
Közlekedési Múzeum, Budapest.

Italy
Museo Alfa Romeo, Arese.
Museo Nazionale, Mailand.
Padiglione Automobile d'Epoca, Moza.
Centro Storico Fiat, Turin.
Museo dell'Automobile, Turin.

Norway
Norsk Teknisk Museum, Oslo.

Poland
Muzeum Technicki, Warschau.

Portugal
Museu do Automóvel, Caramulo.

Rumania
Technisches Museum, Bucharest.

Russia
Polytechnisches Museum, Moscow.

Spain
Museo del Automóvil Claret, Sils.

Sweden
Svardsjo Motorcykelsamling, Hillersboda, Svardsjo.
Industrimuseet, Gothenburg.
Tekniska Museet, Museivagen, Stockholm.
Stokloster Motormuseum, Stockloster.
Svedinos Motormuseum, Ullarp.
Contactus Museum, nr Norrkoping.
Soderstrom Kollektion, Malmo.
Den GamlaBilsalongen, Skelleftea.
AB Scania Vabis, Sodertalje.

Switzerland
Musée de l'Automobile, Grandson.
Verkehrshaus der Schweiz, Lucerne.

UK
Stanford Hall, (nr Rugby), Leicestershire.
Murray's Museum, The Bungalow, Isle of Man.
National Motor Museum, Beaulieu, Hampshire.
Science Museum, South Kensington, London SW7.
Shuttleworth Collection, Old Warden Aerodrome, Biggleswade, Beds.
Caister Castle Motor Museum, Norfolk.
Manx Motor Museum, Crosby, Isle of Man.
East Anglia Transport Museum, Carlton Colville, Lowestoft, Suffolk.
Birmingham Museum of Science and Industry, Newhall Street, Birmingham.
Museum of Technology for the East Midlands, Corporation Road, Leicester.
Transport Department of Liverpool Museums, Liverpool.
Imperial War Museum, London.
Glasgow Museum of Transport, 25 Albert Drive, Glasgow.
Gunnersbury Park Museum, London.
High Barnet Museum, Hertfordshire.
Myreton Motor Museum, Aberlady, East Lothian, Scotland.
Belfast Transport Museum, Witham Street, N. Ireland.
Royal Armoured Corps Tank Museum, Bovingdon Camp, Hertfordshire.
City Museum, Bristol.
Herbert Art Gallery and Museum, Coventry.
Royal Scottish Museum, Edinburgh.
Hull Transport Museum.

Museum of British Transport, London.
Donington Collection, Donington Park, Castle Donington, Derbyshire.

USA
Daytona Speed Museum, Daytona, Florida.
Greenfield Village, Dearborn, Michigan.
Harrah's Automobile Collection, Reno, Nevada.
Pioneer Museum, Nebraska City, Nebraska.
Rodney C. Gott Harley-Davidson Museum, York, Pennsylvania.

W. Germany
BMW Museum, Petuelring 130, Munich.
Deutsches Museum, Museumsinsel, Munich.
Auto-Sammlung Gut Hand, Handerweg 71, Bad Aachen-Richterich.
Norddeutsches Auto- und Motorrad-Museum, Weserstrasse 225, Bad Oeyhausen.
Poddig Automobil Museum Berlin, Sophie Charlotten Strasse 41, Berlin 19.
Auto und Motorrad Museum, Bleichstrasse 18, Burgau.
Schnauferl Stall, Kapuzinerstrasse 237, Burghausen.
Renn und Sportwagenmuseum von Fritz B. Busch, Friedrichshafen Ailingen.
Veteranen Automobil und Motorrad Museum, Bachinger Strasse 68, Gundelfingen.
Auto Museum Hillers, Kurt Schmacher Allee 42, Hamburg.
Oltimer Gasse, Hamburger Strasse, Hamburg.
Verkehrsmuseum Karlsruhe, Werderstrasse 63, Karlsruhe.
Deutsches Auto Museum, Schloss Langenburg, Langenburg.
Fahrzeugmuseum Marxzell, Marxzell.
Deutsches Zweirad Museum, Urbanstrasse, Neckarsulm.
Automuseum Hohenstein/Odenwaldenstetten, Odenwaldstetten.
Automuseum, Story.
Daimler Benz Museum, Mercedesstrasse, Stuttgart Unterturkheim.
Porsche Sammlung, Porsche Werk, Stuttgart Zuffenhausen.
Auto Museum Hillers, Tremsbuttel.
Auto Museum Fritz B. Busch, Schloss Wolfegg, Wolfegg.
Bayerisches Automobil und Motorrad Museum, Untermarkt 64, Wolfratshausen.
Museum der Volkswagenwerk AG, Wolfsburg.
MAN Motoren Museum, Augsburg.
Zweitakt Motorrad Museum, Augustusburg.
Sammlung Gut Hand, Laurensberg.
Verkehrsmuseum, Dresden.
Wartburg Automobil Museum, Eisenach.
KHD Motoren Museum, Cologne.
Auto Museum, Nettelstedt.

Motorcycling Milestones

1869 Michel driven by Perreaux steam engine constructed in France.

1876 Dr N. A. Otto patents his four-stroke engine in Germany.

1880 BSA of UK builds its first road vehicle, the Otto Dicycle.

1881 Sir Thomas Parkyns builds a steam tricycle in England.

1884 Copeland in America builds the first production steam tricycles.

1884 Edward Butler of England patents a horizontal two-stroke tricycle.

1884 Daimler of Germany patents an 800rpm horizontal four-stroke engine.

1885 Gottlieb Daimler's vertical four-stroke single becomes the parent of all modern units.

1894 Millet built by Darracq, France, features five-cylinder rotary engine in rear wheel.

1896 World's first four-cylinder built by Col. Holden of UK.

1898 Royal Enfield, UK, founded.

1899 Matchless, UK, founded.

1900 Joah Phelon of England uses De Dion engines as an integral part of the frame.

1901 Norton production begins in England, using Swiss and French engines.

1901 The first Indian motorcycle appears in the USA.

1901 Development of the British Scott two-stroke begins.

1902 Werner brothers in France mount their engine at the bottom of the front downtube and set the modern trend.

1902 JAP begin engine production in England.

1903 Triumph, England, commence manufacture of their own engines.

1903 Harley-Davidson factory in America founded.

1903 Husqvarna, Sweden, start production.

1903 Hercules factory in Germany founded.

1904 Federation Internationale Motocycliste founded.

1904 Velocette in England commence production.

1904 First international motorcycle race held, the International Coupe Race in France.

1905 The 363cc FN of Belgium features shaft drive, internal expanding rear brake and telescopic forks.

1906 JAP build the first ohv V-twin engines.

1906 Chater-Lea of England pioneer layshaft gearbox.

1906 Douglas of England make the flat-twin a success.

1906 Many factories start to employ magneto ignition.

1907 First Isle of Man TT races held.

1908 Brooklands race track in England opens.

1909 Giuseppe Gilera enters the motorcycle arena, Italy.

1909 Triumph fit hub clutches in their rear wheels.

1909 AJS production begins at Wolverhampton, England.

1910 First wholly BSA made motorcycle built—a belt driven 3.5hp single.

1911 In Italy the six Benelli brothers start manufacture.

1911 Full 'Mountain Course' in the Isle of Man used for the TT.

1912 Sunbeam in England adds its name to the list of manufacturers.

1912 Villiers in England begin production.

1912 Harley-Davidson make the engine clutch a success.

1912 Charlie and Harry Collier (Matchless) use six-speed gearbox for racing.

1913 Peugeot in France use double-overhead camshafts in their 494cc vertical-twin racing engine.

1913 The International Six Days Trial introduced.

1913 Alberto Garelli in Italy designs his first machine, a 346cc double piston two-stroke single.

1914 Indian use dynamo lighting successfully.

1914 BSA produce their own sidecars.

1915 Harley-Davidson create an eight-valve ohv V-twin for racing.

1919 Dunelt, England, design two-stroke single with double diameter piston.

1920 The German Mars features pressed steel frame.

1921 Carlo Guzzi, Italy, designs a 497cc horizontal single.

1921 Sun, England, use rotary valve induction on 247 and 269cc two-stroke engines.

1922 Dolf in Germany builds an eight-port two-stroke.

1923 German BMW flat-twin introduced.

1923 First sidecar TT race held. Freddie Dixon wins with a banking Douglas.

1924 Norton patents an ohc desmodromic valve design.

1925 The German water-cooled 173cc DKW racing two-stroke features charging cylinder at bottom of crankcase.

1926 Chater-Lea build first 347cc ohc singles with face cams.

1927 First ohc 'cammy' AJS produced.

1927 First ohc Norton produced, the 490cc single.

1927 Austrian designer Adalbert Freyler's 347cc ohc single features rotary valve in cylinder head.

1928 BSA's first two-stroke made, the 174cc Model A.

1929 BSA launch ohv V-twin.

1929 Jawa of Czechoslovakia begin production with shaft drive 497cc ohv single.

1931 Matchless of Plumstead, London, buy AJS to form Associated Motor Cycles.

1933 BSA introduce three-wheeler with water cooling and fluid flywheel.

1934 FN produce 1,000cc flat-twin sidecar outfit with driven sidecar wheel and differential as an option.

1935 BSA launch Empire Star range with 18 different models.

1936 AJS 495cc ohc V-four competes in TT.

1937 AMC buy Sunbeam.

1940 BSA buy Sunbeam from AMC.

1944 BSA acquire Ariel.

1945 Vespa scooter designed.

1946 MV Agusta in Italy start production with two-stroke lightweights.

1948 AJS produce 498cc 'porcupine' twin with gear-driven ohc.

1948 Soichiro Honda establishes Honda Motor Co., Japan.

1948 Bantam introduced, BSA's most successful two-stroke.

1949 Kawasaki, Japan, commence motorcycle engine production.

1949 Honda Dream is the first post-war Japanese machine with engine and frame from the same factory.

1949 AJS introduce 348cc ohc single 7R, the 'boy racer'.

1950 Norton use Featherbed frame for first time.

1950 Ducati, Italy, founded.

1951 Honda's first four-stroke, the E-type Dream, produced.

1951 BSA buy Triumph Engineering Co.

1952 Suzuki, Japan, begin production with 50cc motorized bicycle.

1952 Honda Cub 'step thru' lightweight introduced.

1954 Yamaha, Japan, start motorcycle production.

1954 Suzuki build their first motorcycle, the 90cc Colleda two-stroke.

1954 Soichiro Honda visits TT in preparation for road race team.

1957 Honda start to export.

1958 America receives Honda motorcycles for the first time.

1959 Honda enter TT and establish research and development company.

1959 AMC buys US Indian factory.

1960 Honda enter grand prix road racing.

1961	First complete Kawasaki produced.
1961	Honda monthly sales reach 100,000. Factory wins 125 and 250cc world road race championships.
1962	First motorcycle bearing Kawasaki name produced.
1962	Honda win 125, 250 and 350cc world road race titles.
1963	Kawasaki produce moto-cross racer.
1963	Honda established as biggest motorcycle company in the world with 1.25 million annual production. Plant in Belgium opened.
1965	Kawasaki open first overseas office in Chicago, USA.
1965	Suzuki introduce 250cc Super Six (X-6 Hustler).
1966	Honda win all solo road race world championships.
1966	AMC ceases to exist.
1966	Norton Villiers of Wolverhampton set up.
1967	Kawasaki build their first four-stroke, the 650cc WI (Japan's biggest motorcycle) and their first trail bike, the 120cc C2TR.
1967	Honda 50cc Super Cub sales reach 5 million. Factory quits grand prix road racing.
1968	Total Honda production reaches 10 million, with 1 million sales in USA.
1968	Velocette factory closes.
1969	BSA 750cc Rocket-3 introduced.
1969	Honda introduce the four-cylinder CB750 road bike.
1969	Kawasaki introduce 500cc Mach III two-stroke triple and win 125cc world road race championship.
1969	Production of all AJS four-strokes ceases.
1971	Japan now producing nearly 3.5 million motorcycles per annum. Italy next with 617,000.
1971	Last Royal Enfields built in Britain, but production of some models continues in Madras, India.
1971	BSA competition department closes.
1971	Kawasaki create Mach IV H2 750cc two-stroke triple, plus 250 and 350cc version with same engine layout.
1971	Suzuki introduce water-cooled 750–3, their first bike over 500cc.
1972	Kawasaki introduce H2R, racing version of the 750–3.
1973	Total Kawasaki production reaches 1 million.
1973	BSA absorbed by Norton Villiers Triumph.
1973	Yamaha build their first trials bike, the TY250.
1974	Suzuki launch RE5 Wankel engine.
1974	Kawasaki open US plant in Lincoln, Nebraska.
1974	Total production of 50cc Honda Super Cub reaches 10 million. Gold Wing introduced, 1000cc flat-4.
1975	Benelli introduce world's first across-the-frame six-cylinder motorcycle in 750cc form.
1975	Hercules 294cc Wankel-engined W2000 launched commercially.
1975	Honda market 1,000cc flat four water-cooled Gold Wing with shaft drive.
1976	Moto Guzzi of Italy market the V1,000 Convert, a two-speed semi-automatic V-twin with rear and one of two front disc brakes linked.
1978	Honda market 1,050cc transverse six with four valves per cylinder.
1978	Yamaha market 1,100cc double overhead camshaft four.
1978	Turbo Cycle Corporation of America markets 1,000cc Kawasakis fitted with turbochargers.
1979	Kawasaki market 1,300cc water-cooled transverse six.
1981	Yamaha and Honda vie for honours as manufacturers of the first production turbocharged bike with the XJ650T and CX500 Turbo, respectively.

INDEX

Page numbers in italics refer to captions

Acknowledgements

The publishers thank the following organizations and individuals for their kind permission to reproduce the photographs in this book:

All-Sport Photographic Ltd. (D. Morley) 2–3, 4–5, 12–13 above, 49, 54 above, 55 below, 58–59, 72 above, 73, 74 above and below, 77 below, 78–79, 115, 116, 120–121, 121 above right, 122, 126, 136 below, 162, 163, 164–165, 166–167, 170–171, 173, 174 above, (M. Moylan) 16, 153, 154; G. E. Allen 156, 158, 159, 160; Vic Barnes 52 below, 69; P. Behar 143 below; Laurie Caddell 57 above and below, 61 above, 62, 63 below, 64, 65, 66, 67, 68; Champion Sparking Plug Co. Ltd. 12, 45 left; Colorsport 137 above and below; Creed Lane Studio 52 above, 53; Brian Crichton 42, 43 left, 44 left, 46 left, 104, 105, 106, 107 above and below, 108, 110, 112; Diffusion Photo de Presse Internationale 172–173; Douglas (Sales & Service) Ltd. 51; Mary Evans Picture Library 130–131; Foto-Nicholls 76 below, 17, 166, 167, 172–173 above, 176; Jim Greening 72 below, 171, 174–175; Robert Harding Associates 8 below; Dave Hawkins 63 above; Brian Holder 44 right, 45 right, 46 left and right, 174 below; Kawasaki Information Service 56; Steve Kimball 161; Christian Lacombe (*Moto-Journal*) 127; Keith Lee 138–139, 140, 141 above, 142, 142–143 above; London Art Technical Drawings Ltd. 123; Leo Mason 77 above, 141; David Minton 94–95, 98, 100, 136 above; Don Morley 75, 124–125, 129 inset, 168–169; National Motor Museum 6–7; National Motor Museum – Robert Harding Associates 9 above, 11, 12–13, 13 above right, 14–15; Mike Patrick 132–133, 134–135 above and below, 136 above; Pictor International Ltd. 70–71; L. E. Shelley 8 above, 9 below, 114; Rod Sloane 43 right, 113, 128–129, 144; Jasper Spencer Smith 10, 50, 55 above, 60, 76 above; Spectrum Colour Library front and back endpapers, 1; Syndication International 118–119; D. Wilcox 48 left and right; ZEFA 172 above